The Order of Fiction

AN INTRODUCTION

THE ORDER OF
Fiction

AN INTRODUCTION

EDWARD A. BLOOM
Brown University

New York · THE ODYSSEY PRESS · INC.

Acknowledgments

"Gooseberries," reprinted with permission of the publisher from *The Wife and Other Stories* by Anton Chekhov. Copyright 1918 by The Macmillan Company. Renewed 1946 by Constance Garnett.

"The Bride Comes to Yellow Sky," by Stephen Crane. Reprinted by permission of Alfred A. Knopf, Inc. from *Stephen Crane: An Omnibus*, edited by Robert Wooster Stallman, published 1952.

"The Garden-Party," by Katherine Mansfield. Copyright, 1922 by Alfred A. Knopf, Inc. Renewed 1950 by J. Middleton Murry. Reprinted from *The Short Stories of Katherine Mansfield*, by permission of Alfred A. Knopf, Inc.

"The Fur Coat," from *The Man Who Invented Sin* by Sean O'Faolain. Published by the Devin-Adair Company, New York, in 1949.

"The Furnished Room," from *The Four Million* by O. Henry. Reprinted by permission of Doubleday & Company, Inc.

"The Forks," copyright 1947 by J. F. Powers, from *Prince of Darkness and Other Stories* by J. F. Powers. Reprinted by permission of Doubleday & Company, Inc.

"The Glass in the Field," by James Thurber. Reprinted by permission; Copyright © 1939 *The New Yorker* Magazine, Inc.

"Only the Dead Know Brooklyn" (Copyright 1935 F-R Publishing Corporation; renewal copyright © 1963 Paul Gitlin) is reprinted with the permission of Charles Scribner's Sons from *From Death to Morning* by Thomas Wolfe.

Extract from *My Antonia* by Willa Cather is used with permission of Houghton Mifflin Company.

Extract from *Victory* by Joseph Conrad is used with permission of the Trustees of the Joseph Conrad Estate and J. M. Dent & Sons Ltd., Publishers.

Extract from *The Invisible Man* by Ralph Ellison is used with permission of Random House, Inc.

Extract from *The Bear* by William Faulkner is used with permission of Random House, Inc.

Extract from *The Great Gatsby* (Copyright 1925 Charles Scribner's Sons; renewal copyright 1953 Frances Scott Fitzgerald Lanahan) by F. Scott Fitzgerald is used by permission of Charles Scribner's Sons.

Extracts from *Aspects of the Novel* by E. M. Forster are used with permission of Harcourt, Brace & World, Inc.

Selections from *A Farewell to Arms* by Ernest Hemingway (Copyright 1929 Charles Scribner's Sons; renewal copyright © 1957 Ernest Hemingway) are used by permission of Charles Scribner's Sons.

Extract from *Point Counter Point* by Aldous Huxley is used with permission of Harper & Row, Publishers, Inc.

Extract from *A Portrait of the Artist as a Young Man* by James Joyce is used by permission of The Viking Press, Inc.

Extract from *Ulysses* by James Joyce is used by permission of Random House, Inc.

Extract from *Sons and Lovers* by D. H. Lawrence is used by permission of The Viking Press, Inc.

Extract from *Cry, the Beloved Country* by Alan Paton (Copyright 1948 Alan Paton) is used by permission of Charles Scribner's Sons.

Extract from "Mr. Bennett and Mrs. Brown" in *The Captain's Deathbed and Other Essays* by Virginia Woolf is used by permission of Harcourt, Brace & World, Inc.

Extract from "Modern Fiction" in *The Common Reader* by Virginia Woolf is used by permission of Harcourt, Brace & World, Inc.

Extract from *To the Lighthouse* by Virginia Woolf is used by permission of Harcourt, Brace & World, Inc.

Preface

THIS BOOK is addressed to anyone who cares about fiction. As the exposition of a comprehensive critical method, its aim, frankly, is to provide a basis for the study of fiction. But that object, once it has been accomplished, should be regarded as the adjunct of a larger, more important one. The end of fiction is to afford pleasure, both sensuous and mental. While rational, objective study brings its own gratifications, its pursuit is subordinate to the work of art. We study fiction to discover what underlies the superficial impression, and in so doing intensify our grasp and enjoyment. As we increase our ability to criticize constructively—to read closely—we sharpen our responses to the artist's inventiveness and intellect. Criticism is important, then, as an illuminating discipline. And the more rigorous we are in its application, the more light (and, hence, enjoyment) we discover.

The Order of Fiction has emerged out of years of reading, reflection, dialogue, and teaching. The author's debts are many, although he can acknowledge only relatively few of them in the text. The stimulation afforded by innumerable volumes of critical doctrine—even when he has been in disagreement—and fiction is beyond recording. Much of the material in this book has been subjected to the tough scrutiny of students at Brown University who challenged the author to clarify his thoughts on criticism of eighteenth-century and contemporary fiction. He is grateful to those who were not easily satisfied and who made him refine, prune, and amplify, and then start all over again.

But it is particularly agreeable to express gratitude to two colleagues—one professional and one domestic—who have been influential in the construction of this book. For many years the author shared a course in the Contemporary British and American Novel with Professor I. J. Kapstein, an astute and erudite critic. He will recognize here (and, hopefully, approve) the fruit of many hours of discussion and friendly debate, as well as some illustrative material used in English 172. For even more years the author has enjoyed the affectionate but firm and always perceptive critical wisdom of his wife Lillian D. Bloom. Nothing in this book has escaped her editorial vigilance. But if blunders appear, let the reader charge them to the author, who assumes final responsibility for everything stated here.

E. A. B.

Contents

The Meaning of Fiction

The Nature of Fiction

CHAPTER I

Introduction

MANY habitual readers of prose fiction would deny that it is a serious mode of literary expression entitled to serious critical consideration. Indeed, these same people feel that novels and short stories are pleasant anodynes after more important matters have been resolved, a retreat into Poictesme or Shangri-La where all thought and striving may be suspended. This view, popular as it is, has arbitrary and enervating limitations. For to read fiction with maximum enjoyment, one must be conscious of its artistic properties. One must think about fiction as an important medium of art—disciplined, imaginative, provocative—standing firmly in a triad with poetry and drama. To initiate understanding of the nature of fiction, that is, its esthetic and technical order, and the kinds of emotion and meaning of which it is capable, is the purpose of this book. Its further purpose is to stimulate critical attention to fiction. That means establishing standards of judgment and evaluation, but without for one moment waiving the pleasure which is the inherent responsibility of all art.

The term *fiction* as used here is a comprehensive one, embracing such prose aspects of the narrator's art as the short story, the novella or novelette, and the novel. All these manners of storytelling share basic ingredients—plot, character, setting, and the like. But the novel in its various manifestations will be the main concern here. The novel is more massive, more capable of accommodating complexities of action, character, emotion, and meaning than are the short story and novelette. Therefore, the novel poses certain problems, if of physical magnitude alone, that are perhaps more conveniently though not more easily resolved in the briefer forms. That is not to say these forms are of lesser consequence, complexity, or intensity. It is, rather, to say that they proceed from different motives and toward different ends. Regardless of such distinctions, however, many common problems of order and even of meaning can be demonstrated through direct access to the short forms of fiction. This practice is for convenience, not for comparison. A ballad is not to be compared with an epic, nor a *lied* with a sonata, even as a short story is not to be compared with a novel. At the same time, the pairs may be seen profitably as units in a common genus.

Poetry and drama enjoy a cultural advantage over prose fiction because they are so deeply rooted in human traditions—even the religious ones—that any attempt to justify them is presumptuous. Naturally, individual poems and plays are subject to criticism, but the genres—poetry and drama *qua* poetry and drama—seldom require warrant any more than do, say, the Bible or the United States Constitution. Fiction has been less fortunate, having acquired its prestige so late and out of such dubious circumstances. The temptation to apologize for it, as though for a poor relative, is not always resisted. The very word *fiction*, although now generally respectable enough, is a reminder of the shadowy origins of the novel. For anyone who cares about the English language and about the novel as a brand of verbal art, there is still something vaguely misleading about joining *fiction* synonymously with *novel*.

An obsolete meaning of *fiction*, extracted from the *New English Dictionary*, characterizes the morally unwholesome quality originally associated with the prose narrative: "Feigning, counterfeiting; deceit, dissimulation, pretence." As related to literary activity, *fiction* continued for a long time to have a debased connotation. For instance: "The action of 'feigning' or inventing imaginary incidents, existences, states of things, etc., whether for the purpose of deception or otherwise . . . invention as opposed to fact." Puritanical objections to the excessive, melodramatic qualities of early fiction (the *romance*) were often motivated by the "lies" with which much imaginative prose was stubbornly identified. A serious writer like Daniel Defoe therefore hoped to avoid the stigma by pretending his novels were "True Relations," and by assuming in them a realistic-biographical attitude.

Literary implications had been evident in the term *fiction* as early as the seventeenth century. Not until nearly half way through the eighteenth century, however, was it seriously equated with literary performance rather than mere fabrication: "The species of literature which is concerned with the narration of imaginary events and the portraiture of imaginary characters; fictitious composition." Even so, to refer to "a work of fiction" is still regarded in some circles as depreciatory. And to read fiction, that is, novels, is thought to be frivolous if not mildly wicked.

In its origins, the word *novel* had a happier connotation and consequently was less likely to alienate overly righteous readers. Derived from the French *nouvelle* (short story) or Italian *novella*, *novel* has a meaning suggestive of "news." Again, in the attempt to avoid any semblance of fabrication, writers of this particular kind of fiction found in the word *novel* a useful clue to their professed aims. They would, they implied, write prose narratives based upon incidents which had happened (hence were true) recently. This was the impression Defoe intended to make. Even a pretense of truth was more acceptable than an avowal of imaginative art or construction. Actually, *novel* did not become the objective descriptive term we understand in English today until the middle of the eighteenth century. Yet as late as 1778 Fanny Burney could make the timid and self-depreciatory statement in her preface to *Evelina:* "In the republic of letters, there is no member of such inferior rank, or who is so much disdained by his brethren of the quill, as the humble Novelist: nor is his fate less hard in the world at large, since, among the whole class of writers, perhaps not one can be named of which the votaries are more numerous but less respectable. . . ."

No genre as complex as the novel will lend itself to ready definition. That in the *New English Dictionary,* however, is a useful start: "A fictitious prose narrative or tale of considerable length (now usually one long enough to fill one or more volumes), in which characters and actions representative of the real life of past or present times are portrayed in a plot of more or less complexity." We are further advised that in the seventeenth and eighteenth centuries *novel* was frequently contrasted with *romance,* "as being shorter than this, and having more relation to real life."

A volume full of definitions will of course not replace the individual experience of reading novels or successfully give us yardsticks by which to measure intensity of emotion and meaning. There are, however, certain considerations, both tangible and intangible, an apprehension of which will enhance the pleasure and understanding to be derived from reading novels. The Victorian critic George Saintsbury stated the principle many years ago (in *The English Novel*), rather impressionistically, but with a sureness that is no less valid now than in his own day:

> For the novel appeal is not, after all, to a mere blind animal thirst for something that will pass and kill time, for something that will drug or flutter or amuse. Beyond and above these things there is something else. The very central cause and essence of it—most definitely and keenly felt by nobler spirits and cultivated intelligences, but also dimly and unconsciously animating very ordinary people—is the human delight in humanity—the pleasure of seeing the men and women of long past ages living, acting, speaking as they do—but in each case with the portrayal not as a mere copy of particulars, but influenced with that spirit of the universal which is the secret and charm of art.

This is not the kind of precise literary criticism that twentieth-century commentators on literature have taught us to expect. But beneath the eloquent prose, we are amply aware, Saintsbury has reached out to the activating motive responsible for most art: man's identification with mankind. Apart from technical or structural considerations, the novelist shares with other artists a conviction that human joys and dilemmas of all times and places have certain universally true equations. Further, he assumes the responsibility of translating or interpreting his conviction in terms which make disparate experiences similar, unfamiliar experiences recognizable, unshared experiences personal.

Saintsbury's observations on the appeal of the novel are still fresh, if we compare his remarks with these by a contemporary reviewer in the *London Times Literary Supplement* (June 8, 1962): "What we seek in fiction is a realization of ourselves not as (possibly) immortal beings but as people living here and now amid neighbours who are 'such creatures as we are, in such a world as the present one' whom we would wish to understand, like, and, no doubt, for such is human nature, judge." The language of this statement is more austere than Saintsbury's, but the concept is generally the same: the subject of fiction is man and, by implication, universal man. Only one significant idea, the right to judge, has been added. That final idea, however, merely hints at the whole question of judgment, which comes up repeatedly in the creative process and is an integral part of all critical thinking. For the moment, at least, that question must be set aside and the inner nature of fiction discussed.

Those early critics of fiction-writing who complained that it is an act of dissimulation or deception contrary to fact missed the point entirely. While fact and truth would certainly seem to be associable, they are not necessarily interdependent. An author may or may not deal with facts, but—if he is an artist—he always deals with truth. Upton Sinclair, writing a novel (1906) based upon deplorable conditions in the Chicago stockyards, went directly to his source, as a chemist might go to his laboratory. What he saw and then recorded is factual; that is, Sinclair's data were empirically valid. To the extent that his report is verifiable and (within certain limits) objective, his novel *The Jungle* is also truthful. But like a good many *naturalistic* writers, Sinclair documented excessively, virtually effacing the line between fiction and journalism.

For most novelists, however, fiction is something more than a depiction of facts so realistic that, figuratively, we can reach out and touch them, saying: "This is true; it really happened." Fiction, as denotation alone would tell us, is a mode of thinking or of saying that serves a purpose other than the purely factual. Of course, many readers admire the kind of representation that *seems* to be real but that common sense tells them is not. A vase of wax flowers that seem real enough to give off a perfume, or a painting that imparts an illusion of three dimensions belong to this category. The owners of these objects display them not because, after a momentary impression, they will be taken to be real; but because they are pleased with their *appearance* of realism. The appeal of such quasi-art is its ingenuity.

Similarly, many people read and enjoy novels—say, historical, biographical, or documentary—because "they seem to be so real," often preferring them to volumes of history or biography. Obviously, not all realistic fiction or factually based fiction will qualify as good art. But the best fiction of this order satisfies an esthetic need which only exceptional documentary works—for instance, Carl Sandburg's biography of Abraham Lincoln—satisfy. That need, simply stated, is the intangible quality of imagination. Through the reconstructive power of imagination, an author may deal with materials that are not ostensibly factual and yet have the ring of truth to them. Or he may recast materials based upon actual occurrences and individuals, softening, hardening, or otherwise disguising the original lines (e.g., Budd Schulberg's novel about F. Scott Fitzgerald, *The Disenchanted*). For the reader, there may still be a pleasurable shock of recognition; but this exterior reaction is less compelling than the inner, esthetic experience, the awareness of subtle artistic truth.

The craft of the novelist is too complex and too much a matter of individual practice and vision to admit of easy critical generalizations. But in spite of the varieties of technical, emotional, and thematic experience which the novel is capable of accommodating, there are certain common reservoirs available to the novelist, either extrinsically or inherently. Roughly, they can be classified as matters of technical and structural value; and as matters of intellectual, spiritual, and esthetic value. They are the lessons to be learned from other novelists and practice. They are the effects of creative talent —the imaginative, experimental urge—which distinguishes each artist from all others. Ultimately, the extrinsic and the intrinsic are fused, for the novel is not a group of blocks and panels joined at visible seams. It is a single, organically inevitable composition in which all parts, influences, and attitudes matter only as parts of the whole.

The general reader, indeed, is usually concerned only with the totality, reading novels in anticipation of the pleasure—intellectual as well as esthetic—that they may afford him. He is not necessarily indifferent to such particulars of artistry and skill as symbols, subtle emotional tones, special devices of characterization. But these are incidentals for him. Unless he is trained in critical method or happens to be unusually sensitive to the deployment of minute parts and their inter-operations, his attention is absorbed by massive or unified impressions, by the achieved result. Like the owner of a fine watch, he relishes the accuracy and outer physical beauty of the instrument rather than its complex interior action. The general reader of novels tends to be exhilarated by progressive movement in which there is an interplay of emotions, ideas, and esthetic appeal.

The novelist also, for that matter, must not let his attention wander from his large goal. Naturally, he must have complete awareness of the working parts, as it were, that go into the construction of a novel. He must be in control of his materials at all times. For the novelist, as for the reader, no single element in relation to the whole is unimportant. But once the novelist has a plan firmly in mind and a body of materials—actions, people, theme—to fulfill his plan, details are subsumed under or crystallized in the total concept.

One element more than any other bears the responsibility for welding all the parts into a satisfying whole. That is the imagination, which is basic to every fictional utterance. It is through the imagination that the novelist conceives his novel, and it is through the imagination that he selects, orders, interprets, and finally shapes his work into an artistic, unitary composition. The imagination makes the ordinary unique, the familiar new. The novelist does not differ from non-artists in possessing imagination: everyone has this faculty to a certain degree. He differs, rather, by the refined state of his imagination and by his ability to exercise it in a disciplined way toward a controlled end. For the serious artist, this end will coincide with an inner vision, and it will be manifested in the completed novel as an interpretation of that vision.

Novels, obviously, may and do grow out of facts which have been experienced or observed by the novelist. Facts, if these happen to be the substance of a particular novel, may be as real as those learned about in this morning's newspaper. They may be founded upon historical events or upon the careers of men significant in the daily news and in history books. Whatever the case, they are proper aspects of fiction only as they have undergone mutation by the novelist. That is, they cease to be authentic reports and become the novelist's interpretation of their meaning. It is at this point that fact, in the sense that a newspaper reporter or even an editorial writer might deal with fact, ceases to be adequate, except as it supplies an analogy for timeless assumptions about the human condition.

In order to provide credible references or checkpoints consistent with temporal experience, the novelist localizes his imagination. That is to say, he invents data which seem to be real but which actually are the expression of his creative talent. Facts, according to the cliché, are seldom as interesting as fiction. What we take for granted in our daily existence—whether it is squalid or beautiful—must be given a patina of interest; its significance must be symbolized or expatiated. The novelist, toward this end, probes below the surface, unearthing what most uncritical people would probably fail to see. In the early history of the novel, this inventive practice was regarded as a form of fabrication, as lies, because it went beyond fact. Today, however, we recognize that inventive imagination is an essential part of artistry and compatible with truth. Fact is no more than a scaffolding around which the artist builds his structure of truth.

For all the license we give the novelist, however, we insist that he stay within a believable range. *Credibility*, as we call that insistence upon believing, is the acceptance of situations, events, and the like, as bearing a probable relationship to existence, while conceding that they need not have happened in fact. Credibility, in artistic terms, is the extension of fact for purposes of interpretation and conclusion.

The novel, after all, is not a mere carbon copy of life or a substitute for the morning newspaper. What would be the interest or entertainment in that? Indeed, how could one even justify as art the work that proposes to be a direct reproduction of life? The novel is a symbolic representation which helps us to understand and interpret aspects of reality that we have been exposed to within our own experiences, or that we could credibly be exposed to. Each novel, in a manner that strives to be distinctive and memorable, intends to capture and record some of these experiences.

Every view of life is bound to be a fragment of the whole, for no one could take in all of it. But within limits determined by the interests and capabilities of their authors, novels are adaptable to great differences of experience. One novel may, if the imagination of the author is in a state of properly active control, find a satisfy-ing center in an account of the San Francisco earthquake or the Chi-cago fire; another in a depiction of Alice and her friends. Yet we do not want the first to be sheer propaganda or documentary realism; nor do we want the second to be exclusively charming fantasy. In each instance of serious fiction, we may admire the verisimilitude with which details are treated, or we may delight in rompings of an ethereal or unrealistic kind. But we always insist upon the control of a shaping, interpretive imagination.

A sordid or utterly realistic subject—say, for example, that of Theodore Dreiser's *An American Tragedy*—would hardly be more illuminating than a series of lurid news reports, without inventive-ness to amplify its inner meaning. A novel about inexplicable go-ings-on—the kinds of actions which characterized eighteenth-cen-tury Gothic fiction—can have little appeal beyond initial shock ef-fect, unless the author treats his materials in such a way that there continues to be a believable or probable connection with the reality of human existence.

In the absence of any formula for achieving this goal, the author must depend upon his own critical and creative judgment. Doubt-less, he has assimilated techniques and ideas from other writers, for each must undergo his own apprenticeship. But what has been as-similated and what is the fruit of the individual's imagination be-come inseparable. Such a union of old and new obviously goes be-yond mere copywork and emerges as original composition. The art-ist enriches his native materials by blending them—consciously or unconsciously—with what has been borrowed, until the distinc-tions have faded away and his own vision has been fulfilled.

Every novel, then, must be transcribed into an idiom of meaning and structure, of content and form, that is most appropriate for the best and clearest illumination of the author's purpose. Every novel, whether it is read solely for pleasure or for critical analysis and eval-uation, must prove itself as the individual expression of an individ-ual artist. Only in elementary details, such as the formal existence of plot and character, would any two novels be alike. The word *novel* conveys general notions of the properties relevant to the genre. Yet it accommodates itself to such a variety of fictional discourse that it must always be taken in the most liberal or flexible sense. *Novel*, then, like any literary term, provides useful associations and points of critical departure. But any essential definition (barring, of course, common and inherent details of plot, character, setting, and so forth) must grow out of individual works.

Consider, for example, that the term *novel* embraces books as disparate in time and purpose as Henry Fielding's *Tom Jones* and Franz Kafka's *The Trial;* or Charles Dickens' *Great Expectations* and Marcel Proust's *Remembrance of Things Past.* Although the pairs are separated by long spans of time and by preoccupations ranging from the realistic and panoramic to the symbolic and the introverted, they share technical properties which justify their being fitted into a single category. On the other hand, two novels may be written in relatively the same period of time and in broadly similar techniques, but still represent widely diversified experiences.

The examples of Virginia Woolf and James Joyce would be instructive to anyone wishing to see distinctions as well as likenesses in the technique known as stream-of-consciousness or interior monologue. Again, novels written on a common subject are often separated by a variety of considerations: authors' attitudes, control of materials, power of imagination, and so forth. Perhaps we need do no more than mention three novels based on World War I, analysis of which would readily reveal this schism: Ernest Hemingway's *A Farewell to Arms,* John Dos Passos' *Three Soldiers,* and E. E. Cummings' *The Enormous Room.* On the whole, comparisons have a limited value, for each writer has his own purpose, his own technique, and his own vision.

Insofar as the novelist's personality has any interest for us, we may be inclined to think of him as a solitary figure on the stage. In this role he addresses himself as a monologist might to an audience which does not have the opportunity to respond verbally. Some novelists, for reasons which will be taken up under *point-of-view,* do project their personalities and attitudes upon the printed page beyond the normal expectations of art. Most, however, are content to submerge their personalities in their writings, letting the characters and actions assume the responsibility of transmission. The novelist is the dynamic source, obviously, of everything that occurs in the book, but his hand is seldom visible. His voice, likewise, though it will at times be heard among other voices in the book, does not drown them out.

Since the novelist can assume any disguise he wishes, he is in effect speaking in a multitude of roles. His public personality, having been sacrificed to his art, ceases to have any overt significance for us. Simultaneously, with the depersonalization of the creative agent, the masks behind which he speaks become all-important to the reader. Viewed in this way, the novel is a form of narrative discourse in which various characters (as distinguished from the novelist) sustain and advance the issues. As the discourse progresses, the reader responds to it emotionally and intellectually. Ceasing thus to be the passive auditor who cannot be drawn into the monologue, he is transfigured into an active participant.

The fictional experience, in other words, is between the novel and the reader, the novel serving as a vehicle for the communication and interpretation of a complex body of ideas, attitudes, and experiences. For those who are fearful of such encroachments upon the creative spirit as the so-called "fallacy of communication" or "heresy of communication," a word or two of comfort may be helpful. *Communication* is not intended to mean anything more than the effective literary transfer of the created materials. Communication does not here imply "message," instructive theme, or any kind of functional device of transmission. Communication is the employment and fusion of all qualities—intangible and overt, verbal and tacit—within the novel for the inevitable purpose of relaying the created materials to the reader.

Communication is not a form of art; rather, it is an agency of art causing the critical reader to speculate about the novel: What is it communicating? How does it communicate? What effect has the communication had upon the reader? Has the communication in general been successful? These are some of the questions, answers to which are intimately associated with the critical evaluation and judgment of fiction. These and other related questions are directed toward the examination of fiction as a unified literary achievement. From them we determine whether content and form have been brought together in a satisfying or appropriate fusion; and we obtain insights into the connections between novel and reader.

These warrantably demanding questions can be asked profitably only by readers who are willing to commit themselves to a critical discipline which will help provide answers. Only by establishing methods and criteria of judgment are we able to distinguish between the good and the bad, or even between the mediocre and the good. Indeed, the reward for critical reading is a double one: we enhance our capacity for esthetic pleasure by being discriminating readers; but we also acquire an intellectual pleasure from the stimulation that comes with the close application of reason and method to literature.

Thus, we are palpably entitled to make value judgments, estimating the worth of the work we have read. But before we praise or condemn, we should be reasonably certain that we have employed every critical test that is applicable. Having done this, we have perhaps added a new intellectual, emotional, or cultural experience to the permanent store already within us. But if, after judicious critical deliberation, we find the new experiences somehow wanting, we are free to reject them. Under any circumstances, we still profit because we have compared two sets of experience—the author's and our own—and have arrived at a mature decision.

Additionally, the novel may induce an active awareness of problems from which hitherto we have remained passively aloof. It may be a means of causing us to become enlightened or more humane individuals in consequence of the intensified activity of our feelings and thoughts. For example, we may be but hazily aware of chaotic or conflicting values in the twentieth century until novelists, like George Orwell or Samuel Beckett, awaken our sensibilities to them, giving us an otherwise unrealized perception. The importance of this insight is almost too obvious for comment. We cannot help acknowledging that we are members of a society more or less moral, and that as such are intimately affected by its problems.

But no matter how absorbing a moral or social theme may be, its effect upon the reader is diminished if it does not encourage a pleasurable response. All too often we are enthusiastic to "profit" from literature, and faultily (even guiltily) assume that what is good for us should not cause pleasure. We may, indeed, learn a useful lesson from a novel dealing with the Depression Years, racial attitudes in South Africa, or pioneer settlements of the West. These are all ad-

mittedly serious problems, and as such they are proper concerns of
fiction. We expect them to be treated persuasively, to be sure, but
also interestingly and artistically so as to give pleasure. Their symbolic manifestations may be sober, even tragic; but they may also
be light or comic. What matters is the earnest meaning with which
they have been invested.

The sources of pleasure in fiction are, of course, too numerous to
be detailed here. But generally speaking, as we have observed before, they are both intellectual and sensory, preferably in combination. They may, for instance, be related to important ideas, to moral
attitudes, to social dilemmas, to unusual situations or characters,
and many other qualities and things. Consider, for example, the
place of the artist in contemporary society. As a fictional subject,
this has important implications touching upon the practical and the
esthetic, society and the individual. It is also a subject which lends
itself to a variety of treatments and interpretations. The artist of
D. H. Lawrence's *Sons and Lovers* borders tragedy; the leading figure of James Joyce's *A Portrait of the Artist as a Young Man* is
lyrical; that of Joyce Cary's *The Horse's Mouth* is exuberantly
comic. Each novel, dedicated to the visionary spirit in a hostile society, elicits its own kind of pleasurable reaction.

The attitudes and impressions evoked by the fictional rendering
of a given subject are the gauge of the reader's pleasure. His grati-
fication will not always have a tangible outlet (sensuous entertainment or amusement, for instance, may be entirely alien to the situation), but the depth and energy of his response will be an adequate
token of the satisfaction he has derived. In any event, the capacity
to give pleasure is an essential characteristic of fiction. At the same
time, however, we should remind ourselves that this attribute is not
the chief end of fiction. The end, rather, is the total work, the uni-
fication of all elements.

Like any serious art form, the novel brings together very complex,
often highly disparate materials. These, in their original and isolated states—roughly, the "stuff of existence"—seldom show the
organic connections or the symbolic patterns that distinguish representation from the prototypes, the real thing. The artist must not
only be the steward of a creative vision, but he must also project—

that is to say, invent symbols and interpret—his vision. For this task, he must control his materials, confining them within a limited space, yet giving them the appearance of boundlessness; he must place his materials in an order, yet hide all traces of artificial restraint and contrivance.

The ordering of fiction is a synthesizing discipline, but one which has not always been acknowledged as such. Until relatively recent times, writing at the highest level was seen as a kind of *mystique*. Technique was expected to be a spontaneous rather than carefully considered aspect of writing. The contemporary attitude, however, contradicts this position, denying the possibility that a work of fiction may be considered in terms of content or theme exclusively, or that technique is accidental. "Technique alone objectifies the materials of art; hence technique alone evaluates those materials."

Mark Schorer, who made this observation, also has the following to say about technique: "When we speak of the technique, then, we speak of nearly everything. For technique is the means by which the writer's experience, which is his subject matter, compels him to attend to it; technique is the only means he has of discovering, exploring, developing his subject, of conveying its meaning, and, finally, of evaluating it. And surely it follows that certain techniques are sharper tools than others, and will discover more; that the writer capable of the most exacting technical scrutiny of his subject matter will produce works with the most satisfying content, works with thickness and resonance, works which reverberate, works with maximum meaning."

To a large extent, the succeeding pages will be concerned with technique as the author's means "of discovering, exploring, developing his subject, of conveying its meaning, and, finally, of evaluating it." Technique, the controlling principle of the order of fiction, will be examined in its particular modes and with relevance to specific works. As Schorer's statement implies, technique is not a mere tool useful to larger issues; it is an inevitable part of those larger issues.

The Materials of Fiction

CHAPTER 2

Character

IN FICTION, to oversimplify, the author attempts to eliminate the extraneous, isolate and emphasize the significant, and order the chaotic. Keenly observant of everything that goes on about him, he has a capacity for detachment; his paradoxical aloofness permits him to stand aside, as it were, and evaluate experiences to be shared with his readers. "Art," as John Crowe Ransom reminds us, "always sets out to create an 'aesthetic distance' between the object and the subject, and art takes pains to announce that it is not history." Because he is exceptionally appreciative of perspective, the artist gets a clearer image of what life is all about than those of us whose practical involvement promotes clouded or distorted vision.

The critical reader, consequently, will make a rendezvous with the author. He will, if the author has been even partially successful, feel a compulsion to advance toward him and discover as much as he can of his essential meaning and artistry. Reading, like writing, becomes a dynamic process and a repudiation of literalism. Dynamic reading will soon reveal whether the artist has seriously attempted to come to terms with his obligation, namely, the search for the meaning of reality. For art is an illusion of reality somehow founded upon the facts of experience, and projected in such a way as to make the illusion credible or probable.

The beginning critical reader will be puzzled for a way of approaching the author's purpose or *intention*. If there were a simple formula for writing all stories, then there would undoubtedly be a formula for reading—which is to say, analyzing and criticizing—them. But apart from special kinds of stylized techniques—the fiction of De Maupassant, O. Henry, and their followers; detective stories and Westerns—formulas do not generally accommodate themselves to the requirements of literature. Each tale must be read as a unique literary experience.

As a point of departure, however, it may be said that all of us have certain expectations when we read fiction. Mainly, we are concerned with people and the way in which they conduct themselves in given circumstances. It is useful, at this point in critical development and discrimination, to identify the people and see what happens to them under the pressures of events—in the context, that is, of *action* and *plot*. What we want initially is *character* and movement; and, then, related complexities. Furthermore, we want the sense of reality which comes with physical location. As in life, fictional characters undergo their trials and enjoy their triumphs in time and space. There is by no means an absolute approach to the study of fiction, but—barring departures from accepted order—critical logic justifies a primary examination of *character*, *plot*, and *setting*.

It is obvious that mankind is made up of a great variety of people with differing temperaments, values, and attitudes (social, moral, political, esthetic, religious, and so on). It is also obvious that people are similar to each other in their ability to suffer and to enjoy life, although at the same time there may be infinite shadings in their responsiveness to experience. The mutations of human nature are sources of perpetual wonder to the novelist, whose obligation it is to record his impressions and in so doing to create probable human beings.

When they are not probable, they may be what E. M. Forster calls "flat" or two-dimensional figures, tending to be stereotypes rather than individuals. While being perfectly clear to us as agents for representative ideas or emotions, they remain incomplete as human beings. They lack the variability, to say nothing of surprise, of which each person is capable. Thus, a Thwackum (*Tom Jones*) is, as his name implies, a stock pedant, one who belabors his pupils. A Lieutenant Bowling (*Roderick Random*) is a typical, crusty seaman. A Dobbin (*Vanity Fair*) is the epitome of patient, plodding endurance. Undergoing no important changes, these characters may

be described as minor, secondary, or even static. Each one, texturally interesting though he may be in revealing human attributes or
in supporting issues and characters larger than himself, is seldom capable of standing alone. He is an adjunct, not an entity. Jane Austen's Mr. Woodhouse (*Emma*), as an instance, is an entertaining
character; yet his role is minor and complementary. Embodying
what Lionel Trilling calls "a principle of perfect *stasis*," Mr. Woodhouse is active in an amusingly negative and invariable way, for
his ruling passion is inertness.

More satisfying characters are those described by Forster as
"round," which is to say, three-dimensional and complete. If successfully delineated, they display the variability and complexity of
which any human being is capable. They are not symbolic ideas or
emotions or appetites, but individuals having ideas or emotions or
appetites which they express credibly in response to certain situations. Unlike flat characters, the round ones, having an opportunity
for development and change, are organic. They are not limited to a
fixed place or purpose in the *structure* and *theme* for the illumination of a single issue. They may, to be sure, be limited by a preoccupation, such as the guilt feelings of a Raskolnikov (*Crime and
Punishment*), or the pity of a Major Scobie (*The Heart of the Matter*). But the preoccupation will be the motivating impulse for a
chain of actions and reactions involving them. They are people
whom we come to know and even somehow, sympathetically or adversely, with whom we are able to associate ourselves.

The novelist uses people as his models, describing them physically and psychologically. With certain liberties allowable to the
artist, he treats them as a group of beings who have familiar attributes of action and thought. They are his actors or characters, responsible for a significant element of the vitality and credibility which
can make stories important shared experiences for their readers. But
human nature as translated by the author means more than mere
physical delineation or psychological response. It is also the complicated representation of moral or ethical standards, the identification of social or religious responsibilities, and conduct consistent
with that identification. If human nature, for instance, means the
brutish and instinctive attitudes of a McTeague or a Lennie (*Of*

Mice and Men), it also means the sophisticated and intellectualized attitudes of a Christopher Newman (*The American*) or of an Isabel Archer (*The Portrait of a Lady*). Both the exterior and interior, the instinctive and rational, play their role in character and *characterization*.

In our own casual associations, we are relatively indifferent to complexities beneath the social, public manner. Consequently, we see the surface appearance and, perhaps, take in such matters as speech, idiosyncrasies of movement, details of dress, political opinions, and the like, but little more. Only through the intimacies of family and friendship or any other unusually close relationship do we come to understand the less accessible, more profound nature of individuals and the motivations which distinguish them from others. The novelist, on the other hand, acquires an intimate understanding of each of his dynamic (that is, "rounded") characters. He learns everything about those he has created. The surface manner is only the beginning for him, and it is by far the least interesting manifestation of personality. Obviously, not all authors have this kind of subcutaneous insight. But those who do enrich the experiences of their readers with surprise and understanding.

The consequences of an action to a character or a group of characters provoke us instinctively to wonder how that same action might affect us. Only a very dull author will permit his audience to be dissociated, and only a very dull reader will permit himself to be so. Like playgoers, we tend to transplant our personalities in terms of actions and characters, aligning ourselves sympathetically or antithetically, for or against certain characters and the actions in which they are involved. It is difficult for a sensitive reader to be indifferent unless the author himself has been indifferent. And indifference hardly makes for satisfactory fiction. Authors, of course, know this principle very well, and they direct much of their effort toward the establishment of moods which will elicit active responses from their readers.

Fictional characters represent living beings whose actions are notable to the degree in which they excite either identifications or aversions. The novelist—no matter how inventive, symbolic, or impressionistic—seldom wanders from the probable limits of human behavior and emotion. This attention to credibility, ironically, becomes one of the hazards of authorship, for readers often lose sight of the margin between the real and the fictional and overextend their personal commitments. Attitudes and actions which parallel our own or which we would like to share make favorable claims upon us; while attitudes and actions contrary to those in which we would be willing to engage or are likely to engage probably earn our reproaches and even contempt. A stay-at-home bookkeeper may participate to the hilt in the hard-drinking exploits of a Hemingway character. A housewife bound to her domestic chores may closely identify herself with a lurid adventuress. The bookkeeper and the housewife who find a vicarious activity in fiction are straining the intention of literature.

Total identification may be a tribute to the author's ability to mesmerize an audience. But hypnotic or narcotic effects and responses are not consistent with critical, evaluative reading. When we become so much a part of the fictional situation that the illusion *is* the reality, then we are reading with only one part of our minds. *Empathy* is, of course, a valuable aspect of fiction, for the empathic reader enters directly into the mood of the work. The danger of empathy, however, is that it may impair the reader's ability to make objective judgments about the reality which lies outside of fiction. Such a reader is likely to see romanticized or escapist arguments for reading fiction, to place a value on the illusion which is disproportionate to the artistic elements of the story.

Thus, unless we are dealing with a traditional genre such as romance, epic, or tragic drama, we should beware of terms like *hero* and *villain* (there are some exceptions in fiction: e.g., *A Portrait of the Artist as a Young Man*, the artist-hero being Stephen Dedalus, or Stephen Hero originally). Tradition justifies monumental representations like Odysseus or Beowulf, Iago or Satan. But these are understood to be distortions or magnifications, inflations of human attributes for special reasons. We may admire their superhuman endurance, their spectacular capacity for good or evil; but we do not really associate their actions with ours. We let them act for us. A hero is larger than life-size, better than human. His identification as hero implies qualities of talent, courage, and morality, for instance, which few human beings could possibly hope to emulate.

A villain, by implication, acts in such a depraved manner that most human beings are obliged to detest him. *Hero* and *villain* become terms for value judgment rather than believable descriptions. Generally, to think of heroes and villains as the contending forces of fiction is to nullify its experiential nature.

Since the time of Henry Fielding and Samuel Richardson, at least, fictional characters have been created life-size and human. It is better, consequently, to rely upon the familiar terms borrowed from antiquity—*protagonist* and *antagonist*—as descriptions of the roles played by conflicting characters. The protagonist, simply, is the chief actor. Strictly speaking, thus, there can be but one protagonist and one antagonist. As a matter of convenience, however, and for the avoidance of unduly fussy terminology, *protagonist* and *antagonist* may be extended to embrace several characters. The complexity of some novels (Aldous Huxley's *Point Counter Point*, for example) is such that they contain several leading characters. At the same time it should be noted that a protagonist may be fundamentally unadmirable (e.g., Thackeray's Becky Sharp or John O'Hara's Pal Joey) and an antagonist fundamentally admirable (e.g., Hardy's Farfrae). Furthermore, the antagonist may be a generalized group of people, "society" (as in *An American Tragedy*), or society plus forces of nature (as in Willa Cather's *O Pioneers!* or John Steinbeck's *The Grapes of Wrath*).

In the main, those fictional characters are most gratifying who convey an impression of being true to life; those who have the three-dimensional or rounded quality admired by Forster. Yet certain characters are necessarily two-dimensional or even generalized. All characters, no matter how realistic, are products of the author's imagination and correlatives of ideas or emotions which he wishes to project. Characterization, like every other inventive aspect of the novel, is intended to be its own justification but also to "stand for" something else. Characters, thus, have *symbolic* as well as literal meaning. Tom Jones is a particular youth—amiable and ready to satisfy his healthy appetites. He is also a symbolic figure—the epitome of the benevolent, natural man. Gulley Jimson (of *The Horse's Mouth*) is an enormously talented painter—totally dedicated to his art, personally comic, slipshod, and profane. Symbolically, he is art incarnate, Joyce Cary's representation of the eternal conflict between the artist and society, of the artist's invincible struggle to express himself. Both Tom and Gulley, however, stand on their own feet without regard to symbolic necessity. The symbolic aspects of their creation enrich the novels in which they appear but do not overwhelm the reader.

Each character presents its own creative problems, and each novelist must cope with them in terms of his intention. There is no formula to guide him or test his results. Only after the character has been created within a specific context are we able to determine the method of creation and judge its rightness. In anticipation of our critical reading, however, we may be alert to various ways in which characterization is achieved and thus consider how well the author has fulfilled his aims. In the broadest possible sense, thus, characters are either *dynamic* or *static*. Dynamic characters are *structural* agents—protagonistic or antagonistic—directly involved in advancing the action of the story, in promoting complications, and generally in affording a movement or progression. They are capable of undergoing changes within themselves or of contributing to change within others and in the story. Static characters are predominantly *textural*, important for the effects created by their presence. They may on occasion initiate a progression but are not central to it.

It could be argued that Mrs. Wilcox in *Howard's End* is dynamic because of the great importance of her role in the novel. Nevertheless, she does not really act in her own person; rather, she provides the motivation for action. This is an exceptional occurrence, for Mrs. Wilcox's presence is exceptionally vibrant. Static characters ordinarily are not so important, but they must always be considered in relation to dynamic characters, as symbolic reflections of them or as causes of action by them. (Note, for example, the Widow Douglas or the Duke and King in *Huckleberry Finn*.) It is conceivable that a novel will provide only dynamic characters; but not that it will provide only static ones.

One of the most interesting methods of revealing character (and also of developing plot) is that of *dialogue*. Conversation—if it is artistically relevant and controlled—may tell us a great deal about the speakers' personalities. Choice of words, responses, tempo, and the like, characterize mental states and reduce the need for expository description. Dialogue brings greater immediacy to the narrative situation and exemplifies the traits of the characters within it. Furthermore, as an adjunct of plot, dialogue establishes relationships between characters and dramatizes the occasion which has brought them together. (Note, as an illustration, how in Sean O'Faolain's story "The Fur Coat" or in Stephen Crane's "The Bride Comes to Yellow Sky" the contrasting personalities and their conflicts are expressed through utterance.)

Dialogue must be consistent; that is, it must be of a kind which we may reasonably expect of such persons. At the same time, it must not be a mere echo or copy of ordinary conversation. Artistic need imposes on the author an obligation to direct it, to attune it interestingly to a specific narrative purpose. As a rule, fictional dialogue should consist of short speeches, for this is the way most conversations are conducted: brief exchanges, frequently idiomatic, sometimes uncompleted or interrupted—such is the normal conversational pattern. (O'Faolain reveals this very well, but the generally acknowledged master of the mode is Hemingway.) On the other hand, it would be a mistake to insist arbitrarily upon short speeches, for extensive monologues or prolonged statements may very well be an effective part of an author's technique. For verification, we may consider the flowing discourse of characters depicted by Henry James or William Faulkner, or, more closely at hand, the monologue of the protagonist in Chekhov's "Gooseberries." These, to be sure, are exceptions; yet, in any event, we must pay close attention to dialogue for its contribution to character, plot, and intention.

Depending upon the author's intention, characters may be drawn explicitly or implicitly. In *explicit* characterization (e.g., Dreiser's *Sister Carrie*) the individual is revealed overtly, in all of his manifestations. The reader is told about his physical appearance, about his attitudes, thoughts, aspirations, fears. The character's dress may be described, idiosyncracies of speech, movement, and gesture detailed. The author employs his expository license to introduce the reader to the character in numerous representative situations. *Implicit* characterization, on the other hand (e.g., Conrad's *Lord Jim* or Faulkner's Gavin Stevens), is achieved largely by suggestion. Although details such as those relevant to explicit characterization are not barred, they are less important than implication.

It is more essential in these instances of implicit characterization that we infer the interesting qualities of the individual than that we know from direct statement. Subtle hints, conversational allusions, an occasional gesture, juxtaposition to contrasting characters, conduct in certain situations—all these may play their part. The chief technical difference between explicit and implicit characters—since specific details may be presented for both—is occasioned by the fullness or reduction of exposition, the directness or indirectness of portraiture. There can be no quarrel about which, objectively speaking, is the better kind of characterization. Suitability to the author's purpose is after all the real test.

What that purpose should be, however, is not readily determined or agreed upon. Accordingly, Virginia Woolf could argue that she was writing about real life, denying that the reality she saw was the same as that seen by her immediate predecessors, the major Edwardian novelists: H. G. Wells, John Galsworthy, and Arnold Bennett. In her essay "Mr. Bennett and Mrs. Brown," she opposed her view of character as an aspect of reality to that of the Edwardians. Dramatizing the distinction, Mrs. Woolf visualized a typical Englishwoman, Mrs. Brown, traveling in a railroad carriage with Wells, Galsworthy, and Bennett. These writers, she complained, were so busy with external concerns that they failed to see an infinitely more important subject, their fellow passenger. "The Edwardians have laid an enormous stress upon the fabric of things. They have given us a house in the hope that we may be able to deduce the human beings who live there. To give them their due, they have made that house much better worth living in."

But meanwhile, "There [Mrs. Brown] sits in the corner of the carriage—that carriage which is traveling, not from Richmond to Waterloo, but from one age of English literature to the next, for Mrs. Brown is eternal, Mrs. Brown is human nature, Mrs. Brown changes only on the surface, it is the novelists who get in and out—there she sits and not one of the Edwardian writers has so much as looked at her. They have looked very powerfully, searchingly, and sympathetically out of the window; at factories, at Utopias, even at the decoration and upholstery of the carriage; but never at her, never at life, never at human nature. And so they have developed a technique of novel writing which suits their purpose; they have made tools and established conventions which do their business. But those tools are not our tools, and that business is not our business."

Such objective, particularized examinations do not suit Mrs. Woolf, because she rejects the notion that the truth of existence is to be found in a logical, orderly process. Metaphorically (in the essay "Modern Fiction"), she makes the point: "Life is not a series of gig lamps symmetrically arranged; life is a luminous halo, a semi-transparent envelope surrounding us from the beginning of consciousness to the end." The novelist concerned with character, according to Mrs. Woolf's *impressionistic* view of experience, must look for reality in the elusive inner condition of human nature, in the "unknown and uncircumscribed spirit," however complex and irrational. Her technique of characterization, then, depends upon subtleties of psychological and spiritual discoveries, disclosing the mind of the character as it "receives a myriad impressions—trivial, fantastic, evanescent, or engraved with the sharpness of steel."

And yet, while many novelists have viewed life and character as Mrs. Woolf did—inferentially and penetratingly—many others (indeed many more) have approached their material from outward signs. It is not our function as readers of fiction to generalize about the value of intrinsic as contrasted with explicit creative development. We may be content for now to acknowledge that such a distinction exists and that both methods are useful. The writer who wishes to make an overt point—as, say, Frank Norris did in *The Pit*, Arnold Bennett in the *The Old Wives' Tale*, or Richard Wright in *Native Son*—will serve his purpose best by the explicit use of details and character development. The writer, on the other hand, whose concern is with individual personality rather than socioeconomic affairs is committed to greater nuances of language and psychological interpretation in order to develop his fictional people.

Success in fiction is determined by the way technique and talent are applied in relation to the end result. Generalizations about character are useful only when they are applied to specific works. In the short stories which follow, some of the principles of characterization (certainly not all) will become both apparent and demonstrable. Other stories of diversified nature should be selected for continued practice in critical method and for the discovery of the innumerable varieties of characterization. The reader who enjoys Dickens' *David Copperfield* or James Farrell's *Studs Lonigan* may derive equal pleasure from Sterne's *Tristram Shandy,* Nathanael West's *Miss Lonelyhearts,* Joyce's *Ulysses,* or Kafka's *The Trial.*

The Fur Coat

by SEAN O'FAOLAIN

When Maguire became Parliamentary Secretary to the Minister for Roads and Railways his wife wound her arms around his neck, lifted herself on her toes, gazed into his eyes and said, adoringly:

"Now, Paddy, I must have a fur coat."

"Of course, of course, me dear," Maguire cried, holding her out from him admiringly; for she was a handsome little woman still, in spite of the graying hair and the first hint of a stoop. "Get two fur coats! Switzer's will give us any amount of tick from now on."

Molly sat back into her chair with her fingers clasped between her knees and said, chidingly:

"You think I'm extravagant!"

"Indeed, then, I do not. We've had some thin times together and it's about time we had a bit of comfort in our old age. I'd like to see my wife in a fur coat. I'd love to see my wife take a shine out of some of those straps in Grafton Street—painted jades that never lifted a finger for God or man, not to as much as mention the word *Ireland.* By all means get a fur coat. Go down to Switzer's tomorrow morning," he cried with all the innocence of a warm-hearted, inexperienced man, "and order the best fur coat that money can buy."

Molly Maguire looked at him with affection and irritation. The years had polished her hard—politics, revolution, husband in and out of prison, children reared with the help of relatives and Prisoners'

Dependents' funds. You could see the years on her finger tips, too pink, too coarse, and in her diamond-bright eyes.

"Paddy, you big fool, do you know what you'd pay for a mink coat? Not to mention a sable? And not as much as to whisper the word broadtail?"

"Say a hundred quid," said Paddy, manfully. "What's a hundred quid? I'll be handling millions of public money from now on. I have to think big."

She replied in her warm Limerick singsong; sedately and proudly as befitted a woman who had often, in her father's country store, handled thousands of pound notes.

"Do you know, Paddy Maguire, what a really bang-up fur coat could cost you? It could cost you a thousand guineas, and more."

"One thousand guineas? For a coat? Sure, that's a whole year's salary."

"It is."

Paddy drew into himself. "And," he said, in a cautious voice, "is that the kind of coat you had in mind?"

She laughed, satisfied at having taken him off his perch.

"Yerrah, not at all. I thought I might pick up a nice little coat for, maybe, thirty or forty or, at the outside, fifty quid. Would that be too much?"

"Go down to Switzer's in the morning and bring it home on your back."

But, even there, she thought she detected a touch of the bravo, as if he was still feeling himself a great fellow. She let it pass. She said she might have a look around. There was no hurry. She did not bring up the matter again for quite fifteen minutes.

"Paddy! About that fur coat. I sincerely hope you don't think I'm being *vulgar?*"

"How could you be vulgar?"

"Oh, sort of *nouveau riche*. I don't want a fur coat for show-off." She leaned forward eagerly. "Do you know the reason why I want a fur coat?"

"To keep you warm. What else?"

"Oh, well, that too, I suppose, yes," she agreed shortly. "But you must realize that from this on we'll be getting asked out to parties and receptions and so forth. And—well—I haven't a rag to wear!"

"I see," Paddy agreed; but she knew that he did not see.

"Look," she explained, "what I want is something I can wear any old time. I don't want a fur coat for grandeur." (This very scornfully.) "I want to be able to throw it on and go off and be as well dressed as anybody. You see, you can wear any old thing under a fur coat."

"That sounds a good idea." He considered the matter as judiciously as if he were considering a memorandum for a projected by-pass. She leaned back, contented, with the air of a woman who has successfully laid her conscience to rest.

Then he spoiled it all by asking, "But, tell me, what do all the women do who haven't fur coats?"

"They dress."

"Dress? Don't ye all dress?"

"Paddy, don't be silly. They think of nothing else but dress. I have no time for dressing. I'm a busy housewife and, anyway, dressing costs a lot of money." (Here she caught a flicker in his eye which obviously meant that forty quid isn't to be sniffed at either.) "I mean they have costumes that cost twenty-five pounds. Half a dozen of 'em. They spend a lot of time and thought over it. They live for it. If you were married to one of 'em you'd soon know what it means to dress. The beauty of a fur coat is that you can just throw it on and you're as good as the best of them."

"Well, that's fine! Get the ould coat."

He was evidently no longer enthusiastic. A fur coat, he had learned, is not a grand thing—it is just a useful thing. He drew his brief case towards him. There was that pier down in Kerry to be looked at. "Mind you," he added, "it'd be nice and warm, too. Keep you from getting a cold."

"Oh, grand, yes, naturally, cozy, yes, all that, yes, yes!"

And she crashed out and banged the door after her and put the children to bed as if she were throwing sacks of turf into a cellar. When she came back he was poring over maps and specifications.

She began to patch one of the boy's pajamas. After a while she held it up and looked at it in despair. She let it sink into her lap and looked at the pile of mending beside her.

"I suppose when I'm dead and gone they'll invent plastic pajamas that you can wash with a dishcloth and mend with a lump of glue."

She looked into the heart of the turf fire. A dozen pajamas . . . underwear for the whole house . . .

"Paddy!"

"Huh?"

"The last thing that I want anybody to start thinking is that I, by any possible chance, could be getting grand notions."

She watched him hopefully. He was lost in his plans.

"I can assure you, Paddy, that I loathe—I simply loathe all this modern show-off."

"That's right."

"Those wives that think they haven't climbed the social ladder until they've got a fur coat!"

He grunted at the map of the pier.

"Because I don't care what you or anybody else says, Paddy, there *is* something vulgar about a fur coat. There's no shape to them. Especially musquash. What I was thinking of was black Indian lamb. Of course, the real thing would be ocelot. But they're much too dear. The real ones. And I wouldn't be seen dead in an imitation ocelot."

He glanced sideways from the table. "You seem to know a lot about fur." He leaned back and smiled benevolently. "I never knew you were hankering all this time after a fur coat."

"Who said I'm hankering! I am *not*. What do you mean? Don't be silly. I just want something decent to wear when we go out to a show, or to wear over a dance frock, that's all. What do you mean— hankering?"

"Well, what's wrong with that thing you have with the fur on the sleeves? The shiny thing with the what-do-you-call-'ems—sequins, is it?"

"*That!* Do you mean *that?* For heaven's sake, don't be talking about what you don't know anything about, I've had *that* for fourteen years. It's like something me grandmother wore at her own funeral."

He laughed. "You used to like it."

"Of course, I liked it when I got it. Honestly, Paddy Maguire, there are times when . . ."

"Sorry, sorry, sorry. I was only trying to be helpful. How much is an ocelot?"

"Eighty-five or ninety—at the least."

"Well, why not?"

"Paddy, tell me honestly. Honestly, now! Do you seriously think that I could put eighty-five pounds on my back?"

With his pencil Maguire frugally drew a line on the map, reducing the pier by five yards, and wondered would the county surveyor let him get away with it.

"Well, the question is: will you be satisfied with the Indian lamb? What color did you say it is? Black? That's a very queer lamb."

Irritably he rubbed out the line. The wretched thing would be too shallow at low water if he cut five yards off it.

"It's dyed. You could get it brown, too," she cried. "You could get all sorts of lamb. Broadtail is the fur of unborn Persian lambs."

That woke him up: the good farmer stock in him was shocked.

"Unborn lambs!" he cried. "Do you mean to say that they . . ."

"Yes, isn't it awful? Honest to Heaven, Paddy, anyone that'd wear broadtail ought to be put in prison. Paddy, I've made up my mind. I just couldn't buy a fur coat. I just won't buy it. That's the end of it."

She picked up the pajamas again and looked at them with moist eyes. He turned to devote his full attention to her problem.

"Molly, darling, I'm afraid I don't understand what you're after. I mean, do you or do you not want a fur coat? I mean, supposing you didn't buy a fur coat, what else could you do?"

"Just exactly what do you mean?"—very coldly.

"I mean, it isn't apparently necessary that you should buy a fur coat. I mean, not if you don't really want to. There must be some other way of dressing besides fur coats? If you have a scunner against fur coats, why not buy something else just as good? There's hundreds of millions of other women in the world and they all haven't fur coats."

"I've told you before that they dress! And I've no time to dress. I've explained all that to you."

Maguire got up. He put his back to the fire, his hands behind him, a judicial look on him. He addressed the room.

"All the other women in the world can't all have time to dress. There must be some way out of it. For example, next month there'll be a garden party up at the President's house. How many of all these women will be wearing fur coats?" He addressed the armchair. "Has Mrs. de Valera time to dress?" He turned and leaned over the turf basket. "Has Mrs. General Mulcahy time to dress? There's ways and means of doing everything." (He shot a quick glance at the map of the pier; you could always knock a couple of feet off the width of it.) "After all, you've told me yourself that you could purchase a black costume for twenty-five guineas. Is that or is that not a fact? Very well then," triumphantly, "why not buy a black costume for twenty-five guineas?"

"Because, you big fathead, I'd have to have shoes and a blouse and hat and gloves and a fur and a purse and everything to match it, and I'd spend far more in the heel of the hunt, and I haven't time for that sort of thing and I'd have to have two or three costumes—Heaven above, I can't appear day after day in the same old rig, can I?"

"Good! Good! That's settled. Now, the question is: shall we or shall we not purchase a fur coat? Now! What is to be said for a fur coat?" He marked off the points on his fingers. "Number one: it is warm. Number two: it will keep you from getting cold. Number three . . ."

Molly jumped up, let a scream out of her, and hurled the basket of mending at him.

"Stop it! I told you I don't want a fur coat! And you don't want me to get a fur coat! You're too mean, that's what it is! And, like all the Irish, you have the peasant streak in you. You're all alike, every bloody wan of ye. Keep your rotten fur coat. I never wanted it . . ."

And she ran from the room sobbing with fury and disappointment.

"Mean?" gasped Maguire to himself. "To think that anybody could say that I ... Mean!"

She burst open the door to sob:

"I'll go to the garden party in a mackintosh. And I hope that'll satisfy you!" and ran out again.

He sat miserably at his table, cold with anger. He murmured the hateful word over and over, and wondered could there be any truth in it. He added ten yards to the pier. He reduced the ten to five, and then, seeing what he had done, swept the whole thing off the table.

It took them three days to make it up. She had hit him below the belt and they both knew it. On the fourth morning she found a check for a hundred and fifty pounds on her dressing table. For a moment her heart leaped. The next moment it died in her. She went down and put her arms about his neck and laid the check, torn in four, into his hand.

"I'm sorry, Paddy," she begged, crying like a kid. "You're not mean. You never were. It's me that's mean."

"You! Mean?" he said, fondly holding her in his arms.

"No, I'm not mean. It's not that. I just haven't the heart, Paddy. It was knocked out of me donkeys' years ago." He looked at her sadly. "You know what I'm trying to say?"

He nodded. But she saw that he didn't. She was not sure that she knew herself. He took a deep, resolving breath, held her out from him by the shoulders, and looked her straight in the eyes. "Molly, tell me the truth. You want this coat?"

"I do. O God, I do!"

"Then go out and buy it."

"I couldn't, Paddy. I just couldn't."

He looked at her for a long time. Then he asked:

"Why?"

She looked straight at him and, shaking her head sadly, she said in a little sobbing voice:

"I don't know."

Critical Commentary on *The Fur Coat*

Through a simple, almost commonplace, domestic situation, Sean O'Faolain has exemplified the profound truth that the magic of dreams has a way of being dissipated by the reality of experience. "The Fur Coat," consequently, unfolds as a fairy tale *manqué*, a wish unfulfilled, with Molly Maguire nerveless to accept the transition from hardship to good fortune. Too many years of yearning have cancelled the moment of fulfillment, and Cinderella without knowing why remains bound to her hearth. The modest fur coat, though well within her means now, is as inaccessible as an ermine robe. Providing a narrative center and conflict, the coat is crucial to the structure of the story. But it also has symbolic properties related to the abstract meaning of "The Fur Coat": the inability to transcend one's own past.

Worked out through the colloquy between husband and wife, the conflict effects their emergence as "rounded" characters. To be sure, we witness but a single concrete incident in their relationship, but it is enough to establish their dominant traits, or at least those traits which O'Faolain considers most interesting. Furthermore, in this single incident we are drawn closer—that is, more sympathetically—to Molly than to Paddy. If we (like Paddy) are tempted to dismiss her vacillation impatiently as typical female behavior, O'Faolain brings us up short with the subtle implication that much more than a fur coat is at stake here. In fact, what he suggests is that time past is Molly's overpowering enemy, that it will not really let her escape into the successful present. "You could see the years on her finger tips, too pink, too coarse, and in her diamond-bright eyes."

For the essence of Molly's character we must see her in contrast with Paddy. Their married life, through all the uncertainties and desperation of revolution and now at the start of well-earned comfort, has been a good one. But Paddy can accommodate himself to success, as Molly cannot, because his career has been one of cautious action and progression; and his current eminence reflects the sober, steady diligence that has carried him to it. As a man who has helped to effect change, he is always prepared for it. Molly, on the other hand, has been the loyal watcher, satisfied with her subordinate role of wife and mother. Polished hard by the years of waiting and enduring, she has become conditioned to, even rigid in, a pattern of acceptance. Success takes her by surprise, and she is frightened by the possibility that she may now determine an easier and more gracious way of life for herself. After all, she has long been habituated to the inflexible mold of endurance. It is one thing to dream of elegance, but another disconcerting one to experience it.

O'Faolain has drawn Molly as a woman of variable and mercurial temperament. On the surface, thus, she is "typical"; she can't make up her mind. Beneath the superficial manner, however, she is the custom-hardened watcher, the woman who long ago learned to guard herself against vicissitudes and to be wary of the favorable circumstance that in the next moment might turn out to be an illusion. The fur coat is an object of infinite desirability; and yet in a scheme of values dictated by petty economies it is unacceptably alien. Hence, even before she comes to the sad if impalpable realization that she could never wear such a socially aristocratic garment, she rationalizes its possession in terms of utility. What she wants, she pretends to herself and Paddy, is something she can put on any old time. "You see, you can wear any old thing under a fur coat." At the same time, however, she angrily rejects Paddy's agreement that a fur coat is a useful thing. She knows, of course, that she cherishes the thought of possessing the coat not because it is practical but because it connotes her transition into a new social stratum. Fearful of the transition, she irrationally accuses Paddy of meanness, transferring the source of her frustration from herself to him.

Meanwhile Paddy, though a devoted husband and happy to see Molly clad in a symbol of their prosperity, fails to understand her shifts of mood. He is too preoccupied with his own work to assess her deeply ingrained reluctance. As far as he is concerned, a fur coat will arouse envy in his acquaintances and please his wife. Beyond this, however, it is a relatively trivial matter. If the cost of the coat awakens his natural caution, he relies on Molly to do nothing foolish. He sees her desire as a harmless and even agreeable vanity, but not as much more than that. It is ironical that these two, having come through such hard times together, can communicate about the practicalities of existence which have bound them together but not about the intangibilities of dreams. In fact, he is not a dreamer at all but a man of methodical achievement for whom the present is the reality to be counted on. Molly, contrarily, is a woman of dreams who has patiently borne the reality of the past and, unlike the girl in the fairy tale, discovers that the dream is more satisfying than its imminent realization.

The disposition of this story is one of near equilibrium, with Molly and Paddy as counterweights. That is to say, there is no histrionic exterior disturbance of action or emotion. Certainly there is movement to hold the attention, but it is always one of steady, gradual ascent. When Molly, the activating force, threatens to become too explosive, the sympathetic calm of Paddy reasserts the balance. We cannot help being deeply affected by her dilemma; yet we appreciate O'Faolain's capacity for proportion in not letting her moments of imbalance get out of hand. The level of apprehension is distinctly higher at the end of the story than at the beginning. The climb toward enlightenment, however, has never defied the law of artistic gravity: whatever happens, happens within the expectations of normality and credibility.

The crisis is in a minor key, but the advance toward it is inevitable and valuable. By the time it has been reached—and there is no wasteful rhetoric or detail toward its attainment—the couple have learned things about themselves and their relationship that they have not known before. And the reader shares in the discovery. For Molly the essential revelation is her own incapacity to shake off the past. For Paddy it is the obscure realization that his volatile wife has somehow been crippled by experience and that the material fact of prosperity is incalculably beyond her enjoyment. Even with this knowledge, kind though he is, he mistakes the power of a bank check. Taking her loyalty and endurance for granted, as he always has in the past, he cannot now muster an understanding that is spiritual or psychic rather than practical. The failure is his to a large extent, but it is an utterly human one.

We have no reason to believe that the impasse over the coat will effect any serious alteration in their future relationship. Indeed, if anything it will bring them closer together, at least in the external features of their married life. Even in her inarticulate cry, "I don't know," Molly has exposed a side of her character to Paddy that neither had suspected before. Given his compassionate nature and her selflessness, they have deepened the dimensions of their union by a common need to reconcile her bondage to the past. For the first time, perhaps, Paddy is made aware that there are limits to his wife's reliable steadfastness and that his obligation is one of husband as well as of patriot and public figure.

O'Faolain has created a dual portrait that is as economical as it is satisfying. Everything that we need to know about this middle-aged couple is presented through dialogue, precisely the kind of talk we might expect to overhear in the privacy of a home. It is, above all else, affectionate and unpretentious. Not even Molly's outbursts of vexation and sorrow, nor Paddy's mocking and impatient rejoinders, efface the familiarity of the scene. It is the dialogue that controls the even, upward flow of action, that creates a balance between warmth and acerbity. It is the dialogue that gives us sharp insights into the past and present of the Maguires, that brings the crisis into the open, and then isolates the despair of Molly. Through dialogue O'Faolain has fixed his credible portraiture, imbuing it with the roundness or completeness of life itself.

There are few times when he feels called upon to announce his own manipulation of the story. For instance, he tells—and only very briefly—that the years had polished Molly hard. And he is the interpreter who says, Paddy "was evidently no longer enthusiastic." In the main, however, O'Faolain lets his principals work out their problem with only subtle intervention from himself. It is a deft author's touch which causes Paddy to listen inattentively to Molly's protestations while, characteristically, giving himself over to the more urgent business of maps and specifications. By implication here we learn a good deal about Paddy. And again we learn much about him when his wife's chatter concerning relatively small sums of money is reflected in the changes he attempts to make in the size of the pier. As a public man he is more meticulous about his obligations to the county than he is about the question of a fur coat or an outmoded dress. On the other hand, Molly is obsessed by her desire for the coat, which she can afford, but the pile of family mending is the reality she wrestles with. Each in his own way is more comfortable with the practical realities than with the symbol of new status.

O'Faolain, then, makes us see and understand his characters in their normal environment, and in so doing he brings us directly into their lives. Never obtrusive in his presentation nor extraneous in his details—the latter, indeed, being absolutely minimal—he compels the reader to make a sympathetic commitment to his characters and their situation. His imagination and technique exact a high degree of participation from the audience.

Gooseberries

by ANTON CHEKHOV

The whole sky had been overcast with rain-clouds from early morning; it was a still day, not hot, but heavy, as it is in gray dull weather when the clouds have been hanging over the country for a long while, when one expects rain and it does not come. Ivan Ivanovich, the veterinary surgeon, and Burkin, the high school teacher, were already tired from walking, and the fields seemed to them endless. Far ahead of them they could just see the windmills of the village of Mironositskoe; on the right stretched a row of hillocks which disappeared in the distance behind the village, and they both knew that this was the bank of the river, that there were meadows, green willows, homesteads there, and that if one stood on one of the hillocks one could see from it the same vast plain, telegraph-wires, and a train which in the distance looked like a crawling caterpillar, and that in clear weather one could even see the town. Now, in still weather, when all nature seemed mild and dreamy, Ivan Ivanovich and Burkin were filled with love of the countryside, and both thought how great, how beautiful a land it was.

"Last time we were in Prokofy's barn," said Burkin, "you were about to tell me a story."

"Yes; I meant to tell you about my brother."

Ivan Ivanovich heaved a deep sigh and lighted a pipe to begin to tell his story, but just at that moment the rain began. And five minutes later heavy rain came down, covering the sky, and it was hard to tell when it would be over. Ivan Ivanovich and Burkin stopped in hesitation; the dogs, already drenched, stood with their tails between their legs gazing at them feelingly.

"We must take shelter somewhere," said Burkin. "Let us go to Alehin's; it's close by."

"Come along."

They turned aside and walked through mown fields, sometimes going straight forward, sometimes turning to the right, till they came out on the road. Soon they saw poplars, a garden, then the red roofs of barns; there was a gleam of the river, and the view opened onto a broad expanse of water with a windmill and a white bathhouse: this was Sofino, where Alehin lived.

The watermill was at work, drowning the sound of the rain; the dam was shaking. Here wet horses with drooping heads were standing near their carts, and men were walking about covered with sacks. It was damp, muddy, and desolate; the water looked cold and malignant. Ivan Ivanovich and Burkin were already conscious of a feeling of wetness, messiness, and discomfort all over; their feet were heavy with mud, and when, crossing the dam, they went up to the barns, they were silent, as though they were angry with one another.

In one of the barns there was the sound of a winnowing machine, the door was open, and clouds of dust were coming from it. In the doorway was standing Alehin himself, a man of forty, tall and stout, with long hair, more like a professor or an artist than a landowner. He had on a white shirt that badly needed washing, a rope for a belt, drawers instead of trousers, and his boots, too, were plastered up with mud and straw. His eyes and nose were black with dust. He recognized Ivan Ivanovich and Burkin, and was apparently much delighted to see them.

"Go into the house, gentlemen," he said, smiling; "I'll come directly, this minute."

It was a big two-storied house. Alehin lived in the lower story, with arched ceilings and little windows, where the bailiffs had once lived; here everything was plain, and there was a smell of rye bread, cheap vodka, and harness. He went upstairs into the best rooms only on rare occasions, when visitors came. Ivan Ivanovich and Burkin were met in the house by a maidservant, a young woman so beautiful that they both stood still and looked at one another.

"You can't imagine how delighted I am to see you, my friends," said Alehin, going into the hall with them. "It is a surprise! Pelageya," he said, addressing the girl, "give our visitors something to change into. And, by the way, I will change too. Only I must first go and wash, for I almost think I have not washed since spring. Wouldn't you like to come into the bathhouse? And meanwhile they will get things ready here."

Beautiful Pelageya, looking so refined and soft, brought them towels and soap, and Alehin went to the bathhouse with his guests.

"It's a long time since I had a wash," he said, undressing. "I have got a nice bathhouse, as you see—my father built it—but I somehow never have time to wash."

He sat down on the steps and soaped his long hair and his neck, and the water round him turned brown.

"Yes, I must say," said Ivan Ivanovich meaningly, looking at his head.

"It's a long time since I washed . . ." said Alehin with embarrassment, giving himself a second soaping, and the water near him turned dark blue, like ink.

Ivan Ivanovich went outside, plunged into the water with a loud splash, and swam in the rain, flinging his arms out wide. He stirred the water into waves which set the white lilies bobbing up and down; he swam to the very middle of the millpond and dived, and came up a minute later in another place, and swam on, and kept on diving, trying to touch bottom.

"Oh, my goodness!" he repeated continually, enjoying himself thoroughly. "Oh, my goodness!" He swam to the mill, talked to the peasants there, then returned and lay on his back in the middle of the pond, turning his face to the rain. Burkin and Alehin were dressed and ready to go, but he still went on swimming and diving. "Oh, my goodness! . . ." he said, "Oh, Lord, have mercy on me! . . ."

"That's enough!" Burkin shouted to him.

They went back to the house. And only when the lamp was lighted in the big drawing-room upstairs, and Burkin and Ivan Ivanovich, attired in silk dressing-gowns and warm slippers, were sitting in armchairs; and Alehin, washed and combed, in a new coat, was walking about the drawing-room, evidently enjoying the feeling of warmth, cleanliness, dry clothes, and light shoes; and when lovely Pelageya, stepping noiselessly on the carpet and smiling softly, handed tea and jam on a tray—only then Ivan Ivanovich began on his story, and it seemed as though not only Burkin and Alehin were listening, but also the ladies, young and old, and the officers who looked down upon them sternly and calmly from their gold frames.

"There are two of us brothers," he began—"I, Ivan Ivanovich, and my brother, Nikolay Ivanovich, two years younger. I went in for a learned profession and became a veterinary surgeon, while Nikolay sat in a government office from the time he was nineteen. Our father, Chimsha-Himalaisky, was the son of a private, but he himself rose to be an officer and left us a little estate and the rank of nobility. After his death the little estate went in debts and legal expenses; but, anyway, we had spent our childhood running wild in the country. Like peasant children, we passed our days and nights in the fields and the woods, looked after horses, stripped the bark off the trees, fished and so on. . . And, you know, whoever has once in his life caught perch or has seen the migrating of the thrushes in autumn, watched how they float in flocks over the village on bright, cool days, he will never be a real townsman, and will have a yearning for freedom to the day of his death. My brother was miserable in the government office. Years passed by, and he went on sitting in the same place, went on writing the same papers and thinking of one and the same thing—how to get into the country. And this yearning by degrees passed into a definite desire, into a dream of buying himself a little farm somewhere on the banks of a river or a lake.

"He was a gentle, good-natured fellow, and I was fond of him, but I never sympathized with this desire to shut himself up for the rest of his life in a little farm of his own. It's the correct thing to say that a man needs no more than six feet of earth. But six feet is what a corpse needs, not a man. And they say, too, now, that if our intellectual classes are attracted to the land and yearn for a farm, it's a good thing. But these farms are just the same as six feet of earth. To retreat from town, from the struggle, from the bustle of life, to retreat and bury oneself in one's farm—it's not life, it's egoism, laziness, it's monasticism of a sort, but monasticism without good works. A man does not need six feet of earth or a farm, but the whole globe, all nature, where he can have room to display all the qualities and peculiarities of his free spirit.

"My brother Nikolay, sitting in his government office, dreamed of how he would eat his own cabbages, which would fill the whole yard with such a savory smell, take his meals on the green grass, sleep in the sun, sit for whole hours on the seat by the gate gazing at the fields and the forest. Gardening books and the agricultural hints in calendars were his delight, his favorite spiritual sustenance; he enjoyed reading newspapers, too, but the only things he read in them were the advertisements of so many acres of arable land and a grass meadow with farmhouses and buildings, a river, a garden, a mill and millponds, for sale. And his imagination pictured the garden-paths, flowers and fruit, starling cotes, the carp in the pond, and all that sort of thing, you know. These imaginary pictures were of different kinds according to the advertisements which he came across, but for some reason in every one of them he always had to have gooseberries. He could not imagine a homestead, he could not picture an idyllic nook, without gooseberries.

" 'Country life has its conveniences,' he would sometimes say. 'You sit on the veranda and you drink tea, while your ducks swim on the pond, there is a delicious smell everywhere, and . . . and the gooseberries are growing.'

"He used to draw a map of his property, and in every map there were the same things—(a) house for the family, (b) servants' quarters, (c) kitchen-garden, (d) gooseberry-bushes. He lived parsimoniously, was frugal in food and drink, his clothes were beyond description; he looked like a beggar, but kept on saving and putting money in the bank. He grew fearfully avaricious. I did not like to look at him, and I used to give him something and send him presents for Christmas and Easter, but he used to save that too. Once a man is absorbed by an idea there is no doing anything with him.

"Years passed: he was transferred to another province. He was over forty, and he was still reading the advertisements in the papers and saving up. Then I heard he was married. Still with the same object of buying a farm and having gooseberries, he married an elderly and ugly widow without a trace of feeling for her, simply because she had filthy lucre. He went on living frugally after marrying her, and kept her short of food, while he put her money in the bank in his name.

"Her first husband had been a postmaster, and with him she was accustomed to pies and homemade wines, while with her second husband she did not get enough black bread; she began to pine away with this sort of life, and three years later she gave up her soul to God. And I need hardly say that my brother never for one moment imagined that he was responsible for her death. Money, like vodka, makes a man queer. In our town there was a merchant who, before he died, ordered a plateful of honey and ate up all his money and lottery tickets with the honey, so that no one might get the benefit of it. While I was inspecting cattle at a railway-station a cattle-dealer fell under an engine and had his leg cut off. We carried him into the waiting-room, the blood was flowing—it was a horrible thing—and he kept asking them to look for his leg and was very much worried about it; there were twenty roubles in the boot on the leg that had been cut off, and he was afraid they would be lost."

"That's a story from a different opera," said Burkin.

"After his wife's death," Ivan Ivanovich went on, after thinking for half a minute, "my brother began looking out for an estate for himself. Of course, you may look about for five years and yet end by making a mistake, and buying something quite different from what you have dreamed of. My brother Nikolay bought through an agent a mortgaged estate of three hundred and thirty acres, with a house for the family, with servants' quarters, with a park, but with no orchard, no gooseberry-bushes, and no duck-pond; there was a river, but the water in it was the color of coffee, because on one side of the estate there was a brickyard and on the other a factory for burning bones. But Nikolay Ivanovich did not grieve much; he ordered twenty gooseberry-bushes, planted them, and began living as a country gentleman.

"Last year I went to pay him a visit. I thought I would go and see what it was like. In his letters my brother called his estate 'Chumbaroklov Waste, alias Himalaiskoe.' I reached 'alias Himalaiskoe' in the afternoon. It was hot. Everywhere there were ditches, fences, hedges, fir-trees planted in rows, and there was no knowing how to get to the yard, where to put one's horse. I went up to the house, and was met by a fat red dog that looked like a pig. It wanted to bark, but was too lazy. The cook, a fat, barefooted woman, came out of the kitchen, and she, too, looked like a pig, and said that her master was resting. I went in to see my brother. He was sitting up in bed with a quilt over his legs; he had grown older, fatter, wrinkled; his cheeks, his nose, and his mouth all stuck out—he looked as though he might begin grunting into the quilt at any moment.

"We embraced each other, and shed tears of joy and of sadness at the thought that we had once been young and now were both grayheaded and near the grave. He dressed, and led me out to show me the estate.

" 'Well, how are you getting on here?' I asked.

" 'Oh, all right, thank God; I am getting on very well.'

"He was no more a poor timid clerk, but a real landowner, a gentleman. He was already accustomed to it, had grown used to it, and liked it. He ate a great deal, went to the bathhouse, was growing stout, was already at law with the village commune and both factories, and was very much offended when the peasants did not call him 'your Honor.' And he concerned himself with the salvation of his soul in a substantial, gentlemanly manner, and performed deeds of charity, not simply, but with an air of consequence. And what deeds of charity! He treated the peasants for every sort of disease with soda and castor oil, and on his name-day had a thanksgiving service in the middle of the village, and then treated the peasants to a gallon of vodka—he thought that was the thing to do. Oh, those horrible gallons of vodka! One day the fat landowner hauls the peasants up before the district captain for trespass, and next day, in honor of a holiday, treats them to a gallon of vodka, and they drink and shout 'Hurrah!' and when they are drunk bow down to his feet. A change of life for the better and being well fed and idle develop in a Russian the most insolent self-conceit. Nikolay Ivanovich, who at one time in the government office was afraid to have any views of his own, now could say nothing that was not gospel truth, and uttered such truths in the tone of a prime minister. 'Education is essential, but for the peasants it is premature.' 'Corporal punishment is harmful as a rule, but in some cases it is necessary and there is nothing to take its place.'

" 'I know the peasants and understand how to treat them,' he would say. 'The peasants like me. I need only to hold up my little finger and the peasants will do anything I like.'

"And all this, observe, was uttered with a wise, benevolent smile. He repeated twenty times over 'We noblemen,' 'I as a noble'; obviously he did not remember that our grandfather was a peasant, and our father a soldier. Even our surname Chimsha-Himalaisky, in reality so incongruous, seemed to him now melodious, distinguished, and very agreeable.

"But the point just now is not he, but myself. I want to tell you about the change that took place in me during the brief hours I spent at his country place. In the evening, when we were drinking tea, the cook put on the table a plateful of gooseberries. They were not bought, but his own gooseberries, gathered for the first time since the bushes were planted. Nikolay Ivanovich laughed and looked for a minute in silence at the gooseberries, with tears in his eyes; he could not speak for excitement. Then he put one gooseberry in his mouth, looked at me with the triumph of a child who has at last received his favorite toy, and said:

" 'How delicious!'

"And he ate them greedily, continually repeating, 'Ah, how delicious! Do taste them!'

"They were sour and unripe, but, as Pushkin says:

> *Dearer to us the falsehood that exalts*
> *Than hosts of baser truths.*

"I saw a happy man whose cherished dream was so obviously

fulfilled, who had attained his object in life, who had gained what he wanted, who was satisfied with his fate and himself. There is always, for some reason, an element of sadness mingled with my thoughts of human happiness, and, on this occasion, at the sight of a happy man I was overcome by an oppressive feeling that was close upon despair. It was particularly oppressive at night. A bed was made up for me in the room next to my brother's bedroom, and I could hear that he was awake, and that he kept getting up and going to the plate of gooseberries and taking one. I reflected how many satisfied, happy people there really are! What an overwhelming force it is! You look at life: the insolence and idleness of the strong, the ignorance and brutishness of the weak, incredible poverty all about us, overcrowding, degeneration, drunkenness, hypocrisy, lying . . . Yet all is calm and stillness in the houses and in the streets; of the fifty thousand living in a town, there is not one who would cry out, who would give vent to his indignation aloud. We see the people going to market for provisions, eating by day, sleeping by night, talking their silly nonsense, getting married, growing old, serenely escorting their dead to the cemetery; but we do not see and we do not hear those who suffer, and what is terrible in life goes on somewhere behind the scenes. . . Everything is quiet and peaceful, and nothing protests but mute statistics: so many people gone out of their minds, so many gallons of vodka drunk, so many children dead from malnutrition . . . And this order of things is evidently necessary; evidently the happy man only feels at ease because the unhappy bear their burden in silence, and without that silence happiness would be impossible. It's a case of general hypnotism. There ought to be behind the door of every happy, contented man someone standing with a hammer continually reminding him with a tap that there are unhappy people; that however happy he may be, life will show him her jaws sooner or later, trouble will come for him—disease, poverty, losses, and no one will see or hear, just as now he neither sees nor hears others. But there is no man with a hammer; the happy man lives at his ease, the trivial daily cares faintly agitate him like the wind in the aspen-tree—and all goes well.

"That night I realized that I, too, was happy and contented,"

Ivan Ivanovich went on, getting up. "I, too, at dinner and at the hunt liked to lay down the law on life and religion, and the way to manage the peasantry. I, too, used to say that science was light, that culture was essential, but for the simple people reading and writing was enough for the time. Freedom is a blessing, I used to say; we can no more do without it than without air, but we must wait a little. Yes, I used to talk like that, and now I ask, 'For what reason are we to wait?' " asked Ivan Ivanovich, looking angrily at Burkin. "Why wait, I ask you? What grounds have we for waiting? I shall be told, it can't be done all at once; every idea takes shape in life gradually, in its due time. But who is it says that? Where is the proof that it's right? You will fall back upon the natural order of things, the uniformity of phenomena; but is there order and uniformity in the fact that I, a living, thinking man, stand over a chasm and wait for it to close of itself, or to fill up with mud at the very time when perhaps I might leap over it or build a bridge across it? And again, wait for the sake of what? Wait till there's no strength to live? And meanwhile one must live, and one wants to live!

"I went away from my brother's early in the morning, and ever since then it has been unbearable for me to be among people. I am oppressed by peace and quiet; I am afraid to look at the windows, for there is no spectacle more painful to me now than the sight of a happy family sitting round the table drinking tea. I am old and am not fit for the struggle; I am not even capable of hatred; I can only grieve inwardly, feel irritated and vexed; but at night my head is hot from the rush of ideas, and I cannot sleep. . . Ah, if I were young!"

Ivan Ivanovich walked backwards and forwards in excitement, and repeated: "If I were young!"

He suddenly went up to Alehin and began pressing first one of his hands and then the other.

"Pavel Konstantinovich," he said in an imploring voice, "don't be calm and contented, don't let yourself be put to sleep! While you are young, strong, confident, be not weary in well-doing! There is no happiness, and there ought not to be; but if there is a meaning and an object in life, that meaning and object is not our happiness, but something greater and more rational. Do good!"

And all this Ivan Ivanovich said with a pitiful, imploring smile, as though he were asking him a personal favor.

Then all three sat in armchairs at different ends of the drawing-room and were silent. Ivan Ivanovich's story had not satisfied either Burkin or Alehin. When the generals and ladies gazed down from their gilt frames, looking in the dusk as though they were alive, it was dreary to listen to the story of the poor clerk who ate gooseberries. They felt inclined for some reason to talk about elegant people, about women. And their sitting in the drawing-room where everything—the chandeliers in their covers, the armchairs, and the carpet under their feet—reminded them that those very people who were now looking down from their frames had once moved about, sat, drunk tea in this room, and the fact that lovely Pelageya was moving noiselessly about was better than any story.

Alehin was fearfully sleepy; he had got up early, before three o'clock in the morning, to look after his work, and now his eyes were closing; but he was afraid his visitors might tell some interesting story after he had gone, and he lingered on. He did not go into the question whether what Ivan Ivanovich had just said was right and true. His visitors did not talk of groats, nor or hay, nor of tar, but of something that had no direct bearing on his life, and he was glad and wanted them to go on.

"It's bedtime, though," said Burkin, getting up. "Allow me to wish you good night."

Alehin said good night and went downstairs to his own domain, while the visitors remained upstairs. They were both taken for the night to a big room where there stood two old wooden beds decorated with carvings, and in the corner was an ivory crucifix. The big cool beds, which had been made by the lovely Pelageya, smelt agreeably of clean linen.

Ivan Ivanovich undressed in silence and got into bed.

"Lord forgive us sinners!" he said, and put his head under the quilt.

His pipe lying on the table smelt strongly of stale tobacco, and Burkin could not sleep for a long while, and kept wondering where the oppressive smell came from.

The rain was pattering on the windowpanes all night.

Critical Commentary on *Gooseberries*

As narrator of the story-within-the-story, Ivan Ivanovich has two major roles to play in "Gooseberries." Initially, Chekhov presents him as one of the four characters who are brought together on the farm known as Sofino and who supply the narrative movement of the outer story. After a few pages, however, Ivan is placed in the foreground, and from this point on, he commands the reader's interest with his melancholy account of Nikolay. Chekhov thus achieves a semblance of "esthetic distance" or objectivity for his authorial purposes; and he creates in Ivan a complex protagonist. Taken together these roles subtly extend Chekhov's view of man's tendency to delude himself about his apathetic relation to society and, on occasion, to suffer remorse for his deception. Even though Nikolay is the subject of the monologue, we are less concerned with his problems than with Ivan's reactions to them. "But the point just now," he himself reminds us, "is not he, but myself. I want to tell you about the change that took place in me during the brief hours I spent at his country place."

The change is his repudiation of human happiness, which he can no longer regard as anything other than a false, hypnotic state. Like Nikolay's greedy appetite for gooseberries, he thinks, well-being is a selfish mirage. The man who believes himself happy "lives at his ease, the trivial daily cares agitate him like the wind in the aspen-tree—and all goes well." Indifferent to the fact that the fruit is sour and unripe, Nikolay is so "satisfied with his fate and himself" that he has no real love or charity for those less materially fortunate. Like the pigs with which he is compared, Nikolay wallows in self-contentment and apathy. Observing his brother, Ivan suddenly discovers his own notions of happiness have been equally delusory and void of altruism. The discovery is almost more than he can bear, for he feels that he is now too old for sharing, for "good works." Consequently, in pleading with Alehin to "Do good!" Ivan is both accusing himself and abrogating a responsibility he and Nikolay had failed to assume. Without concern for "something greater and more rational," the good of others, human happiness as bitterly seen by Ivan is no more than complacent self-interest.

The tragic source of his pessimism, then, is the belated knowledge that he is as self-deceptive as all people who profess happiness. The faults which he had attributed to Nikolay are also his and those of mankind in general. This revelation, however, gives Ivan no more than a partial understanding of himself, for he continues to be the victim of self-deception. As in *dramatic irony*, Ivan is unable to estimate himself as fully as the reading audience is able to do. Even before the visit to Nikolay's farm, he had preached a doctrine of social action. "To retreat from town, from the struggle, from the bustle of life, to retreat and bury oneself in one's farm—it's not life, it's egoism, laziness, it's monasticism of a sort, but monasticism without good works."

To mourn that, at the time of the narration in Sofino, he is too old to enter into the struggle, is to rationalize his lifelong apathy. In fact, he had always been egoistic and aloof from human problems. Witness, for example, his occupation as veterinary surgeon, a calling dissociated from such matters as equality and freedom. Like Nikolay, Ivan has always loved the land for the personal happiness it brings him. The attitude is *foreshadowed* in the opening paragraph, and then made explicit in his sensuous enjoyment at the millpond. Yet, in the latter scene, his exclamation of piety conveys the feeling of guilt aroused by such simple, natural pleasure. Again, in the conclusion, the fearful prayer—"Lord forgive us sinners!"—is that of a guilt-ridden man. Each instance is accompanied by a symbolic act of withdrawal: Ivan's presumably futile attempt to touch bottom in the pond; his burying his head under the quilt.

Of the four exterior characters in "Gooseberries," only Ivan would satisfy the requirements of "roundness." That is, he is dynamic and central. Only he undergoes change and only his motivation is the issue. The other characters are "flat," important not for themselves but for the ways in which they complement Ivan or are in contrast with him. Although as static, supporting figures—deliberately shown by Chekhov on a plane surface—their significant traits are general rather than personal, they are nevertheless essential to the structure of the story. In addition, Nikolay must be regarded as a minor character who even more than the others helps us to understand Ivan. The presentation of Ivan and those about him is implicit, for they emerge out of a gradual accumulation of suggestive details rather than from overt, conclusive portraiture. The motif of self-deception, fully explored in Ivan, is decipherable in fragmentary form—though unaccompanied by the sense of guilt—as we meet the lesser characters.

Coming from the same peasant origins, both Ivan and Nikolay have rejected their pasts. Each aspires to an ideal of "freedom," and each misuses the ideal. But Nikolay's revolt from the past— granted that it is thoroughly unadmirable—is plain and open. He has sought freedom for himself alone, treating his own servants in an arrogant, aristocratic fashion. His egoism, then, underscores the self-deception of the elder brother, for Ivan had professed sensitivity to humane relationships long before the change incidental to visiting his brother. Yet, recognizing the faults of selfishness and repressiveness, he ignores them until too late. First, he had mouthed platitudes about individual rights, but—like his brother—had felt superior to the peasants, of whom he was one. Then, with revelation, he resorts to the retreat of nerveless pessimism and evaded responsibility.

As readers, we understand what Ivan does not: that pessimism is his way of rationalizing apathetic inaction (which is perhaps no worse than his brother's escape from responsibility) and guilt (which his brother has never felt). Thus, Nikolay has fulfilled his aims, no matter how narrow they are, while Ivan has condemned himself to frustration and despair because he cannot abide the revaluation of the standards by which he has lived. His delayed recognition of failure is attached to a pessimistic denial of happiness. Furthermore, this awareness has not brought wisdom, only more self-deception, the delusion of what he might have done if he were young again.

The remaining characters enlighten the reader further about Ivan's character and at the same time counterbalance his extreme pessimism. Alehin, for example, is of the landed gentry, and yet he works alongside his peasants in simple, unaffected dignity. One infers Ivan's mild contempt—or at least disapproval—that a gentleman should toil like a peasant. And Ivan's vigorous bathing is, in part, an unspoken reproach, a vestige perhaps of his own aristocratic yearnings as well as a repudiation of the peasant state. Like Alehin, Burkin does not speculate about what is unpleasant or what might have been; and he chooses to face life as he sees it on the surface. It is he who tells Ivan he has been in the millpond long enough and who brings him back to his discourse with the dry, realistic remark, "That's a story from a different opera." It is also he who thinks enough time has been spent in storytelling. And then there is the serenely passive, beautiful servant Pelageya, who "was better than any story," a story Alehin and Burkin do not especially care to hear.

In these three—Alehin, Burkin, and Pelageya—Chekhov represents three elements of Russian society, from high to low, whose contentment is a tacit rejection of Ivan's misanthropic attitude. And yet, we are not obliged to assume that Ivan's judgment is incorrect. All three, after all, accept life as it is, without troubling themselves about such matters as vex Ivan. In the comfortable environment of Sofino, indeed, it is difficult to share his dark view. Certainly, the fine ladies and gentlemen in the portraits are alien to the pessimistic tale of Nikolay. Pelageya gives every sign of a servant class that is well treated. After hard, honest work, Alehin is not satisfied with an exceedingly realistic story that tells of a sordid and, possibly, unfamiliar side of life. Nor is Burkin, who is oppressed by Nikolay's greed even as he is by the fact of Ivan's stale tobacco.

Most people, Chekhov seems to say, are like Alehin, "who did not go into the question whether what Ivan Ivanovich had just said was right and true." Alehin does not enjoy the account of delusive happiness, but he listens disinterestedly because it has no bearing on his life. To be sure, the recalled elegance of those who once lived in his house or the attractive presence of Pelageya would be preferable subjects. Even the depressing story, however, serves to take his mind off the day's routine. It is for him a story and nothing else; he feels no commitment to another man's problems. Burkin similarly wishes to remain aloof. In this sense, Alehin and Burkin are further evidence of the selfishness exemplified in Ivan's story.

Although Chekhov avoids stating absolute conclusions, he implies agreement with Ivan that no man should think happiness is a true condition as long as he fails to exercise an altruistic attitude. Too many of us tend to assume that because we enjoy personal tranquillity, we can dissociate ourselves from concerns that do not seem to touch us. Happy lives may be "like still weather, when all nature seemed mild and dreamy." But it is folly to ignore the threat of storm. Human happiness is transitory, but at least we fulfill our own lives when we think of those of others.

CHAPTER 3

Plot

WHEN Aristotle defined the meaning and func-
tion of plot, he was thinking of the Greek drama—especially tragic
drama—of his day. But what he had to say is applicable to prose
fiction as well. Now, more than 2,000 years later, we still respect his
authority while allowing for the cultural-esthetic gap between his
age and ours. Plot, he said, "is the *imitation* of the action:—for by
plot I here mean the arrangement of the incidents." Reduced to its
simplest elements, plot is indeed "the arrangement of the incidents."
The action with which we are concerned in fiction is not a copy of
real action. It is, rather, a symbolic representation of probable or
credible occurrences. The action is such as we might expect to take
place under a given set of circumstances posited by the author, and
it lends itself to meanings consistent with the author's view of experience. So regarded, plot has its own surface interests and sur-
prises; but its end in serious fiction is to disclose the interior meaning and to convey an interpretation, not a direct statement, of experience.

The *selection* and *arrangement*—the ordering—of the incidents
of the plot continues to be of great importance, for interpretation is
based upon a process of intelligent and imaginative discrimination.
That in life which is extraneous or irrelevant to large issues must
be set aside by the author. That which is significant must be identified, enlarged, ordered—even reordered—and juxtaposed to proper
associations. Again, Aristotle is instructive: "For Tragedy," he
says, "is an imitation, not of men, but of an action and of life—of
happiness and misery; and happiness and misery consist in action,

the end of human life being a mode of action, not a quality. Now the characters of men determine their qualities, but it is by their actions that they are happy or the reverse." The actions of a plot must be associated in such a way, given such continuity, as will reveal "happiness and misery." More broadly and explicitly, the actions must be given relationships which illuminate life; it is the writer's self-appointed task to isolate and then harmonize the meaningful connections.

We can no longer agree with Aristotle, however, that "most important of all is the structure of the incidents." Actions in which men engage—no matter how salutary or destructive—are seldom more important than the men themselves. Primary attention to universal moral issues is consistent with Aristotle's view of a general world-order. Today, however, the place of the individual in that order tends to take precedence in our attention over large, widely embracing concepts. We are inclined, that is, to narrow and particularize our concerns, and to think of the ways in which individuals have been affected or are likely to be affected by the world about them. The shift is one of emphasis rather than of value.

It is not necessarily that we elevate the man above his social group or his environment. And it is not even that ultimately we have a greater respect for the microcosmic personality than for the vast organization of which he is part. Rather, man *qua* man has become more interesting to us, perhaps as a matter of simple self-identification, perhaps as the result of growing awareness of human complexity. The sum of the actions—the plot—need not be less interesting than the people in the plot. But as readers who are prepared to share the complexities of the human condition set forth in fiction, we are generally even more responsive to people than to things and actions.

To shift Aristotle's initial emphasis from plot to character is thus reasonable for the contemporary reader; and it is a shift which has been practiced with increased frequency in the last hundred or so years of fictional development. Plot, in the best fiction, will work harmoniously with character. As W. Somerset Maugham advises, plot will give direction to our curiosity about characters. "It is," he says, "a natural desire in the reader to want to know what happens to the people in whom his interest has been aroused and the plot is the means by which you gratify this desire. . . . It should have coherence and sufficient probability for the needs of the theme; it should be of a nature to display the development of character, which is the chief concern of fiction at the present day, and it should have completeness, so that when it is finally unfolded no more questions can be asked about the persons who took part in it."

As a storyteller in the classical sense, Maugham places more emphasis upon the "completeness" of a story—the beginning, middle, and end insisted upon by Aristotle—than do a good many other contemporary writers. We may, in fact, admire this kind of completeness because it satisfies a need in us to see things through to their resolutions. The position taken by Maugham, however, may seem old-fashioned to a generation brought up on fiction in which self-evident resolutions are no longer regarded as imperative.

Concepts of what fiction should do change all the time in answer to the concerns of the ages which give birth to them. Thus, it is possible to enjoy a "complete" novel—one in which there is a satisfying resolution—but also to enjoy another one which is closer to the unsettled urgencies of our own age. The "existentialists" (e.g., Albert Camus, Jean-Paul Sartre, Samuel Beckett, Gabriel Fielding) or the "angry young men" (e.g., Kingsley Amis, Alan Sillitoe, John Braine) dedicate themselves, indeed, to a resolution that there can really be no resolution. For that matter, some of the same inconclusive strain is at times evident in older writers like Aldous Huxley and Evelyn Waugh. If novels like Maugham's *Of Human Bondage* answer all the questions we wish to ask, other novels may fulfill an equally valuable function in forcing us to ask our own questions and even to answer them. Hemingway, Faulkner, or Durrell, for instance, leave a burden upon their readers to a certain extent, but we do not admire them the less for it.

In any event, the committed reader participates in the fictional experience. Toward this end, Maugham points out, the plot "is a line to direct the reader's interest. That is possibly the most important thing in fiction, for it is by direction of interest that the author carries the reader along from page to page and it is by direction of interest that he induces in him the mood he desires. The author always loads his dice, but he must never let the reader see that he has done so, and by the manipulation of his plot he can engage the reader's attention so that he does not perceive what violence has been done him."

We readers become personally absorbed in the consequences of an action to a person or to a group of people. Our response, then, is likely to be an identifying, affective one causing us to feel affinity to certain of the characters, and to others pity, aversion, or some other emotion regulated by the author. Writers plant the basic emotions into their delineations of plot and character, but it is up to the reader—granted that the novelist has done his work well—whether those emotions will be brought to maximum fruition. The author-reader partnership has been well stated by Laurence Sterne, who, for all his eccentricities of manner, was never indifferent to it.

> Writing, when properly managed, (as you may be sure I think mine is) is but a different name for conversation: As no one, who knows what he is about in good company, would venture to talk all;—so no author, who understands the just boundaries of decorum and good breeding, would presume to think all: The truest respect which you can pay to the reader's understanding, is to halve this matter amicably, and leave him something to imagine, in his turn, as well as yourself.

All art is conscious, and nowhere in the art of fiction is the conscious impulse more apparent than in the construction of plot. Novels produced by widely separated talents and purposes enable us to recognize that there can be nothing accidental in the architecture of plot. Although some artists scorn critical explanations of their work, demonstrable results of the creative process attest to their technical care. Any good novel reflects the author's need to order and manage his materials, to fuse them coherently, harmoniously, and persuasively into a progression from cause to effect. The importance of conscious rendering is further clarified by those novelists who are not reluctant to speak about their techniques. The value of such statements is enhanced when otherwise discrete writers subscribe to related theories of fictional intent.

As we have already seen, Maugham speculates that plot is the author's way of directing interest, his theory strongly implying full authorial awareness of what goes into plot and where the plot is going. Elizabeth Bowen, whose fiction is most unlike Maugham's, has a comparable sense of her duty to advance plot and know how it must be advanced. "Plot," she says, "is the knowing of destination," the means by which the matter of fiction is moved. She goes on to note, "Plot must not cease to move forward. . . . The *actual* speed of movement must be even. *Apparent* variations in speed are good, necessary, but there must be no actual variations in speed. To obtain those apparent variations is part of the illusion—task of the novel. Variations in texture can be made to give the effect of variations in speed. Why are *apparent* variations in speed necessary? For the sake of internal evenness, for its own sake. Perfection of evenness = perfection of control. The tautness of the taut string is equal (or even) all along and at any part of the string's length."

Miss Bowen clearly goes far beyond Maugham in her rational analysis of plot control, although both agree that such conscious control is necessary. Where Maugham generalizes pleasantly, Miss Bowen shrewdly particularizes on the plot as a vehicle between author and reader. Control and progression are uppermost in her mind. The happenings of a novel must always move "towards an end not to be foreseen (by the reader) but also towards an end which, having *been* reached, must be seen to have been from the start inevitable." The plot, she insists, must be reasoned. Her notion of "completeness" is less rigidly prescribed than Maugham's, but it is also more profound in its implications. And she is at least as rigorous in her attitude toward providing answers to questions which she has raised about her fictional characters. Miss Bowen, in short, probes more deeply, searches more acutely for the hidden cause or motive; yet she is always conscious of her obligation to command and direct the reader's attention and interest. Thus, she exploits tension, surprise, and movement, controlling fluidity of narrative and the illusion of time related to action.

Plot and character, then, are correlatives, organically inseparable. They thrive, as the above passage implies, on paradoxical conditions of inevitability (which is hardly distinguishable from probability or credibility) and illusion. The paradox is one which can be reconciled only in art, for art insists upon identifying its materials with "reality"—insofar as the artistic situation has a source in experience—and upon transfiguring that reality or experience through imagination and invention. Thus, a novel will never be a precise report of experience, but it may seem to be: it could happen that way and, because the novelist has prepared us to accept his vision or interpretation, we are not outraged by a disparity between reality and illusion. Indeed, the successful novelist has given us a new understanding of reality. Experience, it should be noted, consists as much in reflections upon life as it does in physical manifestations.

The need to reconsider and transfigure reality, to combine in the new reality that which is actually experienced and that which is imagined, is well represented in Henry James. "I have always fondly remembered," he wrote, "a remark that I heard fall years ago from the lips of Ivan Turgenev in regard to his own experience of the usual origin of the fictive picture. It began for him almost always with the vision of some person or persons, who hovered before him, soliciting him, as the active or passive figure, interesting him and appealing to him just as they were and by what they were. He saw them, in that fashion, as *disponibles* [at his disposal; available], saw them subject to the chances, the complications of existence, and saw them vividly, but then had to find for them the right relations, those that would most bring them out; to imagine, to invent and select and piece together the situations most useful and favourable to the sense of the creatures themselves, the complications they would be most likely to produce and feel."

A Turgenev tale (and, similarly, one by James), according to this account, brings the actual and the imagined into such close conjunction that the differences vanish and a wholly new experience emerges. As in most modern fiction, character was of primary interest to Turgenev, but it was an interest to be shown only in connection with plot. He told James: "If I watch them [the characters] long enough I see them come together, I see them *placed*, I see them engaged in this or that act and in this or that difficulty. How they look and move and speak and behave, always in the setting I have found for them, is my account of them." Turgenev, that is, did not repudiate reality and experience. Rather, he improvised upon them, shaped them to exemplify something he had to say in terms of action and character.

In *The Portrait of a Lady* (the preface to which contains the remarks on Turgenev) and other novels, James practices the same kind of refined actuality: a character is *seen* and then *placed* in situations created by the novelist. Reality obviously contributes, or there would be no credibility. But the novelist must select, transfigure, and order those views of reality that he wishes to use fictionally. "As regards plot," Ivy Compton-Burnett complains, "I find real life no help at all. Real life seems to have no plots." The complaint, it must be assumed, is a whimsical one, for if life provided plots—contrived, interrelated, ordered—then the novelist would not have novels to write, only experiences to report.

Life is the source of the raw materials. Drawing upon this store the fiction-writer then supplies imagination, intelligence, and emotional attitudes, the creative tools for shaping a structure of people and incidents. It is up to the novelist to find for his characters "the right relations, those that would most bring them out; to imagine, to invent and select and piece together the situations most useful and favourable to the sense of the creatures themselves, the complications they would be most likely to produce and feel."

Ordinary life as experienced by most individuals is comprised of sequential events varying in magnitude and significance. Although they may not be related to each other by any perceptible logic, they are related in time. The individual is aware of successive events taking place during the passing moments of his own day; yet he does not customarily identify them with events taking place simultaneously in the next street or house or room. A man entering his car to keep an appointment does not know that at this very instant his friend, on his way to the same appointment, has slipped on an icy sidewalk and broken a leg. What matters to the average individual at each moment is the occurrence—trivial, singular, significant—within his conscious range. The meaning of each event, if it is to be assessed by the individual, comes more gradually—unless, of course, the import is immediate and obviously worth evaluation. Even a planned routine is subject to interruption, but we seldom anticipate the interruption.

Forster was thinking of the steady flow of activities marking normal experience when he distinguished *story* from *plot*. A story, he wrote (in *Aspects of the Novel*), "is a narrative of events arranged in their time-sequence—dinner coming after breakfast, Tuesday after Monday, decay after death, and so on." These are successions in time for which we have been prepared by experience, "and what the story does is to relate the life in time." Time-sequence Forster states to be "the lowest and simplest of literary organisms." He concedes that "in daily life the allegiance [to time] may not be necessary: we do not know, and the experience of certain mystics suggests, indeed, that it is not necessary, and that we are quite mistaken in supposing that Monday is followed by Tuesday, or death by decay. It is always possible for you and me in daily life to deny that time exists and act accordingly even if we become un-intelligible and are sent by our fellow citizens to what they choose to call a lunatic asylum."

The novelist, however, may never "deny time inside the fabric of his novel: he must cling however lightly to the thread of his story." Time, then, when translated from normal experience to fiction becomes "the highest factor common to all the very complicated organisms known as novels." Forster's insistence upon time-awareness—upon some kind of chronology—may appear to preclude unconventional treatments of the "time-sense" we find in fiction-writers like Sterne, Joyce, Mrs. Woolf, Proust, Conrad, Ford Madox Ford, Conrad Aiken, and many others. Time—like character, action, and place—after all connects experience with fiction. It should be noted, therefore, that there may be apparent variations in time-sequence (even as Miss Bowen allows for apparent variations in the speed or movement of plot). But actual time-sequence—regardless of structural organization—must exist within the novel. A novelist may have special, justifiable reasons for treating time-sequence in an unexpected manner, but its permanent abandonment is alien to human experience and desire for order.

For Forster, the inclusion of values and causality distinctively elevate plot over mere story. "A plot is also a narrative of events, the emphasis falling on causality. 'The king died and then the queen died,' is a story. 'The king died, and then the queen died of grief,' is a plot. The time-sequence is preserved, but the sense of causality overshadows it. Or again: 'The queen died, no one knew

why, until it was discovered that it was through grief at the death
of the king.' This is a plot with a mystery in it, a form capable of
high development. It suspends the time-sequence, it moves as far
away from the story as its limitations will allow. Consider the death
of the queen. If it is in a story we say 'and then?' If it is in a plot
we ask 'why?' That is the fundamental difference between these
two aspects of the novel. A plot cannot be told to a gaping audience of cave men or to a tyrannical sultan or to their modern descendant, the movie-public. They can only be kept awake by 'and
then—and then—' they can only supply curiosity. But a plot demands intelligence and memory also." As is true for Maugham, the
plot must reveal answers to certain questions which it has raised.
As is true for all good novelists, the plot must have the reader's interested participation. Ultimately, the effects must emerge from
causes; they must convey meanings which have acquired symbolic
support from plot and character.

Although every novelist must determine his own strategy for fulfilling his aims as a writer of fiction, his strategy embraces certain
principles shared by all writers of fiction. That is, each fictional
intention is promoted by a plot and by characters, but—as we have
already seen in relation to characters, and now will see in relation
to plot—the kinds of plots and characters are dictated by the artistic
need which first impelled the creative act. "Plot," says Miss Bowen,
"might seem to be a matter of choice (and the same is so of character). It is not. The particular plot for the particular novel is something the novelist is driven to. It is what is left after the whittling-
away of alternatives. The novelist is confronted, at a moment . . .
by the impossibility of saying what is to be said in any other way."

Contingent upon his artistic need, the novelist creates a narrative
situation whose action is dynamic—i.e., forward-moving—and generally *complicated* in such a manner as to cause surprise and (for
some authors) necessitate *resolution*. Plot intricacies (for example,
subplots)—not for their own sakes but for the illumination and emphasis they contribute to the controlling purpose of the novel—engage the critical reader's emotions and intelligence. But such intricacies as the novelist chooses to employ must eventually come
to a head, or *climax*. Thereafter, whether the unraveling is explicitly

described or implicitly suggested, the events must be concluded in a manner which will not outrage credibility.

Furthermore—and perhaps most urgently—the novelist is engrossed in the *conflict* between opposed characters, forces or wills. Conflict in narrative, as in life, is a principle upon whose outcome depends success or failure, victory or defeat. We are keenly aware of the fictional struggle and in all likelihood identify our hopes with those of the contestant who has our sympathy. The conflict may be an inner one, within a single character; it may be an external one, between a character and his society or environment, or between two characters—the protagonist and antagonist. In any event, the conflict entails a clash of forces, characters, or wills—intellectually, physically, emotionally. The clash initiates and heightens tension, creating *suspense* while the outcome is awaited.

Not all novelists, of course, feel an obligation to exploit with equal intensity the elements touched upon in the preceding paragraph. Camus in his brief novel *The Stranger*, for example, has created a protagonist who is passive toward all external events and in whom, consequently, conflict is nonexistent. Nevertheless, he is an object of outside conflicting forces if he is not one of the conflicting forces himself. His emotional and intellectual dormancy does not preclude suspense, climax, and resolution (or at least finality): he initiates these by his mere presence; he cannot be said to be a source of dynamic action except insofar as he exists and commits an inexplicable crime.

Kafka in his novel *The Trial* similarly has created a character who is a protagonist by virtue of his existence. What happens, happens around him and to him but not overtly because of him. K's conflict is less passive than Meursault's, but it never—except for his confusion and wonder—is made explicit, nor does it reach a resolution that is clear in the rational sense of that term. In either instance, the character is a fixed point, but one inevitably destroyed by a sequence of events which have little to do with his participation in them.

The kinds of plot are as variable as the application of plot materials just discussed. They range from the most simple structural organization to the most complex, from externalized, strict chronology to the indirection of time-shifts and stream-of-consciousness. Each fictional development has its own values and is to be judged in terms of its relevance. What, we ask, has the author attempted to do? And has he been successful in relating form to intention? Complexity for its own sake is not to be praised.

One of the most familiar kinds of plot is that which we may call *linear*. This is a form which resembles the unfolding of a stage-play and proceeds, generally, in a chronological fashion. As in the drama, this conventional plot lays an expository foundation (to explain events or people prior to the opening of the narration), and then advances the action with appropriate complications upward toward the climax. After the climax, the action descends—probably swiftly—toward the resolution. Thus we have rising action and falling action.

Linear plot is, in its simplest construction, laid out on the narrative surface. The novelist, that is, presents all essential details overtly and explicitly: action, characters, motivation, conflict, and so on, are set forth in such a way that narrative and theme are clearly before the reader. The result is one of cumulative effects and advancing narration. Such a process in the hands of a consummate artist like, say, Jane Austen, may be profoundly engaging for the reader, even though there are few gaps for him to bridge, few hints for him to make concrete. We know everything about Emma that we need to know—her background, family loyalties, her meddling in the lives of others, and the consequences. Linear plot, for all its seeming simplicity, may be an exacting imaginative and technical form. It is the narrative form most nearly akin to the customary view of life, for it takes maximum advantage of time-sequence.

We may agree in this connection with George Eliot's remark, that "the only true stories life presents to us in an orderly way are those of our autobiography, or the careers of our companions from our childhood upwards, or perhaps of our own children. But it is a great art to make a connected strictly relevant narrative of such careers as we can recount from the beginning." This is the method described by Sterne (borrowing from Horace) as *ab ovo*. Additionally, chronological directness makes for an interpretive vehicle which may penetrate the complexities of cause and effect. For instance, Ar-

nold Bennett in *The Old Wives' Tale* begins his novel with the lives
of two sisters in conjunction, separates them, traces their lives separately, and then after a long span of years brings them together
again.

Obviously, no plot can or should account for every moment in
the life of a protagonist. Irrelevancies obstruct the view of what is
important, thinning out the narrative and weakening the reader's
interest. Many novelists, therefore, block out their materials in
units of meaningful dramatic actions, in *scenes* which emphasize effects and values, while assuming that the reader will prefer to ignore details not reasonably relevant to the intention. Henry James,
though an indifferent dramatist, reveals in his fiction a brilliant
grasp of dramatically scenic highlights.

Discussing his own practice in *What Maisie Knew*, James wrote:
"Going over the pages here placed together has been for me, at all
events, quite to watch the scenic system at play. The treatment of
'scene,' regularly, quite rhythmically occurs; the intervals, the massing of the elements to a different effect and by quite other law, remain, in this fashion, all preparative, just as the scenic occasions
in themselves become, at a given moment illustrative, each of the
agents, true to its function, taking up the theme from the other very
much as the fiddles, in an orchestra, may take it up from the cor-
nets, flutes, or the wind instruments take it up from the violins. The
point, however, is that the scenic passages are *wholly* and logically
scenic, having for their rules of beauty the principle of the 'conduct,' the organic development, of a scene—the entire succession
of values that flower and bear fruit on ground solidly laid for them.
The great advantage for the total effect is that we feel, with the
definite alteration, how the theme *is* being treated."

James and other novelists who employ a scenic treatment assign
the major effects to dramatic moments rather than to all moments.
The moments between—the "intervals"—link the scenes and pre-
pare us for them. The scenes are complete units of action, though
not self-sufficient. They depend on what precedes and what follows, contributing cumulatively to the values or meanings and effects that the author intends to impart through the entire novel.
Willa Cather maintained that scenic usage is all-important, al-

though she insisted more specifically than James that its essence is emotional. "The 'scene' in fiction is not a mere matter of construction, any more than it is in life. When we have a vivid experience in social intercourse, pleasant or unpleasant, it records itself in our memory in the form of a scene; and when it flashes back to us, all sorts of apparently unimportant details are flashed back with it."

The kind of writer Miss Cather admired and the kind she aspired to become creates scenes intensively to represent strong or revelatory experiences in which he participates with his characters. Only scenic writing, as she described it, could produce the emotional, pictorial depth she esteemed. It would have been interesting to get her reaction to Lawrence or Durrell, whose technical practice accords very closely with her theory but whose thematic interests are entirely at variance with her own. Durrell's narrative evocation of decaying Alexandrian life in *Justine* undoubtedly would be unpleasant for her taste. Nevertheless, Durrell builds upon a succession of scenes in the way she admired. His vivid social and emotional experience "records itself in our memory in the form of a scene; and when it flashes back to us, all sorts of apparently unimportant details are flashed back with it."

In the early history of the novel, before the dramatic possibilities of fiction were fully realized, plots tended to move along a horizontal rather than a gradually rising line. Novelists were more concerned with entertainment to be supplied by rapid action—or with outright edification by series of exempla—than with symbolic values or meanings of action. Development of character was less appealing to early audiences of fiction than adventures and escapades. Or, as the concept of the novel grew more serious, loosely related pieces of action became a means of asserting moral purpose, again with less regard to the way a protagonist might be affected than to abstract principles of justice, humanity, and the like. Such novels could be called linear only by the most liberal construction of that term. More accurately they were *episodic*.

Now an episodic plot is one consisting of episodes loosely held together, generally deriving such unity as it may have from a central character or two and a rudimentary situation. Episodes—unlike the scenes of a Jamesian novel—are largely self-sufficient. That is, blocks of action, each complete in itself, are yoked one after the other without necessarily arriving at a climax. Ingenuity and variety of action are all. Such novels, presumably, could go on indefinitely, their stopping point determined not by the solution of a problem but by the limits of the author's imagination. The episodes—as in Alain-René Le Sage's *picaresque* novel *Gil Blas*—have no very serious or probable causal relationship with the other episodes, nor any compelling reasons for their particular location within the novel's structure.

With maturing literary tastes, entertainment and edification were implanted in dramatically constructed linear plots; or episodic plots became both more subtle and flexible, verging upon the linear kind. The weakness of episodic storytelling was traced as long ago as Aristotle to the desire for mere entertainment or to artistic ineptitude. "Of all plots and actions," he stated, "the epeisodic are the worst. I call a plot 'epeisodic' in which the episodes or acts succeed one another without probable or necessary sequence."

Many good novelists, however, have managed to build novels upon episodes which, delineating conflict, ultimately develop character and meaning. In the strict Aristotelian sense, to be sure, these authors are not writing episodic novels as such. Thus, Daniel Defoe used a series of self-contained episodes to propagate Moll Flanders' moral and economic conflict, and through them fixed her failure and redemption. Henry Fielding's *Joseph Andrews* and *Tom Jones*, Tobias Smollett's *Roderick Random*, have bead-like successions of episodes. But these episodes contain the ascending properties of conflict and climax, as well as satisfying if not necessarily reasonable resolutions. Mark Twain made Huck Finn an unforgettable human being through the medium of episodes in series. In modern times Saul Bellow has done the same for Augie March and Willa Cather for Bishop Latour.

Of Fielding and Smollett, especially, it could be argued that their episodes are only loosely probable, that sequence or causal relationships are forced, not inevitable. The artistic skill of these writers is such, however, that, working close to the picaresque, episodic mode, they nevertheless achieved completeness of character, action, and meaning. Twain, Bellow, and Cather, infinitely better versed in the art and technique of fiction, achieved large dramatic effects in single episodes, but subordinated these units to the harmonious effects and values of their total structures.

A novel like Dickens' *Pickwick Papers* more closely resembles the now discredited episodic tradition. But Dickens, it should be recalled, had adapted his technique to the publishing fashion of his day. Writing the novel as a monthly serial, he found it useful to present each installment as a complete unit of action, bound only by the presence of the Pickwickians. (In other novels by him published under the same serial scheme, however—and this was true of other novelists as well: e.g., Thackeray—the episodic effects were ultimately centralized with the appearance of the whole novel; causality—the rising results of conflict—finally imbued each episode with the serious controlling purpose of the whole.)

The episodic method as used by most novelists in the last few hundred years can be artistically advantageous. That is, it can be justified in terms of massed narrative effects which are a part of the even larger effects of the total work of fiction. Each segment of *Huckleberry Finn*, for instance, offers an illusion of completeness. Each reveals a dominant aspect of Huck's personality and his ability to cope with the crises confronting him. Individual episodes run their course, from beginning to end, and have a capacity for particularized interest. Their massing of details, if the artist has worked well—as Twain has—enables the reader to linger over implications almost as though he were reading short stories.

At the same time, it is understood that these implications are not isolated from the main structure but are a contributory element of it. It is understood, in other words, that no episode is conclusive, that each is contributing in a progressive manner to the total effect. When Anthony Trollope says, therefore, "There should be no episodes in a novel," we think he must be mistaken or, at least, is over-zealous in his formal requirements of the novel. In fact, he appears to be so insistent upon a linear plot development as to disqualify any other form. "Every sentence, every word, through all those pages, should tend to the telling of the story." That, of course, is one important way of writing a novel, but not the only way.

Trollope regards as episodic *any* fictional element (including dialogue) which is not clearly and directly relevant. We may question his taste and literary judgment in deploring certain bypaths of Cervantes and Fielding. But he is critically correct in terming as episodes their respective interior tales "*Curioso Impertinente*" (accepting the common mistranslation, "The Curious Impertinent") and "The History of the Man of the Hill." Narrative detours such as those by Cervantes and Fielding (which are defensible) may, indeed, disrupt the main flow of the plot, and for one hostile to an episodic structure the fault is serious.

Trollope's preference for complex, linear plotting is summed up in the statement: "Though his story should be all one, yet it may have many parts. Though the plot itself may require but few characters, it may be so enlarged as to find its full development in many. There may be subsidiary plots, which shall tend to the elucidation of the main story, and which will take their places as part of one and the same work—as there may be many figures on a canvas which shall not to the spectator seem to form themselves into separate pictures." Significant as a condensation of Trollope's critical views, these remarks also promote interesting speculation on the associated matters of relevance and digression.

What is or is not relevant can be determined only in the context of specific novels: stipulations, as always in creative matters, are not very helpful. Miss Bowen goes so far as to believe that relevance cannot be judged rationally, relying upon intuition as a means of checking whether certain details belong and are useful. While this may be true for the novelist, the critical reader needs something more than a sixth sense. He needs experience in reading a novel, of course, and sensitivity. But he also needs critical intelligence to determine that the novel contains nothing irrelevant to the development of character and plot, meaning and mood.

There must be nothing extraneous. For instance, dialogue which does not assist in the exemplification of character or furthering of plot is, as Miss Bowen says, "a cloud and a drag on, a weakener of the novel. It dilutes meaning. Relevance crystallizes meaning." Scenes must contain no elements which are not integral to the purpose of the novel. Details of place, descriptions, and so on must support or even foster the mood; they must have a bearing upon the action; they may, indeed, illuminate the expository elements of the novel. Textural matters introduced without relevance to the structure become digressive, supernumerary. Meanwhile, the reader should remember, relevance need not become immediately apparent. A good novel develops gradually and builds toward the conclusion. Thus, what appears to be irrelevant in the early chapters of a narrative may very well assert its relevance in the later ones.

Digressiveness without artistic purpose leads to esthetic failure. But digressions are often a valuable part of the author's intention, reflecting his desire to capture the interruptions and divergences that we experience in life. How often is a storyteller reminded of one incident while relating another? Or how often does an auditor break in on a conversation with matters either irrelevant or somehow parallel to the subject at hand? When an author consciously interrupts himself—if his interruption is aimed at a useful narrative purpose— he is not to be accused of irrelevance. Being out of sympathy with what he is doing, we may be irritated by the digression, but we have an obligation to understand, critically at least.

The digressions in a novel like *Tristram Shandy* are whimsical but not unconsciously so. Of his own, admittedly extreme, method, Sterne said: "Digressions, incontestably, are the sunshine;—they are the life, the soul of reading;—take them out of this book for instance,—you might as well take the book along with them;—one cold eternal winter would reign in every page of it; restore them to the writer;—he steps forth like a bridegroom,—and bids All hail; brings in variety, and forbids the appetite to fail." The digressions may be spasmodic parentheses in thought or conversation, like the drunken maunderings of Malcolm Lowry's Consul in *Under the Volcano*. They may be longer, coherent narrative asides—as in the story of La Fever (*Tristram Shandy*), "The Man of the Hill" (*Tom Jones*), "*Curioso Impertinente*" (*Don Quixote*). Or they may be extensive interruptions having closer affinities with the main story— as in Faulkner's *Intruder in the Dust* or *The Bear*. The point is that they are congruous with their respective authors' aims and hence belong.

The more sophisticated the art of fiction becomes, the more integral seeming digressions are. "A good novel," Ford Madox Ford

reminds us, "needs all the attention the reader can give it." But the
digression which is obviously so makes "a patch over which the
mind will progress heavily." The author must, Ford insists, "appear
to digress. This is the art which conceals your art. The reader, you
should premise, will always dislike you and your book. He thinks
it an insult that you should dare to claim his attention, and if lunch
is announced or there is a ring at the bell he will welcome the digression. So you will provide him with what he thinks are digressions—with occasions on which he thinks he may let his attention
relax. . . . But really not one single thread must ever escape your
purpose." If Ford appears to be unduly hostile toward, even con-
temptuous of, his audience, the issue is not altered. The novel is,
after all, between him and his readers. He digresses with purpose,
because this is his concept of the way fiction must be written.

The digressions, then, are only seeming ones, and the good
reader—that is, the attentive one—will be aware that he must not
really relax his attention or skip over what may later prove to be essential to the entire structure. Similarly, Sterne, Fielding, Thackeray,
Joyce, Proust—as well as all those authors who practice less sophisticated forms of digression—must be watched carefully lest we
trick ourselves into missing something vital.

One of the most skillful, seemingly digressive methods of plot is
the "time-shift," as employed by Ford and his friend Joseph Conrad. The device, notably employed in such novels as *The Good
Soldier* and *Lord Jim*, is also sometimes known as "looping chronology." It is based upon an assumption that strong narrative interest
does not necessarily follow an upward linear path. The novelist
who would use plot for the delineation of character must establish
a compelling attraction early in the novel. To do that, according to
Ford, "you must first get him with a strong impression, and then
work backwards and forwards over his past." This means deserting
chronology in its accepted sense and maneuvering normal time-
order. Time-sequence, as Forster insisted upon it, is still present.
But the novelist has let important pieces of action and reaction influence the organization of his book. That is, what happens at 10:00
a.m. and 3:00 p.m. may have a narrative interdependence; and
what happens at ten and three may then become clearer in the light

of what happened at 8:30 a.m., and so forth. Action temporarily, thus, loops forward and backward through time. At the conclusion, however, the whole action may be seen in proper time-order, from beginning to end, from cause to effect, with which it began.

"There is nothing startling in the method," Ford says. "It is that of every writer of workmanlike detective stories. . . . It is, in fact, indispensable to the detective-writer. He begins the story with the words: ' "He is dead," she said.' Then he gives some details of the past of him and her. He returns to the present to introduce the sleuths and the district attorney. The chief sleuth delves for pages into the past of him or her, going back thirty years to 'his' past in Muddy Creek or Pekin. He returns to lunch with the District Attorney who is trying to doublecross him and then back and back and back. . . . And back once more to the '15th March 19—'. Eventually the final clue is given, but something that happened in 1922, and you return to the present for half a page to dispose of the sleuth and the dashing young lady . . . that technique is identical with that of all modern novelists, or of myself. . . . Or Proust."

The "time-shift" is not the technique of all modern novelists, but its development has had a profound influence on the writing of fiction. The novel ceases to be a biographical-historical record and becomes a treatment of associated causes and effects. The detective-story technique then moves from the elemental thriller to the exploration of a character's innermost conflicts and their resolutions. This is what Ford does in *The Good Soldier* and Conrad in *Lord Jim*. As the treatment grows more intensive, or as the concern with the mind becomes more absorbing than with the external or public life, the "time-shift" may supersede though never entirely supplant normal time-order.

In *Mrs. Dalloway*, for instance, the reader is always aware of the passing of time through the symbolic tolling of Big Ben. But Mrs. Woolf sees simultaneous events in time as no average individual would, or she temporarily dissolves time in the consciousness of her characters, letting associations of ideas—stream-of-consciousness—prevail. Yet Big Ben never lets us forget the sequence of time. Even farther removed from the progression of time, writers like Sterne,

Joyce, and Proust seem to take their events and characters out of
time-order. Their "digressions," however, are for the purpose of emphasizing states of mind and emotions, not for that of denying actual continuity. The continuity in the writing of such novelists,
thus, is seen whole only when the novels are seen whole.

Another contrived disruption of continuity, for emotional or thematic emphasis, inheres in *anacoluthon*. Less familiar than other
seemingly eccentric rearrangements of time in fiction, the device is
represented in Willa Cather's *Shadows on the Rock*. Strictly speaking, anacoluthon is a rhetorical mannerism involving change of
grammatical construction within a unit of thought, like a sentence.
For example: "The foolhardiness of trying to cross the lake at
night—but let's not think of it." Without conscious purpose, anacoluthon is a grammatical blunder, the dangling participle. But
when deliberate and controlled, it helps the author to achieve valuable figurative effects.

Willa Cather, consequently, conceiving of anacoluthon as a plot
technique, amplified it beyond the rhetorical and figurative. Her
aim was to evoke emotional and moral effects through a temporary
suspension of completeness—that is, like a series of minor sus-
penses—within the individual actions of the novel. She attained
the seeming disjunction implied in anacoluthon by initiating actions, suspending them for other actions which were then likewise
temporarily interrupted. At the appropriate moment in the novel,
the resolution of each action is disclosed. Through an accumulation of related textural effects, the unitary intention of the novel is
fully achieved. The questions are posed, and we are induced to wait
for answers which the postponement has made all the more satisfying.

It must be amply apparent that plot method or form develops,
in each instance, out of the author's creative necessity. Thus, the
narration may go straight forward, as in the account of a life. It may
proceed by blocks of action, episodically; by dominant impressions,
scenically or through reorganized concepts of time; and so forth.
The more complex or intricate the fictional problem, the more complex and intricate the shape of the novel. To accommodate their notions of the variability of existence, for example, André Gide (e.g.,

The Counterfeiters) and Aldous Huxley (e.g., *Antic Hay* and *Point Counter Point*) hit upon the form identifiable as the *contrapuntal* novel. The term musically, as in counterpoint, implies a pluralism of melody—melody added to melody, that is, a series of related but independent melodies within a single musical structure.

Philip Quarles, a novelist in *Point Counter Point,* is (like Gide's Edouard in *The Counterfeiters*) made to conceptualize the form as "the musicalization of fiction." Reflecting on the possibilities, he writes: "Meditate on Beethoven. The changes of moods, the abrupt transitions. . . . Comedy suddenly hinting at prodigious and tragic solemnities in the scherzo of the C sharp minor Quartet. More interesting still, the modulations, not merely from one key to another, but from mood to mood. A theme is stated, then developed, pushed out of shape, imperceptibly deformed, until though still recognizably the same, it has become quite different." So it is in *Point Counter Point,* a "novel of ideas" built with mutations upon a single controlling theme. For convenience, let us call it the aridity or wastefulness of human values in the twentieth century; the devaluation of man's obligations and incentives.

Permitting Quarles to explain the process he himself uses, Huxley has his fictional character speculate: "Get this into a novel. How? The abrupt transitions are easy enough. All you need is a sufficiency of characters and parallel, contrapuntal plots. While Jones is murdering a wife, Smith is wheeling the perambulator in the park. You alternate themes. More interesting, the modulations and variations are also more difficult. A novelist modulates by reduplicating situations and characters. He shows several people falling in love, or dying, or praying in different ways—dissimilars solving the same problem. Or, *vice versa,* similar people confronted with dissimilar problems. In this way you can modulate through all the aspects of your theme, you can write variations in any number of different moods. Another way: The novelist can assume the god-like creative privilege and simply elect to consider the events of the story in their various aspects—emotional, scientific, economic, religious, metaphysical, etc. He will modulate from one to the other—as from the aesthetic to the physico-chemical aspect of things, from the religious to the physiological or financial."

What emerges is a novel whose theme is single but ramified by situations (and characters) different in mood but parallel or contiguous in their connections with that theme. In John Dos Passos' trilogy *USA*, as an instance, a good many actions and people, representative of the varied nature of existence as seen by the author, operate toward the fulfillment of a single, major purpose. One might amend the geometrical image of the parallel lines to one of a radial nature. At the center, the axis or the hub is the controlling motif. Lines, each one revelatory of a specific aspect of that motif, radiate from the axis. Each line conveys a specific mood or segment of meaning, perhaps complete in itself but incapable of final assessment without regard to the total structure. In this example, the wheel-like device is whole only in terms of the individual spokes of which it is comprised.

Each of the plot modes discussed—from the simple linear and episodic to the complex contrapuntal—is shaped by a logic of form and meaning. Whether the author's purpose is to create action symbolic of external conditions or of character development, the plot generally operates within certain definable limits. At times, however, these limits become too restrictive to accommodate the author's intention and he must seek a more malleable structure. Many authors, dissatisfied with traditional, logical explanations of character through plot, have resourcefully adopted the tools of psychoanalysis for ways of probing into ordinarily inaccessible aspects of personality. This approach can be a trap, tempting the imitative or novelty-bent writer to sacrifice narration and meaning to artificial effects. But in the hands of an artist, plot based on psychological exploration reveals often unsuspected dimensions and leads to interesting new "shapes." Broadly classifiable as *stream-of-consciousness* or *interior monologue*, the method to be employed is as variable as the authors who employ it.

Stream-of-consciousness is an analytic technique for tracking irrational inner states which psychoanalysis tells us precede or qualify rational communication. The term was invented by William James, in *Principles of Psychology*, as a way of describing the supposedly interminable and erratic flow of thoughts and feelings of the human mind. As a source of fiction, these tumultuous inner states may be analyzed to explain the conflicts, motivations, desires, and the like which make people interesting and individual. The author approximates the illogical interior condition of his characters by creating an illusion of chaotic, random flow. The illusion, it must be emphasized again, is the nature of deliberate art, and must not be confused with aimlessness or lack of control. The shape of the novel may be different from any we have ever experienced, but it is nevertheless a shape—a novel with a form created by the novelist for his purpose.

The popularity of Freud's teachings helped to activate the interior monologue, for Freudian psychology awakened novelists to the fictional possibilities of irrational mental processes, free association, and dreams. But even before Freud placed these matters in a psychoanalytic context, writers had been led to some of them either imaginatively or through other sources. Building upon John Locke's concept of associationism, Laurence Sterne in the eighteenth century created a prototypical novel in *Tristram Shandy*. Later, Browning's dramatic monologues were to reveal the poetic vitality of stream-of-consciousness, and the novels of George Eliot, George Meredith, and Henry James were to contribute to its development, if only tentatively. George Eliot, who admired Sterne, defied tradition by asking: "Why should a story not be told in the most irregular fashion that an author's idiosyncracy may prompt, provided that he gives us what we can enjoy?"

The relation of psychology to fiction, however, is a phenomenon largely of the twentieth century. One of the best-known novels in this mode is Marcel Proust's *A la recherche du temps perdu* (*Remembrance of Things Past*), which employs an extremely digressive technique. Proust's aim was to recapture the whole of his experience and to include any circumstances which came to mind during the course of his narration. Concomitant with his telling of things which had happened and events associated with them, he also intricately set down his present reflections. Digressing on inner states, he at the same time held together the many character-strands of his novel contrapuntally. In English, James Joyce is the best-known practitioner of the interior monologue, a method to which he was inspired by the late nineteenth-century novel of Edouard Dujardin, *Les lauriers sont coupés*. Joyce's *Ulysses*, though brilliantly organized, characteristically renders the illusion of an inner chaos of thoughts and feelings.

Freudian terminology is useful for indicating the levels beneath the conscious self to which the novelist may descend in his exploration of character. At the subconscious level, for example, there is still a connection with outward reality and logic, but the conscious mind releases much of its control over the will. Fiction of this order is exemplified by *Ulysses; Mrs. Woolf's Mrs. Dalloway, To the Lighthouse,* and others; and William Faulkner's *As I Lay Dying* and *The Sound and the Fury.* For further instances of the subconscious in stream-of-consciousness, note may be taken of the writings of Sherwood Anderson and Dorothy Richardson. At the unconscious level, a total separation is effected between the outer world and the irrational self. Fictionally, the artist attempts to approximate the behavior of the physical unconscious in literary style and content by creating an illusion of breaking completely from rational control. The dream-state has provided the framework for explorations into the unconscious in such works as Joyce's *Finnegan's Wake* and Conrad Aiken's *The Great Circle.*

It is obvious that the farther removed the novel is from areas of familiar experience, the more difficult the line of communication between novel and reader is going to be. *Finnegan's Wake,* probably the most extreme instance of separation between physical reality and irrational self, is for all its ingenuity and moments of splendor unreadable as a total fictional experience. Yet while making apparent that successful fiction cannot abandon all ties with reality, it deserves critical attention as an important link in fictional development. The ideal intended by highly introspective fiction is summed up figuratively by Samuel Beckett: "The only fertile research is excavatory, immersive, a contraction of the spirit, a descent." He says, "the heart of the cauliflower or the ideal core of the onion would represent more appropriate tribute to the labors of poetical excavation than the crown of bay." Ultimately, the critical reader will learn by his own experience that he need not limit his preferences to a single mode of plot or characterization. He may be drawn to the very complex contrapuntal or even involuted novel, but at the same time, he should not—at least not without profound critical deliberation—

contemptuously reject (as does Beckett) "the literature that 'describes,' . . . content to transcribe the surface, the facade, behind which the Idea is prisoner."

The Furnished Room

by O. HENRY

Restless, shifting, fugacious as time itself is a certain vast bulk of the population of the red brick district of the lower West Side. Homeless, they have a hundred homes. They flit from furnished room to furnished room, transients forever—transients in abode, transients in heart and mind. They sing "Home, Sweet Home" in ragtime; they carry their *lares et penates* in a bandbox; their vine is entwined about a picture hat; a rubber plant is their fig tree.

Hence the houses of this district, having had a thousand dwellers, should have a thousand tales to tell, mostly dull ones, no doubt; but it would be strange if there could not be found a ghost or two in the wake of all these vagrant guests.

One evening after dark a young man prowled among these crumbling red mansions, ringing their bells. At the twelfth he rested his lean hand-baggage upon the step and wiped the dust from his hatband and forehead. The bell sounded faint and far away in some remote, hollow depths.

To the door of this, the twelfth house whose bell he had rung, came a housekeeper who made him think of an unwholesome, surfeited worm that had eaten its nut to a hollow shell and now sought to fill the vacancy with edible lodgers.

He asked if there was a room to let.

"Come in," said the housekeeper. Her voice came from her throat; her throat seemed lined with fur. "I have the third floor back, vacant since a week back. Should you wish to look at it?"

The young man followed her up the stairs. A faint light from no particular source mitigated the shadows of the halls. They trod noiselessly upon a stair carpet that its own loom would have forsworn. It seemed to have become vegetable; to have degenerated in that rank, sunless air to lush lichen or spreading moss that grew in patches to the staircase and was viscid under the foot like organic matter. At each turn of the stairs were vacant niches in the wall. Perhaps plants had once been set within them. If so they had died in that foul and tainted air. It may be that statues of the saints had stood there, but it was not difficult to conceive that imps and devils had dragged them forth in the darkness and down to the unholy depths of some furnished pit below.

"This is the room," said the housekeeper, from her furry throat. "It's a nice room. It ain't often vacant. I had some most elegant people in it last summer—no trouble at all, and paid in advance to the minute. The water's at the end of the hall. Sprowls and Mooney kept it three months. They done a vaudeville sketch. Miss B'retta Sprowls—you may have heard of her—Oh, that was just the stage names—right there over the dresser is where the marriage certificate hung, framed. The gas is here, and you see there is plenty of closet room. It's a room everybody likes. It never stays idle long."

"Do you have many theatrical people rooming here?" asked the young man.

"They comes and goes. A good proportion of my lodgers is connected with the theatres. Yes, sir, this is the theatrical district. Actor people never stays long anywhere. I get my share. Yes, they comes and they goes."

He engaged the room, paying for a week in advance. He was tired, he said, and would take possession at once. He counted out the money. The room had been made ready, she said, even to towels and water. As the housekeeper moved away he put, for the thousandth time, the question that he carried at the end of his tongue.

"A young girl—Miss Vashner—Miss Eloise Vashner—do you remember such a one among your lodgers? She would be singing on the stage, most likely. A fair girl, of medium height and slender, with reddish, gold hair and a dark mole near her left eyebrow."

"No, I don't remember the name. Them stage people has names they change as often as their rooms. They comes and they goes. No, I don't call that one to mind."

No. Always no. Five months of ceaseless interrogation and the inevitable negative. So much time spent by day in questioning man-

agers, agents, schools and choruses; by night among the audiences
of theatres from all-star casts down to music halls so low that he
dreaded to find what he most hoped for. He who had loved her best
had tried to find her. He was sure that since her disappearance from
home this great, water-girt city held her somewhere, but it was like
a monstrous quicksand, shifting its particles constantly, with no
foundation, its upper granules of to-day buried to-morrow in ooze
and slime.

The furnished room received its latest guest with a first glow of
pseudo-hospitality, a hectic, haggard, perfunctory welcome like the
specious smile of a demirep. The sophistical comfort came in reflected gleams from the decayed furniture, the ragged brocade upholstery of a couch and two chairs, a foot-wide cheap pier glass between the two windows, from one or two gilt picture frames and a
brass bedstead in a corner.

The guest reclined, inert, upon a chair, while the room, confused
in speech as though it were an apartment in Babel, tried to discourse
to him of its divers tenantry.

A polychromatic rug like some brilliant-flowered rectangular, tropical islet lay surrounded by a billowy sea of soiled matting. Upon the
gay-papered wall were those pictures that pursue the homeless one
from house to house—The Huguenot Lovers, The First Quarrel, The
Wedding Breakfast, Psyche at the Fountain. The mantel's chastely
severe outline was ingloriously veiled behind some pert drapery
drawn rakishly askew like the sashes of the Amazonian ballet. Upon
it was some desolate flotsam cast aside by the room's marooned
when a lucky sail had borne them to a fresh port—a trifling vase or
two, pictures of actresses, a medicine bottle, some stray cards out of
a deck.

One by one, as the characters of a cryptograph become explicit,
the little signs left by the furnished room's procession of guests developed a significance. The threadbare space in the rug in front of
the dresser told that lovely woman had marched in the throng. The
tiny finger prints on the wall spoke of little prisoners trying to feel
their way to sun and air. A splattered stain, raying like the shadow
of a bursting bomb, witnessed where a hurled glass or bottle had
splintered with its contents against the wall. Across the pier glass

had been scrawled with a diamond in staggering letters the name "Marie." It seemed that the succession of dwellers in the furnished room had turned in fury—perhaps tempted beyond forbearance by its garish coldness—and wreaked upon it their passions. The furniture was chipped and bruised; the couch, distorted by bursting springs, seemed a horrible monster that had been slain during the stress of some grotesque convulsion. Some more potent upheaval had cloven a great slice from the marble mantel. Each plank in the floor owned its particular cant and shriek as from a separate and individual agony. It seemed incredible that all this malice and injury had been wrought upon the room by those who had called it for a time their home; and yet it may have been the cheated home instinct surviving blindly, the resentful rage at false household gods that had kindled their wrath. A hut that is our own we can sweep and adorn and cherish.

The young tenant in the chair allowed these thoughts to file, soft-shod, through his mind, while there drifted into the room furnished sounds and furnished scents. He heard in one room a tittering and incontinent, slack laughter; in others the monologue of a scold, the rattling of dice, a lullaby, and one crying dully; above him a banjo tinkled with spirit. Doors banged somewhere; the elevated trains roared intermittently; a cat yowled miserably upon a back fence. And he breathed the breath of the house—a dank savour rather than a smell—a cold, musty effluvium as from underground vaults mingled with the reeking exhalations of linoleum and mildewed and rotten woodwork.

Then, suddenly, as he rested there, the room was filled with the strong, sweet odour of mignonette. It came as upon a single buffet of wind with such sureness and fragrance and emphasis that it almost seemed a living visitant. And the man cried aloud: "What, dear?" as if he had been called, and sprang up and faced about. The rich odour clung to him and wrapped him around. He reached out his arms for it, all his senses for the time confused and commingled. How could one be peremptorily called by an odour? Surely it must have been a sound. But, was it not the sound that had touched, that had caressed him?

"She has been in this room," he cried, and he sprang to wrest from it a token, for he knew he would recognize the smallest thing that had belonged to her or that she had touched. This enveloping scent of mignonette, the odour that she had loved and made her own—whence came it?

The room had been but carelessly set in order. Scattered upon the flimsy dresser scarf were half a dozen hairpins—those discreet, indistinguishable friends of womankind, feminine of gender, infinite of mood and uncommunicative of tense. These he ignored, conscious of their triumphant lack of identity. Ransacking the drawers of the dresser he came upon a discarded, tiny, ragged handkerchief. He pressed it to his face. It was racy and insolent with heliotrope; he hurled it to the floor. In another drawer he found odd buttons, a theatre programme, a pawnbroker's card, two lost marshmallows, a book on the divination of dreams. In the last was a woman's black satin hairbow, which halted him, poised between ice and fire. But the black satin hairbow also is femininity's demure, impersonal, common ornament and tells no tales.

And then he traversed the room like a hound on the scent, skimming the walls, considering the corners of the bulging matting on his hands and knees, rummaging mantel and tables, the curtains and hangings, the drunken cabinet in the corner, for a visible sign, unable to perceive that she was there beside, around, against, within, above him, clinging to him, wooing him, calling him so poignantly through the finer senses that even his grosser ones became cognisant of the call. Once again he answered loudly: "Yes, dear!" and turned, wild-eyed, to gaze on vacancy, for he could not yet discern form and colour and love and outstretched arms in the odour of mignonette. Oh, God! whence that odour, and since when have odours had a voice to call? Thus he groped.

He burrowed in crevices and corners, and found corks and cigarettes. These he passed in passive contempt. But once he found in a fold of the matting a half-smoked cigar, and this he ground beneath his heel with a green and trenchant oath. He sifted the room from end to end. He found dreary and ignoble small records of many a peripatetic tenant; but of her whom he sought, and who may have lodged there, and whose spirit seemed to hover there, he found no trace.

And then he thought of the housekeeper.

He ran from the haunted room downstairs and to a door that showed a crack of light. She came out to his knock. He smothered his excitement as best he could.

"Will you tell me, madam," he besought her, "who occupied the room I have before I came?"

"Yes, sir. I can tell you again. 'Twas Sprowls and Mooney, as I said. Miss B'retta Sprowls it was in the theatres, but Missis Mooney she was. My house is well known for respectability. The marriage certificate hung, framed, on a nail over—"

"What kind of a lady was Miss Sprowls—in looks, I mean?"

"Why, black-haired, sir, short, and stout, with a comical face. They left a week ago Tuesday."

"And before they occupied it?"

"Why, there was a single gentleman connected with the draying business. He left owing me a week. Before him was Missis Crowder and her two children, that stayed four months; and back of them was old Mr. Doyle, whose sons paid for him. He kept the room six months. That goes back a year, sir, and further I do not remember."

He thanked her and crept back to his room. The room was dead. The essence that had vivified it was gone. The perfume of mignonette had departed. In its place was the old, stale odour of mouldy house furniture, of atmosphere in storage.

The ebbing of his hope drained his faith. He sat staring at the yellow, singing gaslight. Soon he walked to the bed and began to tear the sheets into strips. With the blade of his knife he drove them tightly into every crevice around windows and door. When all was snug and taut he turned out the light, turned the gas full on again and laid himself gratefully upon the bed.

.   .   .   .

It was Mrs. McCool's night to go with the can for beer. So she fetched it and sat with Mrs. Purdy in one of those subterranean retreats where housekeepers foregather and the worm dieth seldom.

"I rented out my third floor, back, this evening," said Mrs. Purdy, across a fine circle of foam. "A young man took it. He went up to bed two hours ago."

"Now, did ye, Mrs. Purdy, ma'am?" said Mrs. McCool, with intense admiration. "You do be a wonder for rentin' rooms of that kind. And did ye tell him, then?" she concluded in a husky whisper laden with mystery.

"Rooms," said Mrs. Purdy, in her furriest tones, "are furnished for to rent. I did not tell him, Mrs. McCool."

" 'Tis right ye are, ma'am; 'tis by renting rooms we kape alive. Ye have the rale sense for business, ma'am. There be many people will rayjict the rentin' of a room if they be tould a suicide has been after dyin' in the bed of it."

"As you say, we has our living to be making," remarked Mrs. Purdy.

"Yis, ma'am; 'tis true. 'Tis just one wake ago this day I helped ye lay out the third floor, back. A pretty slip of a colleen she was to be killin' herself wid the gas—a swate little face she had, Mrs. Purdy, ma'am."

"She'd a-been called handsome, as you say," said Mrs. Purdy, assenting but critical, "but for that mole she had a-growin' by her left eyebrow. Do fill up your glass again, Mrs. McCool."

Critical Commentary on *The Furnished Room*

"The Furnished Room," by O. Henry (the pseudonym of William Sydney Porter), is a classic example of deliberately contrived plot construction. The author, an American literary descendant of Guy de Maupassant, indulges in trickery of coincidence to create the celebrated "surprise ending" which emphasizes cleverness at the cost of credibility. The O. Henry technique, relying on manipulation of quasi-realistic events and a suspenseful emotional atmosphere, outrages normal assumptions of logic and causality. Character is simply a tool of his emotional effects, human personality being subordinated to the shock of the unexpected.

O. Henry draws upon a situation whose culmination would be realistic and credible enough, if it were confined to the suicide of the young man, and if the histrionics were modified. Seeking to instill added stimulus, however, he goes beyond probable expressions of feeling and beyond the probable narrative terminus. In so doing, he asks us to accept a coincidence of event and setting which plays havoc with reason. Fiction, of course, does not insist upon literal reason; but its materials ordinarily imply a source somewhere in experience. By his sudden shift from the probable to the improbable, O. Henry announces a departure from experience as a fictional motive.

His purpose is to entertain by surprise. While we may be deeply affected by the young man's loss and his fatal response to it, we find it hard to identify ourselves with his personal tragedy. For one thing, he does not exist as a particularly interesting or well-drawn character. Nameless and shapeless, he is more an emotion-wracked ghost looking for another ghost than a bereft human being. All we know of this young man is his passionate despair, and what we know we have discovered from O. Henry's report or from frantic gestures. For another thing, the logical climax and resolution turn out to be false ones; the lover's suicide is diminished, subordinated to the coincidence of the other death in the same room by the same means.

We are intrigued by the author's resourcefulness but can find little other meaning in the story. Tragedy, as we understand it in Western literature, unites the reader with the victim, eliciting great compassion and possibly self-recognition. These we do not experience in "The Furnished Room." Coincidence may contribute heavily to a tragic result, but when coincidence becomes its own end, as here, then we are dealing not with human misfortune but with ingenious accident.

On the other hand, there is no need to believe O. Henry ever had a tragic purpose in mind. At least, it would be a critical comfort to think he had not. The chief impact of "The Furnished Room" inheres in its emotional and atmospheric effects. An important aspect of the story consists in its gothic (that is, deliberately horror-distorted, overcharged), macabre setting, the room itself acting as a major antagonistic force, more clearly defined indeed than the young man. As described by O. Henry, the room is the impersonal tomb of countless tenants other than the young man and his sweetheart.

Poe-like, he evokes an oppressive image of rot on the fetid stair-case. He has his protagonist breathe "the breath of the house—a dank savour rather than a smell—a cold, musty effluvium as from underground vaults mingled with the reeking exhalations of linoleum and mildewed and rotten woodwork." Suddenly, in the midst of this decay, "the room was filled with the strong, sweet odour of mignon-ette." How the scent of his sweetheart's perfume managed to linger for a week remains inexplicable, nor do we care to have it explained as anything more than the result of an overwrought imagination. What does matter is the intensification of neurotic fantasy and the disaster to which it leads.

But more significant even than the macabre atmosphere is the sentimental excess. *Sentimentality* is properly considered an es-thetic fault, because it demands of the reader an emotional response far greater than is justified by the situation as presented. Sentimen-tal writing artificially prompts the reader's feelings, exacting copi-ous tears as a substitute for dignified sadness or grief. We would have to be much closer to the young man than we are allowed to be, if we were to sympathize with his violence of feeling and indulge in it ourselves. O. Henry, having a flair for purple passages, sets the lachrymose mood with his exaggerated tropical metaphors and sim-iles—strangely at odds with the pervasive physical corruption. Vestiges of former tenants enhance the sentimentality, calling forth the pathos of their sorry lives: "lovely woman" on the threadbare rug, "tiny finger prints," "the name 'Marie' " scratched on the mir-ror, hairpins, a handkerchief, and other mute traces of departed ghosts.

But most harrowing of all, emotionally, is the odor of mignonette. We are made to conjure up a vision of the poor girl in this horror of a house clinging to the last reminder of delicacy and gentleness be-fore her death. The sentimentality of this vision, and of the young man's wildly lacerated emotions, is magnified by contrast with the calculating landlady and her friend. Yet, they, for all their coldness and stage-Irish idiom, provide our only connections with reality, the world of experience. The five-month search, ended here, is thus bound up with a turbulence of feeling that tries belief. Experience has been sacrificed to coincidence, sentimentality, and horror.

The Bride Comes to Yellow Sky

by STEPHEN CRANE

I

The great Pullman was whirling onward with such dignity of motion that a glance from the window seemed simply to prove that the plains of Texas were pouring eastward. Vast flats of green grass, dull-hued spaces of mesquite and cactus, little groups of frame houses, woods of light and tender trees, all were sweeping into the east, sweeping over the horizon, a precipice.

A newly married pair had boarded this coach at San Antonio. The man's face was reddened from many days in the wind and sun, and a direct result of his new black clothes was that his brick-colored hands were constantly performing in a most conscious fashion. From time to time he looked down respectfully at his attire. He sat with a hand on each knee, like a man waiting in a barber's shop. The glances he devoted to other passengers were furtive and shy.

The bride was not pretty, nor was she very young. She wore a dress of blue cashmere, with small reservations of velvet here and there, and with steel buttons abounding. She continually twisted her head to regard her puff sleeves, very stiff, straight, and high. They embarrassed her. It was quite apparent that she had cooked, and that she expected to cook, dutifully. The blushes caused by the careless scrutiny of some passengers as she had entered the car were strange to see upon this plain, under-class countenance, which was drawn in placid, almost emotionless lines.

They were evidently very happy. "Ever been in a parlor-car before?" he asked, smiling with delight.

"No," she answered; "I never was. It's fine, ain't it?"

"Great! And then after a while we'll go forward to the diner, and get a big lay-out. Finest meal in the world. Charge a dollar."

"Oh, do they?" cried the bride. "Charge a dollar? Why, that's too much—for us—ain't it, Jack?"

"Not this trip, anyhow," he answered bravely. "We're going to go the whole thing."

Later he explained to her about the trains. "You see, it's a thousand miles from one end of Texas to the other; and this train runs right across it, and never stops but four times." He had the pride of an owner. He pointed out to her the dazzling fittings of the coach; and in truth her eyes opened wider as she contemplated the sea-green figured velvet, the shining brass, silver, and glass, the wood that gleamed as darkly brilliant as the surface of a pool of oil. At one end a bronze figure sturdily held a support for a separated chamber, and at convenient places on the ceiling were frescos in olive and silver.

To the minds of the pair, their surroundings reflected the glory of their marriage that morning in San Antonio; this was the environment of their new estate; and the man's face in particular beamed with an elation that made him appear ridiculous to the negro porter. This individual at times surveyed them from afar with an amused and superior grin. On other occasions he bullied them with skill in ways that did not make it exactly plain to them that they were being bullied. He subtly used all the manners of the most unconquerable kind of snobbery. He oppressed them; but of this oppression they had small knowledge, and they speedily forgot that infrequently a number of travellers covered them with stares of derisive enjoyment. Historically there was supposed to be something infinitely humorous in their situation.

"We are due in Yellow Sky at 3:42," he said, looking tenderly into her eyes.

"Oh, are we?" she said, as if she had not been aware of it. To evince surprise at her husband's statement was part of her wifely amiability. She took from a pocket a little silver watch; and as she held it before her, and stared at it with a frown of attention, the new husband's face shone.

"I bought it in San Anton' from a friend of mine," he told her gleefully.

"It's seventeen minutes past twelve," she said, looking up at him with a kind of shy and clumsy coquetry. A passenger, noting this play, grew excessively sardonic, and winked at himself in one of the numerous mirrors.

At last they went to the dining-car. Two rows of negro waiters, in glowing white suits, surveyed their entrance with the interest, and also the equanimity, of men who had been forewarned. The pair fell to the lot of a waiter who happened to feel pleasure in steering them through their meal. He viewed them with the manner of a fatherly pilot, his countenance radiant with benevolence. The patronage, entwined with the ordinary reference, was not plain to them. And yet, as they returned to their coach, they showed in their faces a sense of escape.

To the left, miles down a long purple slope, was a little ribbon of mist where moved the keening Rio Grande. The train was approaching it at an angle, and the apex was Yellow Sky. Presently it was apparent that, as the distance from Yellow Sky grew shorter, the husband became commensurately restless. His brick-red hands were most insistent in their prominence. Occasionally he was even rather absent-minded and far-away when the bride leaned forward and addressed him.

As a matter of truth, Jack Potter was beginning to find the shadow of a deed weigh upon him like a leaden slab. He, the town marshal of Yellow Sky, a man known, liked, and feared in his corner, a prominent person, had gone to San Antonio to meet a girl he believed he loved, and there, after the usual prayers, had actually induced her to marry him, without consulting Yellow Sky for any part of the transaction. He was now bringing his bride before an innocent and unsuspecting community.

Of course people in Yellow Sky married as it pleased them, in accordance with a general custom; but such was Potter's thought of his duty to his friends, or of their idea of his duty, or of an unspoken form which does not control men in these matters, that he felt he was heinous. He had committed an extraordinary crime. Face to face with this girl in San Antonio, and spurred by his sharp impulse, he had gone headlong over all the social hedges. At San Antonio he was like a man hidden in the dark. A knife to sever any friendly duty, any form, was easy to his hand in that remote city. But the hour of Yellow Sky—the hour of daylight—was approaching.

He knew full well that his marriage was an important thing to his town. It could only be exceeded by the burning of the new hotel. His friends could not forgive him. Frequently he had reflected on the advisability of telling them by telegraph, but a new cowardice had been upon him. He feared to do it. And now the train was hurrying him toward a scene of amazement, glee, and reproach. He glanced out of the window at the line of haze swinging slowly in toward the train.

Yellow Sky had a kind of brass band, which played painfully, to the delight of the populace. He laughed without heart as he thought of it. If the citizens could dream of his prospective arrival with his bride, they would parade the band at the station and escort them, amid cheers and laughing congratulations, to his adobe home.

He resolved that he would use all the devices of speed and plains-craft in making the journey from the station to his house. Once within that safe citadel, he could issue some sort of vocal bulletin, and then not go among the citizens until they had time to wear off a little of their enthusiasm.

The bride looked anxiously at him. "What's worrying you, Jack?"

He laughed again. "I'm not worrying, girl; I'm only thinking of Yellow Sky."

She flushed in comprehension.

A sense of mutual guilt invaded their minds and developed a finer tenderness. They looked at each other with eyes softly aglow. But Potter often laughed the same nervous laugh; the flush upon the bride's face seemed quite permanent.

The traitor to the feelings of Yellow Sky narrowly watched the speeding landscape. "We're nearly there," he said.

Presently the porter came and announced the proximity of Potter's home. He held a brush in his hand, and, with all his airy superiority gone, he brushed Potter's new clothes as the latter slowly turned this way and that way. Potter fumbled out a coin and gave it to the porter, as he had seen others do. It was a heavy and muscle-bound business, as that of a man shoeing his first horse.

The porter took their bag, and as the train began to slow they moved forward to the hooded platform of the car. Presently the two engines and their long string of coaches rushed into the station of Yellow Sky.

"They have to take water here," said Potter, from a constricted throat and in mournful cadence, as one announcing death. Before the train stopped his eye had swept the length of the platform, and he was glad and astonished to see there was none upon it but the station-agent, who, with a slightly hurried and anxious air, was walking toward the water-tanks. When the train had halted, the porter alighted first, and placed in position a little temporary step.

"Come on, girl," said Potter, hoarsely. As he helped her down they each laughed on a false note. He took the bag from the negro, and bade his wife cling to his arm. As they slunk rapidly away, his hang-dog glance perceived that they were unloading the two trunks, and also that the station-agent, far ahead near the baggage-car, had turned and was running toward him, making gestures. He laughed, and groaned as he laughed, when he noted the first effect of his marital bliss upon Yellow Sky. He gripped his wife's arm firmly to his side, and they fled. Behind them the porter stood, chuckling fatuously.

II

The California express on the Southern Railway was due at Yellow Sky in twenty-one minutes. There were six men at the bar of the Weary Gentleman saloon. One was a drummer who talked a great deal and rapidly; three were Texans who did not care to talk at that time; and two were Mexican sheepherders, who did not talk as a general practice in the Weary Gentleman saloon. The barkeeper's dog lay on the board walk that crossed in front of the door. His head was on his paws, and he glanced drowsily here and there with the constant vigilance of a dog that is kicked on occasion. Across the sandy street were some vivid green grass-plots, so wonderful in appearance, amid the sands that burned near them in a blazing sun, that they caused a doubt in the mind. They exactly resembled the grass mats used to represent lawns on the stage. At the cooler end of the railway station, a man without a coat sat in a tilted chair and smoked his pipe. The fresh-cut bank of the Rio Grande circled near the town, and there could be seen beyond it a great plum-colored plain of mesquite.

Save for the busy drummer and his companions in the saloon, Yellow Sky was dozing. The new-comer leaned gracefully upon the bar, and recited many tales with the confidence of a bard who has come upon a new field.

"—and at the moment that the old man fell downstairs with the bureau in his arms, the old woman was coming up with two scuttles of coal, and of course—"

The drummer's tale was interrupted by a young man who suddenly appeared in the open door. He cried: "Scratchy Wilson's drunk, and has turned loose with both hands." The two Mexicans at once set down their glasses and faded out of the rear entrance of the saloon.

The drummer, innocent and jocular, answered: "All right, old man. S'pose he has? Come in and have a drink, anyhow."

But the information had made such an obvious cleft in every skull in the room that the drummer was obliged to see its importance. All had become instantly solemn. "Say," said he, mystified, "what is this?" His three companions made the introductory gesture of eloquent speech; but the young man at the door forestalled them.

"It means, my friend," he answered, as he came into the saloon, "that for the next two hours this town won't be a health resort."

The barkeeper went to the door, and locked and barred it; reaching out of the window, he pulled in heavy wooden shutters, and barred them. Immediately a solemn, chapel-like gloom was upon the place. The drummer was looking from one to another.

"But say," he cried, "what is this, anyhow? You don't mean there is going to be a gun-fight?"

"Don't know whether there'll be a fight or not," answered one man, grimly; "but there'll be some shootin'—some good shootin'."

The young man who had warned them waved his hand. "Oh, there'll be a fight fast enough, if any one wants it. Anybody can get a fight out there in the street. There's a fight just waiting."

The drummer seemed to be swayed between the interest of a foreigner and a perception of personal danger.

"What did you say his name was?" he asked.

"Scratchy Wilson," they answered in chorus.

"And will he kill anybody? What are you going to do? Does this happen often? Does he rampage around like this once a week or so? Can he break in that door?"

"No; he can't break down that door," replied the barkeeper. "He's tried it three times. But when he comes you'd better lay down on the floor, stranger. He's dead sure to shoot at it, and a bullet may come through."

Thereafter the drummer kept a strict eye upon the door. The time had not yet been called for him to hug the floor, but, as a minor precaution, he sidled near to the wall. "Will he kill anybody?" he said again.

The men laughed low and scornfully at the question.

"He's out to shoot, and he's out for trouble. Don't see any good in experimentin' with him."

"But what do you do in a case like this? What do you do?"

A man responded: "Why, he and Jack Potter—"

"But," in chorus the other men interrupted, "Jack Potter's in San Anton'."

"Well, who is he? What's he got to do with it?"

"Oh, he's the town marshal. He goes out and fights Scratchy when he gets on one of these tears."

"Wow!" said the drummer, mopping his brow. "Nice job he's got."

The voices had toned away to mere whisperings. The drummer wished to ask further questions, which were born of an increasing anxiety and bewilderment; but when he attempted them, the men merely looked at him in irritation and motioned him to remain silent. A tense waiting hush was upon them. In the deep shadows of the room their eyes shone as they listened for sounds from the street. One man made three gestures at the barkeeper; and the latter, moving like a ghost, handed him a glass and a bottle. The man poured a full glass of whiskey, and set down the bottle noiselessly. He gulped the whiskey in a swallow, and turned again toward the door in immovable silence. The drummer saw that the barkeeper, without a sound, had taken a Winchester from beneath the bar. Later he saw this individual beckoning to him, so he tiptoed across the room.

"You better come with me back of the bar."

"No, thanks," said the drummer, perspiring; "I'd rather be where I can make a break for the back door."

Whereupon the man of bottles made a kindly but peremptory gesture. The drummer obeyed it, and, finding himself seated on a box with his head below the level of the bar, balm was laid upon his soul at sight of various zinc and copper fittings that bore a resemblance to armor-plate. The barkeeper took a seat comfortably upon an adjacent box.

"You see," he whispered, "this here Scratchy Wilson is a wonder with a gun—a perfect wonder; and when he goes on the wartrail, we hunt our holes—naturally. He's about the last one of the old gang that used to hang out along the river here. He's a terror when he's drunk. When he's sober he's all right—kind of simple—wouldn't hurt a fly—nicest fellow in town. But when he's drunk—whoo!"

There were periods of stillness. "I wish Jack Potter was back from San Anton'," said the barkeeper. "He shot Wilson up once—in the leg—and he would sail in and pull out the kinks in this thing."

Presently they heard from a distance the sound of a shot, followed by three wild yowls. It instantly removed a bond from the men in the darkened saloon. There was a shuffling of feet. They looked at each other. "Here he comes," they said.

III

A man in a maroon-colored flannel shirt, which had been purchased for purposes of decoration, and made principally by some Jewish women on the East Side of New York, rounded a corner and walked into the middle of the main street of Yellow Sky. In either hand the man held a long, heavy, blue-black revolver. Often he yelled, and these cries rang through a semblance of a deserted village, shrilly flying over the roofs in a volume that seemed to have no relation to the ordinary vocal strength of a man. It was as if the surrounding stillness formed the arch of a tomb over him. These cries of ferocious challenge rang against walls of silence. And his boots had red tops with gilded imprints, of the kind beloved in winter by little sledding boys on the hillsides of New England.

The man's face flamed in a rage begot of whiskey. His eyes, rolling, and yet keen for ambush, hunted the still doorways and windows. He walked with the creeping movement of the midnight cat. As it occurred to him, he roared menacing information. The long revolvers in his hands were as easy as straws; they were moved with an electric swiftness. The little fingers of each hand played sometimes in a musician's way. Plain from the low collar of the shirt, the cords of his neck straightened and sank, straightened and sank, as passion moved him. The only sounds were his terrible invitations. The calm adobes preserved their demeanor at the passing of this small thing in the middle of the street.

There was no offer of fight—no offer of fight. The man called to the sky. There were no attractions. He bellowed and fumed and swayed his revolvers here and everywhere.

The dog of the barkeeper of the Weary Gentleman saloon had not appreciated the advance of events. He yet lay dozing in front of his master's door. At sight of the dog, the man paused and raised his revolver humorously. At sight of the man, the dog sprang up and walked diagonally away, with a sullen head, and growling. The man yelled, and the dog broke into a gallop. As it was about to enter an alley, there was a loud noise, a whistling, and something spat the ground directly before it. The dog screamed, and, wheeling in terror, galloped headlong in a new direction. Again there was a noise, a whistling, and sand was kicked viciously before it. Fear-stricken, the dog turned and flurried like an animal in a pen. The man stood laughing, his weapons at his hips.

Ultimately the man was attracted by the closed door of the Weary Gentleman saloon. He went to it and, hammering with a revolver, demanded drink.

The door remaining imperturbable, he picked a bit of paper from the walk, and nailed it to the framework with a knife. He then turned his back contemptuously upon this popular resort and, walking to the opposite side of the street and spinning there on his heel quickly and lithely, fired at the bit of paper. He missed it by a half-inch. He swore at himself, and went away. Later he comfortably fusilladed the windows of his most intimate friend. The man was playing with this town; it was a toy for him.

But still there was no offer of fight. The name of Jack Potter, his ancient antagonist, entered his mind, and he concluded that it would be a glad thing if he should go to Potter's house, and by bombardment induce him to come out and fight. He moved in the direction of his desire, chanting Apache scalp-music.

When he arrived at it, Potter's house presented the same still front as had the other adobes. Taking up a strategic position, the man howled a challenge. But this house regarded him as might a great stone god. It gave no sign. After a decent wait, the man howled further challenges, mingling with them wonderful epithets.

Presently there came the spectacle of a man churning himself into deepest rage over the immobility of a house. He fumed at it as the winter wind attacks a prairie cabin in the North. To the distance there should have gone the sound of a tumult like the fighting of two hundred Mexicans. As necessity bade him, he paused for breath or to reload his revolvers.

IV

Potter and his bride walked sheepishly and with speed. Sometimes they laughed together shamefacedly and low.

"Next corner, dear," he said finally.

They put forth the efforts of a pair walking bowed against a strong wind. Potter was about to raise a finger to point the first appearance of the new home when, as they circled the corner, they came face to face with a man in a maroon-colored shirt, who was feverishly pushing cartridges into a large revolver. Upon the instant the man dropped his revolver to the ground and, like lightning, whipped another from its holster. The second weapon was aimed at the bridegroom's chest.

There was a silence. Potter's mouth seemed to be merely a grave for his tongue. He exhibited an instinct to at once loosen his arm from the woman's grip, and he dropped the bag to the sand. As for the bride, her face had gone as yellow as old cloth. She was a slave to hideous rites, gazing at the apparitional snake.

The two men faced each other at a distance of three paces. He of the revolver smiled with a new and quiet ferocity.

"Tried to sneak up on me," he said. "Tried to sneak up on me!" His eyes grew more baleful. As Potter made a slight movement, the man thrust his revolver venomously forward. "No; don't you do it, Jack Potter. Don't you move a finger toward a gun just yet. Don't you move an eyelash. The time has come for me to settle with you, and I'm goin' to do it my own way, and loaf along with no interferin'. So if you don't want a gun bent on you, just mind what I tell you."

Potter looked at his enemy. "I ain't got a gun on me, Scratchy," he said. "Honest, I ain't." He was stiffening and steadying, but yet somewhere at the back of his mind a vision of the Pullman floated: the sea-green figured velvet, the shining brass, silver, and glass, the wood that gleamed as darkly brilliant as the surface of a pool of oil— all the glory of the marriage, the environment of the new estate. "You know I fight when it comes to fighting, Scratchy Wilson; but I ain't got a gun on me. You'll have to do all the shootin' yourself."

His enemy's face went livid. He stepped forward, and lashed his weapon to and fro before Potter's chest. "Don't you tell me you ain't got no gun on you, you whelp. Don't tell me no lie like that. There ain't a man in Texas ever seen you without no gun. Don't take me for no kid." His eyes blazed with light, and his throat worked like a pump.

"I ain't takin' you for no kid," answered Potter. His heels had not moved an inch backward. "I'm takin' you for a damn fool. I tell you I ain't got a gun, and I ain't. If you're goin' to shoot me up, you better begin now; you'll never get a chance like this again."

So much enforced reasoning had told on Wilson's rage; he was calmer. "If you ain't got a gun, why ain't you got a gun?" he sneered. "Been to Sunday-school?"

"I ain't got a gun because I've just come from San Anton' with my wife. I'm married," said Potter. "And if I'd thought there was going to be any galoots like you prowling around when I brought my wife home, I'd had a gun, and don't you forget it."

"Married!" said Scratchy, not at all comprehending.

"Yes, married. I'm married," said Potter, distinctly.

"Married?" said Scratchy. Seemingly for the first time, he saw the drooping, drowning woman at the other man's side. "No!" he said. He was like a creature allowed a glimpse of another world. He moved a pace backward, and his arm, with the revolver, dropped to his side. "Is this the lady?" he asked.

"Yes; this is the lady," answered Potter.

There was another period of silence.

"Well," said Wilson at last, slowly, "I s'pose it's all off now."

"It's all off if you say so, Scratchy. You know I didn't make the trouble." Potter lifted his valise.

"Well, I 'low it's off, Jack," said Wilson. He was looking at the ground. "Married!" He was not a student of chivalry; it was merely that in the presence of this foreign condition he was a simple child of the earlier plains. He picked up his starboard revolver, and, placing both weapons in their holsters, he went away. His feet made funnel-shaped tracks in the heavy sand.

Critical Commentary on *The Bride Comes to Yellow Sky*

The plot of "The Bride Comes to Yellow Sky" is formal in its linear simplicity and completeness. Four segments of narrative movement, each containing its own scene in place and time, advance the situation logically from the introduction of Jack Potter and his bride to the climactic confrontation with Scratchy Wilson. The first scene reveals the awkwardness of the newlyweds in an alien environment and, in contrast, establishes our respect for Potter. The second, coinciding in time with the approach and arrival of the train, evokes the atmosphere of Yellow Sky, prepares us for Wilson's terrorism, and reconfirms the image of Potter as protector. The third is devoted to the drunken gambols of Wilson and his desire to challenge Potter, "his ancient antagonist." The fourth, in which all the lines converge, brings the opponents face to face for the resolution. Each scene, having its own meaning in relation to the whole, may be considered as follows:

From the outset, we are aware that the self-conscious ungainliness of the couple is not consistent with their natural dignity. Virtually stereotypes of rustic newlyweds, they are uncomfortable in their city clothes and impressed as only the inexperienced would be by their luxurious train accommodations. They are so obviously in a strange setting and so obviously absorbed in their mutual love that they appear incongruous to the supercilious porter and the amused passengers. As they approach Yellow Sky, however, Jack's thoughts wander uneasily from the coach and even his bride. He is "beginning to find the shadow of a deed weigh upon him like a leaden slab." It is at this point that we discover Jack owns an obligation to the community for his private as well as his public actions. More than most men, indeed, he has sacrificed the greatest part of personal self to the public good and its approbation. Understandably, therefore, he suffers the qualms of one who has breached a confidence, almost as though his celibacy is a qualification for office. At the same time, the bride reveals her sensitivity to his dilemma and a willingness to share in it. "A sense of mutual guilt invaded their minds and developed a finer tenderness."

Meanwhile, the patrons of the Weary Gentleman saloon have barricaded themselves upon hearing the report that "Scratchy Wilson's drunk, and has turned loose with both hands." Here we find a situation parallel to the one in the train, the drummer now playing the role of the outsider. His function is to ask questions, answers to which provide essential expository details about the periodic rampages of Scratchy and which show the dependence of the community on Jack Potter. The drummer, further, is a comic coward whose timidity counters the marshal's bravery. None of the others are demonstrably braver than the drummer; but they are inured to this situation, although their anxiety is increased by the knowledge of Potter's absence. As they sit waiting, secure enough behind barred door and window, plenty of liquor at hand, they convey the tenseness of the atmosphere.

The group in the saloon, like a chorus in ancient drama, are more static witnesses of than dynamic participants in the main action. They provide an interlude of suspense, which is broken with the appearance of Scratchy Wilson on the deserted Yellow Sky street. Apart from his drunken misconduct, we are struck by the flamboyance of his attire. In his maroon shirt and fancy boots, he is less the irresponsible adult than the wildly threatening child who wishes to call attention to his antics. Crane himself specifies the childishness of his dangerous game. "The man was playing with this town; it was a toy for him." As must have happened many times in the past, when no one will come out to fight with him, Scratchy looks for Jack Potter. The bad man of the script, he must show his defiance of the best and bravest man in town.

The story moves to its final scene with the reappearance of Jack and his frightened bride. Reverting to his traditional role, Jack momentarily disengages himself from the woman, a symbolic gesture showing that he is accustomed to upholding the law as a figure in isolation. Almost instantaneously, however, he remembers the time for isolation is past—he remembers the honeymoon trip and with it "all the glory of the marriage, the environment of the new estate." Explaining to Scratchy that he is unarmed because he has just come from San Antonio with his bride, he bewilders the gun-waving drunk. Scratchy goes away disconsolate, let down because the game is no longer being played by the familiar rules or code. The game can hardly be played any other way. "He was not a student of chivalry; it was merely that in the presence of this foreign condition he was a simple child of the earlier plains." With custom altered by the woman's intrusion, physical conflict is surrendered to peaceable resolution.

In its surface appearance, "The Bride Comes to Yellow Sky" has many of the clichés of the typical "Western": the tough marshal and shy bride, the colloquial saloon set, the maverick gunman on the open street, the atmosphere of imminent violence. The clichés recede, however, under Crane's carefully controlled tone and intention. The melodramatic circumstances are modified by his gentle irony, by the keen understanding of Wilson's childish nature, and by the ameliorating love—shy and grave, but never mawkish—of the marshal and his wife. The literal elements of the story are a source of excitement, suspense, amusement, and tenderness, but they are treated metaphorically in such a way as to assert much larger issues than a mere "showdown." "The Bride Comes to Yellow Sky" has the heroic and mythic undertones of an Arthurian legend accommodated to an American tradition.

The prevailing theme is a chivalric one, with Potter as a kind of Lancelot whose mission it is to protect the innocent against wanton evil. Unlike Lancelot, Potter retains his purity despite the loss of celibacy, for his marriage is the confirmation of his innate goodness. As a celibate knight, he had exercised an impersonal duty on behalf of "an innocent and unsuspecting community." Now, in marriage, he has a specific obligation to the woman he is protecting. "She was a slave to hideous rites, gazing at the apparitional snake." Although her fears are unwarranted—for Potter is destined to defeat Scratchy —he has to acknowledge that ritualistic combat with his enemy must not be allowed to darken "the environment of the new estate." The innocence of the bride is a profoundly more serious one than the innocence of the community, which is of an altogether different kind. For both Potter and Scratchy, then, the war-like ritual must give way to a peaceful order. Scratchy's disappointment is that of a man who has suddenly been excluded, but he accepts the formalities of a "foreign condition," even though he does not comprehend them.

The mythic allusions are sustained throughout the story, if not always in the heroic Arthurian mold. The saloon setting, for instance, undergoes an interesting metamorphosis from the retreat for congenial fellowship to one of sanctuary against harm. The bar is a place of public access, but in time of crisis it is understood to be an area of isolation, cut off from outside danger. The *bar*keeper thus —methodically performing an accustomed rite—*barred* the door and window, creating in this protective action "a solemn, chapel-like gloom." The conversion of the secular to the mythic is again suggested by Scratchy's primitive howling before Potter's house, which "regarded him as might a great stone god." As in ancient times, an object belonging to a deified person takes on that person's attributes. Scratchy's futile clamor is a forewarning of frustration and defeat.

Still other mythic undertones may be found in the opposed allusions to water. First, there is the fluid impression of the Pullman's interior (the "sea-green" velvet . . . "the wood that gleamed as darkly brilliant as the surface of a pool," albeit, "a pool of oil" recalled by Potter in his moment of decision) and the flowing sensation ascribed to the train. Then, the stop for water, which he reports like "one announcing death." Finally, the bride as a "drooping, drowning woman." Although the water references have a plain enough narrative and descriptive function, they, like numerous other metaphorical statements (e.g., "Potter's mouth seemed to be merely a grave for his tongue.") amplify meaning. In this instance, the water is suggestive of an unstoppable, destined movement. The water is also suggestive of the principles of life and death, of generation and destruction. It is these principles which, combined with the chivalric motif, define the main issues of the story. The quest is for something larger than physical life, something vaguely supernatural.

Yet, if the story reaches out beyond the literal, we are always kept in touch with reality. Crane hovers over the story, so to speak, directing the action at all times as well as the meaning. Unwilling to let the theme become oppressive or too obvious, he frequently exercises his license to intrude, to speak in his own lightly mocking voice. Jack's house, for example, is a "safe citadel" as well as "a great stone god." The dog "had not appreciated the advance of events." "Historically there was supposed to be something infinitely humorous in their situation." Other examples (all reminiscent, incidentally, of Crane's poetic practice) abound. Some of this usage may be attributed to the mannered style of Crane's day which now seems old-fashioned to us. More significantly, however, he uses verbal humor for brief moments of comic respite, to maintain a balance between the melodramatic and the real. He knows that if we smile, it will be uneasily. We cannot long be indifferent to the loneliness of Potter's occupation, to the frenzied brutality of Scratchy, or the tender pathos of the newlyweds. The situation is serious and we respond to it seriously. What seems remote in time and custom becomes immediate.

CHAPTER 4

Setting

CHARACTER and plot, as we have seen, are active symbolic representations of human experience. We do not expect the people and action of fiction to be identical with those of real life; but we do expect probability. No matter how far-fetched—in terms of everyday reality—they remain acceptable as long as the author can convince us that they fall somewhere within the range of human personality, motive, and consequence. While character and plot are the principal sources of interest, they generally require the support of other identifiable details to strengthen their believable qualities and to enhance interest. Since, as Miss Bowen succinctly reminds us, "nothing can happen nowhere," setting is an especially valuable means of furthering credibility. Artistically contrived, "the locale of the happening always colors the happening, and often, to a degree, shapes it."

Setting is the physical background against which the story is projected and of which it is a coherent part. It is the element of place and also of time, for setting may impart a sense of history, the season of the year, or the hour of the day. The setting of a novel is a group of symbols or a single symbol by which the author conveys certain of his own impressions and by which, at the same time, he gives us a more or less specific point of spatial and temporal reference. This may be drawn from any aspect of physical nature: the world of trees, mountains, rivers, oceans, sun, moon, stars, and so forth. It may also be drawn from man-made phenomena like specific cities, streets, houses, rooms, and the like. The value of the physical location will vary in direct proportion to the emphasis that the novelist chooses to attach to the setting.

In this sense, for example, setting may even have the force of a character in the story. E. E. Cummings, to cite an instance, uses the enclosure in *The Enormous Room* both as a place of confinement and as a source of fellowship. The parched land in John Steinbeck's *Grapes of Wrath* evokes a social attitude, but it is also a hostile, impersonal agency for destruction. In *The Naked and the Dead*, Norman Mailer lets the island jungles "stand for" the savagery of war; he also uses them as a dynamic part of his narrative situation. The main thing about setting is that it must contribute to the development of plot and character, and never be extraneous to them. Setting is not merely scenic; it is connected with the happenings of the story. Like character and plot, setting arouses and helps to sustain our thoughts and feelings. It also calls into play our visual imagination.

Setting may be evoked implicitly, through an accumulation or progression of incidents, even though specific details are sparse. Some passages from Jane Austen's *Pride and Prejudice* typify this kind of economy:

> When they left the high road for the lane to Hunsford, every eye was in search of the Parsonage, and every turning expected to bring it in view. The paling of Rosings Park was their boundary on one side. Elizabeth smiled at the recollection of all that she had heard of its inhabitants.
>
> At length the Parsonage was discernible. The garden sloping to the road, the house standing in it, the green pales, and the laurel hedge, everything declared they were arriving. Mr. Collins and Charlotte appeared at the door, and the carriage stopped at the small gate which led by a short gravel walk to the house amidst the nods and smiles of the whole party. In a moment they were all out of the chaise, rejoicing at the sight of each other. Mrs. Collins welcomed her friend with the liveliest pleasure, . . .

                    * * * * * * * * * *

> The dinner was exceedingly handsome, and there were all the servants and all the articles of plate which Mr. Collins had promised; and, as he had likewise foretold, he took his seat at the bottom of the table by her ladyship's desire, and looked as if he felt that life could furnish nothing greater. He carved, and ate, and praised with delighted alacrity; and every dish was commended, first by him and then by Sir William, who was now enough recovered to echo whatever his son-in-

law said, in a manner which Elizabeth wondered Lady Catherine could
bear.

* * * * * * * * * *

She was proceeding directly to her favourite walk, when the recollection of Mr. Darcy's sometimes coming there stopped her, and instead of
entering the park, she turned up the lane, which led farther from the
turnpike-road. The park paling was still the boundary on one side, and
she soon passed one of the gates into the ground.

After walking two or three times along that part of the lane, she was
tempted, by the pleasantness of the morning, to stop at the gates and look
into the park. The five weeks which she had now passed in Kent had
made a great difference in the country, and every day was adding to
the verdure of the early trees. She was on the point of continuing her
walk when she caught a glimpse of a gentleman within the sort of grove
which edged the park; he was moving that way; and, fearful of its
being Mr. Darcy, she was directly retreating.

In each passage cited, Miss Austen gives just enough detail to
engage the reader's imagination, but not so much that he is following an elaborate description. It is noteworthy that each physical
setting blends almost imperceptibly with the action which follows.
First, there is the natural apprehension of detail suited to a parson-
age. Then, there is the small flurry of activity at the dinner table,
interlarded with impressions of the service and Mr. Collins' officiousness. Finally, there is the pleasant country setting contrasted with
Elizabeth's attempt to avoid Mr. Darcy. Descriptive details of the
countryside and the dinner table not only do not intrude upon the
action, they are assimilated within it, giving it a tangible location
and emphasizing the muted, social situations intended by the author. Miss Austen uses setting as a necessary background, depending upon it to support somewhat larger effects incident to the genteel
and prosperous society of which she writes.

Landscape in Jane Austen's novels is a companion to the tranquil,
almost pastoral mood that she intended to depict. Turning to
Thomas Hardy for further evidence of the relationships among character, plot, and setting, we discover the achievement of an opposite
effect. His intention in *The Return of the Native* is to dramatize
the tragic destiny of man. The sunny, well-tended countryside of
Miss Austen becomes the dark threat of Egdon Heath, where the

somber events of the novel take place. In the opening chapter, Hardy puts his setting into a position of overt importance.

> The most thorough-going ascetic could feel that he had a natural right to wander on Egdon: he was keeping within the line of legitimate indulgence when he laid himself open to influences such as these. Colours and beauties so far subdued were, at least, the birthright of all. Only in summer days of highest feather did its mood touch the level of gaiety. Intensity was more usually reached by way of the solemn than by way of the brilliant, and such a sort of intensity was often arrived at during winter darkness, tempests, and mists. Then Egdon was aroused to reciprocity; for the storm was its lover, and the wind its friend. Then it became the home of strange phantoms; and it was found to be the hitherto unrecognized original of those wild regions of obscurity which are vaguely felt to be compassing us about in midnight dreams of flight and disaster, and are never thought of after the dream till revived by scenes like this.

Little analysis is required to point out the obvious, explicit function of setting in *The Return of the Native*. The heath is envisioned as a malignant, overpowering force. When we read that "the storm was its lover, and the wind its friend," we anticipate a destructiveness that operates with almost demoniac intelligence. And, in fact, Hardy throughout the novel stresses the centrality of Egdon Heath, giving it the prominence of a leading antagonist. Setting, then, is specifically correlative with the human characters, and Hardy insists upon this identification.

The setting, apart from this dynamic, explicit role, is also the main source of atmosphere in the novel. That is, the descriptive details are self-sufficient for the narrative purpose. But the setting also gradually assumes a pervasive intangible force whose premonitions of disaster transcend mere physical uneasiness. We see the heath in all its starkness, to be sure, but even more direly we sense its impalpable malevolence. The imagination, as most of us know, can create greater terrors than physical reality. Hardy's ability to educe atmosphere from setting is comparable to that of such celebrated writers as Edgar Allan Poe ("Fall of the House of Usher"), William Faulkner ("A Rose for Emily"), or Emily Brontë (*Wuthering Heights*).

Hardy's use of setting is unusually instructive, for its role in his novels is always an intricate element of structure. Conceived in both physical and moral terms, his settings characteristically amplify the meanings of the actors and their actions. Observe in this brief passage from *The Mayor of Casterbridge* the way in which the protagonists are fitted into the landscape:

> The wife mostly kept her eyes fixed ahead, though with little interest —the scene for that matter being one that might have been matched at almost any spot in any county in England at this time of the year; a road neither straight nor crooked, neither level nor hilly, bordered by hedges, trees, and other vegetation which had entered the blackened-green stage of colour that the doomed leaves pass through on their way to dingy, and yellow, and red. The grassy margin of the bank, and the nearest hedgerow boughs, were powdered by the dust that had been stirred over them by hasty vehicles, the same dust as it lay on the road deadening their footfalls like a carpet; and this, with the aforesaid total absence of conversation, allowed every extraneous sound to be heard.

Here, as in the previous passage, Hardy shows us the countryside, giving it the recognizable descriptive details of a summer scene. He goes beyond the merely descriptive, however, using the landscape as a background for the two silent figures. He calls attention to the neutrality of the countryside and to its late-summer desolation, which complement the detachment of husband and wife. All that they share is a physical location in which the sounds about them magnify their own silence. The dust "deadening their footfalls like a carpet" signifies the aridity of their relationship. Comparably, the dying leaves bring into focus the deterioration of their union. Setting establishes a place and season for the action, but more significantly it creates an atmosphere and a mood. It gives us an undefined presage of something ominous or baleful. More specifically, it causes us to direct our feelings—of wonder and misgiving, perhaps —to the reticent pair. Ultimately, the oppression caused by the dust and the "doomed leaves" is transferred to them.

Hardy's settings are familiar to many of us because they bear a close physical resemblance to landscapes we have seen. Yet, they are capable of producing surprise because they have been transfigured—overshadowed, as it were—by implications which are foreign to normal experience. The author, that is, has interpreted reality in an unexpected manner. The desire for surprise is strong in most readers of fiction, and they are gratified when the seeming commonplace is imbued with the unusual.

Setting, to touch upon a single element, provides an exacting test of the author's ability to embellish familiar details in a way that might escape even a careful observer of nature and yet without violating the truth of what has been observed. An even greater responsibility is assumed by the author whose purposes require an unfamiliar setting, for in addition to maintaining a harmonious structural relationship among character, plot, and setting, he must record unfamiliar places in a way that will make them seem familiar. Joseph Conrad, for example, places his most important novels in exotic, tropical locations where characters far removed from their customary environments are obliged to work out moral or spiritual dilemmas. Setting, thus, emphasizes physical isolation and the lonely struggle for self-recognition. Following are two selections from *Victory*:

> On the nights of full moon the silence around Samburan—the "Round Island" of the charts—was dazzling; and in the flood of cold light Heyst could see his immediate surroundings, which had the aspect of an abandoned settlement invaded by the jungle: vague roofs above low vegetation, broken shadows of bamboo fences in the sheen of long grass, something like an overgrown bit of road slanting among ragged thickets towards the shore only a couple of hundred yards away, with a black jetty and a mound of some sort, quite inky on its unlighted side.

A few paragraphs earlier, Conrad had made this identification between Axel Heyst and his tropical setting:

> He was out of everybody's way, as if he were perched on the highest peak of the Himalayas, and in a sense as conspicuous. Every one in that part of the world knew him, dwelling on his little island. An island is but the top of a mountain. Axel Heyst, perched on it immovably, was surrounded instead of the imponderable stormy and transparent ocean of air merging into infinity, by a tepid, shallow sea; a passionless offshoot of the great waters which embrace the continents of this globe. His most frequent visitors were shadows, the shadows of clouds, relieving the monotony of the inanimate, brooding sunshine of the tropics. His nearest neighbour—I am speaking now of things showing some sort of animation—was an indolent volcano which smoked faintly all day

with its head just above the northern horizon, and at night levelled at
him, from amongst the clear stars, a dull red glow, expanding and col-
lapsing spasmodically like the end of a gigantic cigar puffed at intermittently in the dark. Axel Heyst was also a smoker; and when he
lounged out on his verandah with his cheroot, the last thing before
going to bed, he made in the night the same sort of glow and of the
same size as that other one so many miles away.

Through setting, Conrad has created an image of an aloof, isolated man. In the first passage quoted, Heyst is surrounded in the
night by silence and jungle. The moon-bathed setting is serene and
primitive—except for a "conspicuous object . . . a gigantic black-
board raised on two posts and presenting to Heyst, when the moon
got over that side, the white letters 'T. B. C. Co.' in a row at least
two feet high. These were the initials of the Tropical Belt Coal
Company, his employers—his late employers, to be precise." Here
the identification with the scenery is intimated, not stated, and we
infer in time a similar ambivalence in Heyst's personality: the solitary man whose detachment from society is impinged upon by an
obvious symbol of society.

In the second passage, however, Conrad makes the identification
with nature explicit. Heyst is placed metaphorically on an island
and mountain, and in a sea, obscured by cloud-shadows. The transition from metaphor to fact, with the introduction of the volcano, is
hardly noticed. Like Hardy, Conrad uses the mystery of nature as
a part of his fictional treatment, especially of mood; and like Hardy,
he isolates man in that mystery. But he differs in this respect. He
makes setting a metaphoric key to the understanding of an individual, and thus an element of him; whereas Hardy makes setting a
force of destiny that hovers over him, and thus supreme. In each
instance, however, setting is an inseparable aspect of character and
plot.

The metaphoric possibilities of setting are evident in the fiction
of Willa Cather, who represents the changing seasons in a fugue-
like way. She uses them to promote theme and mood, and at the
same time to reiterate the shifting fortunes of her protagonists. The
transition experienced by the pioneers of *My Ántonia* from extreme

hardship to the beginnings of comfort is dramatized in the return of spring:

> When spring came, after that hard winter, one could not get enough of the nimble air. Every morning I wakened with a fresh consciousness that winter was over. There was none of the signs of spring for which I used to watch in Virginia, no budding woods or blooming gardens. There was only—spring itself; the throb of it, the light restlessness, the vital essence of it everywhere: in the sky, in the swift clouds, in the pale sunshine, and in the warm, high wind—rising suddenly, sinking suddenly, impulsive and playful like a big puppy that pawed you and then lay down to be petted. If I had been tossed down blind-fold on that red prairie, I should have known that it was spring.
>
> Everywhere now there was the smell of burning grass. Our neighbours burned off their pasture before the new grass made a start, so that the fresh growth would not be mixed with the dead stand of last year. Those light, swift fires, running about the country, seemed a part of the same kindling that was in the air.

The pioneers are resurrected in the new season, coming out of the frozen land into the exuberance of teeming life. The setting calls forth joy and parallels the developing narrative situation:

> The Shimerdas were in their new log house by then. The neighbours had helped them to build it in March. It stood directly in front of their old cave, which they used as a cellar. The family were now fairly equipped to begin their struggle with the soil. They had four comfortable rooms to live in, a new windmill—bought on credit—a chicken-house and poultry. Mrs. Shimerda had paid grandfather ten dollars for a milk cow, and was to give him fifteen more as soon as they harvested their first crop.

When spring gives way to summer, the promise of spring is fulfilled, the seeds burst into full and sensuous life. The setting is drawn explicitly into the optimistic theme of the novel:

> July came on with that breathless, brilliant heat which makes the plains of Kansas and Nebraska the best corn country in the world. It seemed as if we could hear the corn growing in the night; under the stars one caught a faint crackling in the dewy, heavy-odoured corn-fields where the feathered stalk stood so juicy and green. If all the great plain from the Missouri to the Rocky Mountains had been under glass, and the heat regulated by a thermometer, it could not have been better for the yellow tassels that were ripening and fertilizing the silk day by day. The cornfields were far apart in those times, with miles of

wild grazing land between. It took a clear, meditative eye like my grandfather's to foresee that they would enlarge and multiply until they would
be, not the Shimerdas' cornfields, or Mr. Bushy's, but the world's corn-
fields; that their yield would be one of the great economic facts, like
the wheat crop of Russia, which underlie all the activities of men, in
peace or war.

The settings at which we have looked thus far utilize natural
phenomena, for the most part, helping to define inner conflicts, to
identify man with his environment, or—in the case of Jane Austen
—to confirm normal social relationships. These by no means exhaust
the possibilities of setting, but only a few more functions may be
illustrated. One of these is practiced by Arnold Bennett, who favored closely detailed description (as Mrs. Woolf complained) that
would coincide with the realism of his fiction. This characteristic
depiction of locale is clearly evident in the following passage from
The Old Wives' Tale:

> The Baines's shop, to make which three dwellings had at intervals
> been thrown into one, lay at the bottom of the Square. It formed about
> one-third of the south side of the Square, the remainder being made up
> of Critchlow's (chemist), the clothier's, and the Hanover Spirit Vaults.
> ("Vaults" was a favourite synonym of the public-houses in the Square.
> Only two of the public-houses were crude public-houses: the rest were
> "vaults.") It was a composite building of three storeys, in blackish-
> crimson brick, with a projecting shop-front and, above and behind that,
> two rows of little windows. On the sash of each window was a red
> cloth roll stuffed with sawdust, to prevent draughts; plain white blinds
> descended about six inches from the top of each window. There were
> no curtains to any of the windows save one; this was the window of
> the drawing-room, on the first floor at the corner of the Square and
> King Street. Another window, on the second storey, was peculiar, in
> that it had neither blind nor pad, and was very dirty; this was the
> window of an unused room that had a separate staircase to itself, the
> staircase being barred by a door always locked. Constance and Sophia
> had lived in continual expectation of the abnormal issuing from that
> mysterious room, which was next to their own. But they were disap-
> pointed. The room had no shameful secret except the incompetence of
> the architect who had made one house out of three; it was just an
> empty, unemployable room. This building had also a considerable
> frontage on King Street, where, behind the shop, was sheltered the par-
> lour, with a large window and a door that led directly by two steps
> into the street. A strange peculiarity of the shop was that it bore no sign-

board. Once it had had a large signboard which a memorable gale had
blown into the Square. Mr. Baines had decided not to replace it. He
had always objected to what he called "puffing," and for this reason
would never hear of such a thing as a clearance sale. The hatred of
"puffing" grew on him until he came to regard even a sign as "puffing."
Uninformed persons who wished to find Baines's must ask and learn.
For Mr. Baines, to have replaced the sign would have been to condone,
yea, to participate in, the modern craze for unscrupulous self-advertise-
ment. This abstention of Mr. Baines's from indulgence in signboards was
somehow accepted by the more thoughtful members of the community
as evidence that the height of Mr. Baines's principles was greater even
than they had imagined.

After the rather impressionistic scenes described by the preceding
authors, Bennett's exactitude is overwhelming. He has given us a
verbal blueprint of the Baines building, of those adjacent to it, and
even ironically of Mr. Baines's attitudes. One may sympathize with
Mrs. Woolf's objection to such particularity, yet acknowledge its
importance to the leisurely, specific realism of Bennett's technique.
By giving us initially a total view of the Square and the shop, he
prepares us to accept the centrality of these physical details in the
novel which gradually unfolds. Mr. Baines's restricted, provincial
outlook fits naturally into the restricted, provincial community of a
past era. Bennett's minute rendering is thus invaluable to his structure. His purpose is to reveal a segment of life—in its totality—as
he sees it.

This method may be compared with that of D. H. Lawrence, who
also uses setting in relation to experience. But Lawrence, as the
following quotation from *Sons and Lovers* shows, is more selective.
His partial intention being social protest, he emphasizes realistic
details to show how man has selfishly despoiled the country with
complete disregard for the esthetic, economic, and social well-being
of the miners who must live there. To a certain extent, then, contrast is an essential feature of Lawrence's technique:

"The Bottoms" succeeded to "Hell Row." Hell Row was a block of
thatched, bulging cottages that stood by the brookside on Greenhill
Lane. There lived the colliers who worked in the little gin-pits two
fields away. The brook ran under the alder trees, scarcely soiled by these
small mines, whose coal was drawn to the surface by donkeys that
plodded wearily in a circle round a gin. And all over the country-side

were these same pits, some of which had been worked in the time of
Charles II, the few colliers and the donkeys burrowing down like ants
into the earth, making queer mounds and little black places among the
corn-fields and the meadows. And the cottages of these coalminers, in
blocks and pairs here and there, together with odd farms and homes of
the stockingers, straying over the parish, formed the village of Best-
wood. . . .

The houses themselves were substantial and very decent. One could
walk all round, seeing little front gardens with auriculas and saxifrage
in the shadow of the bottom block, sweet-williams and pinks in the
sunny top block; seeing neat front windows, little porches, little privet
hedges, and dormer windows for the attics. But that was outside; that
was the view on to the uninhabited parlours of the colliers' wives. The
dwelling-room, the kitchen, was at the back of the house, facing inward
toward the blocks, looking at a scrubby back garden, and then at the
ash-pits. And between the rows, between the long lines of ash-pits, went
the alley, where the children played and the women gossiped and the
men smoked. So, the actual conditions of living in the Bottoms, that
was so well built and that looked so nice, were quite unsavoury because
people must live in the kitchen, and the kitchens opened on to that
nasty alley of ash-pits.

Setting may serve a variety of fictional purposes, but it is never
meaningful unless it is cohesive with the entire work. Sometimes,
as in several passages already cited, it is worked discreetly and unobtrusively—perhaps even symbolically—into the framework of
the novel. Sometimes, and this we have also seen, the setting is virtually spelled out by the author as a functional device in support
of theme or mood. Again, setting may make special demands upon
our attention in consequence of unusually conspicuous presentation.
In illustration of this final point, let us look at two complete, introductory chapters, in which setting acts as a prologue to action. The
first is from Alan Paton's *Cry, the Beloved Country:*

There is a lovely road that runs from Ixopo into the hills. These
hills are grass-covered and rolling, and they are lovely beyond any
singing of it. The road climbs seven miles into them, to Carisbrooke;
and from there, if there is no mist, you look down on one of the fairest
valleys of Africa. About you there is grass and bracken and you may
hear the forlorn crying of the titihoya, one of the birds of the veld.
Below you is the valley of the Umzimkulu, on its journey from the
Drackensberg to the sea; and beyond and behind the river, great hill
after great hill; and beyond and behind them, the mountains of Ingeli
and East Griqualand.

The grass is rich and matted, you cannot see the soil. It holds the rain and the mist, and they seep into the ground, feeding the streams in every kloof. It is well-tended, and not too many cattle feed upon it; not too many fires burn it, laying bare the soil. Stand unshod upon it, for the ground is holy, being even as it came from the Creator. Keep it, guard it, care for it, for it keeps men, guards men, cares for men. Destroy it and man is destroyed.

Where you stand the grass is rich and matted, you cannot see the soil. But the rich green hills break down. They fall to the valley below, and falling, change their nature. For they grow red and bare; they cannot hold the rain and mist, and the streams are dry in the kloofs. Too many cattle feed upon the grass, and too many fires have burned it. Stand shod upon it, for it is coarse and sharp, and the stones cut under the feet. It is not kept, or guarded, or cared for, it no longer keeps men, guards men, cares for men. The titihoya does not cry here any more.

The great red hills stand desolate, and the earth has torn away like flesh. The lightning flashes over them, the clouds pour down upon them, the dead streams come to life, full of the red blood of the earth. Down in the valleys women scratch the soil that is left, and the maize hardly reaches the height of a man. They are valleys of old men and old women, of mothers and children. The men are away, the young men and the girls are away. The soil cannot keep them any more.

The second passage is from Ernest Hemingway's *A Farewell to Arms:*

In the late summer of that year we lived in a house in a village that looked across the river and the plain to the mountains. In the bed of the river there were pebbles and boulders, dry and white in the sun, and the water was clear and swiftly moving and blue in the channels. Troops went by the house and down the road and the dust they raised powdered the leaves of the trees. The trunks of the trees too were dusty and the leaves fell early that year and we saw the troops marching along the road and the dust rising and leaves, stirred by the breeze, falling and the soldiers marching and afterwards the roads bare and white except for the leaves.

The plain was rich with crops; there were many orchards of fruit trees and beyond the plain the mountains were brown and bare. There was fighting in the mountains and at night we could see the flashes from the artillery. In the dark it was like summer lightning, but the nights were cool and there was not the feeling of a storm coming.

Sometimes in the dark we heard the troops marching under the window and guns going past pulled by motor-tractors. There was much traffic at night and many mules on the roads with boxes of ammunition on each side of their pack-saddles and gray motor-trucks that carried men, and other trucks with loads covered with canvas that moved slower in the traffic. There were big guns too that passed in the day drawn by tractors, the long barrels of guns covered with green branches and vines laid over the tractors. To the north we could look across a valley and see a forest of chestnut trees and behind it another mountain on this side of the river. There was fighting for that mountain too, but it was not successful, and in the fall when the rains came the leaves all fell from the chestnut trees and the branches were bare and the trunks black with rain. The vineyards were thin and bare-branched too and all the country wet and brown and dead with the autumn. There were mists over the river and clouds on the mountain and the trucks splashed mud on the road and the troops were muddy and wet in their capes; their rifles were wet and under their capes the two leather cartridge-boxes on the front of their belts, gray leather boxes heavy with the packs of clips of thin, long 6.5 mm. cartridges, bulged forward under the capes so that the men, passing on the road, marched as though they were six months gone with child.

There were small gray motor-cars that passed going very fast; usually there was an officer on the seat with the driver and more officers in the back seat. They splashed more mud than the camions even and if one of the officers in the back was very small and sitting between two generals, he himself so small that you could not see his face but only the top of his cap and his narrow back, and if the car went especially fast it was probably the King. He lived in Udine and came out in this way nearly every day to see how things were going, and things went very badly.

At the start of the winter came the permanent rain and with the rain came the cholera. But it was checked and in the end only seven thousand died of it in the army.

Although their thematic intentions are different, both Paton and Hemingway rely strongly upon setting to open their respective novels. While writers like Hardy, Conrad, Lawrence, and Cather make equally effective and early use of setting, they weave it into their stories in more gradual stages. Paton and Hemingway, on the other hand, pronounce place and season, making them the foreground into which the action will enter. The setting in each is responsible for controlling mood: from rapture to despair in Paton; a deceptive monotony in Hemingway. The other principal similarity inheres in the rhythmic style which each employs to further the initial impression. Paton, especially, appeals to our emotions, by repeating key phrases of description and by gentle religious exhortation. Hemingway's rhythm (which like Paton's has Biblical undertones) is less varied, moving along with a steadiness that emphasizes the military movements.

The sensuous appeal in both authors is predominantly visual, the natural scenery of mountains, hills, and plains dwarfing the labors and strife of the people in them. Paton, however, creates a developing—or more properly, a retrogressive—scene. At first, like Willa Cather, he presents the loveliness of nature, without intimating disaster. He brings the eye from the distant hills to the ground underfoot. Then he looks off, again, to the hills and valleys, noting the change from abundance to desolation. In Hemingway's scenery we are similarly aware of shifting perspective. But unlike Paton, he amplifies his contrasts through change of season, from summer through winter. For Paton, the land is spoiled by man's slovenliness and creates economic disaster. For Hemingway, the land alters with the passage of the seasons and adds to the ugliness of war.

Both authors use color to enhance the significance of setting. Paton's dominant green clashes with the harsh red earth of the ravaged hills. Hemingway's is essentially neutral—the whitened pebbles, the dust-covered roads and leaves (like Hardy's), the rain-blackened trees. The greenery is an illusion, for it is the cut branches and vines which camouflage the guns and simply foretells destruction. This illusion of fertility is furthered by the grotesque image of the soldiers whose gray cartridge-boxes make them look pregnant. We can imagine the colorful crops and fruit-orchards, but even these are illusory, for the brown, bare mountains dominate them.

Paton and Hemingway both focus the reader's attention on setting by contrasting nature at its best and worst; and they relate setting to what is about to occur. Of the two, Paton gives the greater impression of personal involvement. His lyrical style and then his overt denunciation of man's improvidence bring his attitudes immediately to bear upon the situation. In this respect, he is much like Lawrence, who openly states a social criticism of man's abuse of the land. Hemingway seems detached, revealing himself only in the final two sentences, where his irony is inescapable. "At the start of the winter came the permanent rain and with the rain came the cholera. But it was checked and in the end only seven thousand died of it in the army." Different though their purposes are, however, Paton and Hemingway make setting a key to mood and theme.

Samples such as have been included in this chapter can do no more than suggest the varieties and applications of setting. Even within these limits, however, the reader may discover subtleties of which he was not previously aware and for which he should be alert in his subsequent readings. To review briefly, setting may be merely incidental to considerations of theme and structure; but incidental or haphazard representation of place and time is never so satisfying as that which is integrated with the total effect of the novel. Setting works especially well with mood, for it helps to strengthen the emotional responses through visualization. In the short story "Gooseberries," for example, Chekhov manipulates the farm and house in such a way as to enhance the poignancy of Ivan's tale. Jane Austen and Willa Cather control setting to elicit appropriate responses of tranquillity and joy. Further, as we have had occasion to see in *The Mayor of Casterbridge*, setting may extend beyond tangible reality to become absorbed in an intangible atmosphere. Something of this atmospheric effect is to be found also in *Victory* and *Cry, the Beloved Country*.

As a corollary of theme, setting enjoys considerable prominence in several of the preceding quotations (most notably in the Paton and Hemingway pieces). For added evidence, we may consider in "The Bride Comes to Yellow Sky" the dual setting of the elegant Pullman and the crude Western town. Physically they are incompatible; yet symbolically they find a common center in Crane's theme. But where Crane emphasizes setting in relation to an individual's dilemma, Hardy, Lawrence, and Paton are concerned with moral or social problems incorporated in setting. It is obvious that setting may have more than one function in a novel, or that similar settings may have opposed functions in different novels. For instance, the summer scenes in Hardy and Hemingway are physically pretty much alike; yet they contribute to altogether different intentions. Hardy treats the summer as a parched season already dying, doomed as his characters are doomed. These charac-

ters, isolated and alien to each other, seem to be a part of this setting. But Hemingway relishes the fullness of summer, a good season, except for the foreign presence of the troops.

All these and other potentialities of setting have been treated in
enough detail that brief reminders should be sufficient now. One of
the most important characteristics of setting is its close affinity with
development of plot and character. Each of the examples above,
thus, makes full use of this connection. Individual artists, however,
render setting in relation to plot and character distinctively: explicitly, as in Bennett; implicitly, as in Cather, Conrad, and Hemingway; or in combination, as in Hardy, Lawrence, and Paton.
Many authors find setting a useful instrument for enveloping their
attitudes or tone. Jane Austen allows a flourishing countryside or a
dining-room to objectify her social irony; Hemingway is more directly and stringently ironical through evocation of the winter rains.
Lawrence Durrell's exotic depictions of Alexandria in Egypt help to
impart his views of a decadent society. Settings familiar or unfamiliar—an American prairie, an English moor or town, an African
veld, a Dublin apartment—may be a source of sensuous or intellectual illumination. Their purpose, whether to surprise, please, or
disturb, always coincides with the total purpose of the novels to
which they belong.

The Ordering of Fiction

CHAPTER 5

Categories of Order

Selection and Arrangement

ONLY the author is responsible for the unity—the coherent literary totality—of the novel, and the way in which he achieves it is a partial test of his artistry. His task would be difficult enough if he were only to observe life keenly and intelligently, and then set down his report. In fact, however, an ability to collect and transcribe experiences is a primary condition, to be followed by the complexities of judicious choice and disposition of material. In opposition to this view, a self-conscious rebel like Jack Kerouac sneers openly (in *The Subterraneans*) at discriminating selection because he feels it shackles his creative manner. But we need to be reminded by Joyce Cary (in *Art and Reality*) that "life doesn't have a total meaning, it is simply a wild confusion of events from which we have to select what we think significant for ourselves. Look at any morning paper. It makes no sense at all—it means nothing but chaos. We read only what we think important; that is to say, we provide our own sense to the news. We have to do so because otherwise it wouldn't be there. To do this, we have to have some standard of valuation, we have to know whether the political event is more than a murder, or a divorce than the stock market, or the stock market than who won the Derby."

The matter of fiction is experience refined through a long process of selection, invention, and reflection. Furthermore, it is arranged on the page in a manner which the author thinks most appropriate and effective for the purpose underlying the novel's creation. The completed novel, thus, reveals the economy and concentration of art. It also reveals the author's subjectivity, for he has the privilege of stating or implying prejudices and sympathies. All the materials are consciously arranged for the fulfillment of a specific purpose. Time and place, toward this end, may be in keeping with conventional expectations; or they may frustrate our sense of logic and regularity. Characters may be well-balanced, "normal" people; they may be exaggerated or limited in some exceptional way.

The selective principle of fiction is recorded very well by Henry James in his preface to *The Spoils of Poynton*. "Life being all inclusion and confusion, and art being all discrimination and selection, the latter, in search of the hard latent value with which alone it is concerned, sniffs round the mass as instinctively and unerringly as a dog suspicious of some buried bone." Life is the core (the "germ," he calls it) of fiction, but whatever essential meaning is in that core the writer must disclose for himself by his own devices. "If life, presenting us the germ, and left merely to herself in such a business, gives the case away, almost always, before we can stop her, what are the signs for our guidance, what the primary laws for a saving selection, how do we know when and where to intervene, where do we place the beginnings of the wrong or the right deviation? . . . The answer may be after all that mysteries here elude us, that general considerations fail or mislead, and that even the fondest of artists need ask for no wider range than the logic of the particular case."

The selective "logic of a particular case" is exemplified in *The Red Badge of Courage*, which centers on the initiation of Henry Fleming into manhood through warfare. Everything extraneous to that initiation is omitted, and everything relevant to it is compressed and intensified for maximum emotion and meaning. Through a succession of harrowing, credible circumstances, Stephen Crane represents Fleming's growth during his participation in a Civil War campaign. Crane's technique, however, is alien to that of the diarist who faithfully and undiscriminatingly records a calendar of events. Rather, he has reduced the confused totality of war to a number of individual scenes—often giving them a symbolic turn—which are directly consequential to the development of the young man. The massive chaos of war is condensed into Fleming's experiences.

The war details are vivid, but they tend to be impressionistic (as if the isolated Fleming were watching the contour of a steady movement) rather than particularized. The impressionistic effect is enhanced by Henry's relations to shifting groups of soldiers and by an unobtrusive natural setting. The massing of physical and emotional experiences is unified by an almost hazy sense of time's passage. "After complicated journeyings with many pauses, there had come months of monotonous life in a camp. . . . For days he had made ceaseless calculations. . . . The rushing yellow of the developing day went on behind their backs. . . . When another night came the columns, changed to purple streaks, filed across two pontoon bridges." Time is a progressive and unifying quality, discreetly complementing variations of mood and fortune but never important for its own sake.

Crane's selection and ordering of materials is masterly. Yet his procedure represents but one of the countless methods available to the artist. As James said, it may be "that general considerations fail or mislead," and only "the logic of the particular case" is useful. What we can say here is that Crane exemplifies a concern with rigorous selection and an arrangement imparting a sense of direct, uninterrupted movement. Other novelists—say, Thackeray or Bennett or Galsworthy—likewise narrated in a forward flow of time and event. But they deliberately aimed at the inclusiveness of biographical and historical reconstruction. On the other hand, George Eliot's artistic engrossment—the profundity of human nature—demanded a restrictive treatment that might seem lacking in the bulk of *Middlemarch*. "I don't see how I can leave anything out," she fretted, "because I hope there is nothing that will seem irrelevant to my design." Still other novelists have satisfied their intentions by meticulous selection of materials which, however, they have deliberately rearranged out of normal time-sequence (as has been observed in an earlier chapter). The use of the "flashback" or introspective memories or shifting points-of-view—methods exploited in varying manners by Faulkner, Aiken, Joyce, Mrs. Woolf, Conrad, and their numerous successors—suggest the variability of selection and arrangement.

Complex narrative techniques necessitate artistic subtlety, for contrivance must never be obvious. Once the reader is distracted from the story by the author's cleverness, he is more likely to read as though he were playing a game with him than enjoying a literary experience. A restrained technique, such as Crane's, reduces the possible barriers between the writer and his audience. An eccentric technique, such as Sterne's, raises barriers which the reader must be encouraged to surmount for fullest enjoyment. The responsibility becomes mutual, if the novelist takes his art seriously and the reader is willing to extend himself. In *Tristram Shandy*, the author's wildly comic spirit plays havoc with order and direction. Conscious of his parody of normal narrative techniques, Sterne pretends to share his problem with the reader:

> You must know, my uncle *Toby* mistook the bridge as widely as my father mistook the mortars;—but to understand how my uncle *Toby* could mistake the bridge,—I fear I must give you an exact account of the road which led to it;—or drop the metaphor, (for there is nothing more dishonest in an historian, than the use of one,)—in order to conceive the probability of this error in my uncle *Toby* aright, I must give you some account of an adventure of *Trim's*, though much against my will. I say much against my will, only because the story, in one sense, is certainly out of its place here; for by right it should come in, either amongst the anecdotes of my uncle *Toby's* amours with widow *Wadman*, in which corporal *Trim* was no mean actor,—or else in the middle of his and my uncle *Toby's* campaigns on the bowling green,— for it will do very well in either place;—but then if I reserve it for either of those parts of my story,—I ruin the story I'm upon,—and if I tell it here—I anticipate matters, and ruin it there.

Pursuing his mock disturbance, Sterne sets forth reflections on the selective principle which are surprisingly consistent with James' and pertinent to the discussion in this section:

> O ye POWERS! (for powers ye are, and great ones too)—which enable mortal man to tell a story worthy the hearing,—that kindly shew him, where he is to begin it,—and where he is to end it,—what he is to put into it,—and what he is to leave out,—how much of it he is to cast into shade,—and whereabouts he is to throw his light!—Ye, who

preside over this vast empire of biographical freebooters, and see how many scrapes and plunges your subjects hourly fall into;—will you do one thing?

I beg and beseech you, (in case you will do nothing better for us) that wherever, in any part of your dominions it so falls out, that three several roads meet in one point, as they have done just here,—that at least you set up a guidepost, in the center of them, in mere charity to direct an uncertain devil, which of the three he is to take.

Sterne, of course, is being playful in an attempt to make fun of conventional novelists and to disarm readers who might not know what to make of his meandering narrative technique. Under the whimsy, however, is the conscious realization that the selection and arrangement of fictional materials are not to be decided by arbitrary fiat, and that artistic intuition must be respected. James blandly refers to the elusive "mysteries" which may play a part in composition, and Sterne to "POWERS." Fortunately, the supernatural is not a critical problem for our consideration. But we must remind ourselves from time to time that art, unlike science, can resort to very few absolute or clearly infallible rules. On the other hand, we should be reluctant to dismiss such attributes as artistic judgment or common sense, intangible though they may seem.

Working toward an end result, the author must frequently trust to his critical intelligence for the rightness of his decisions. The need to select and to place can be exasperating and even inhibiting, as we are told by the narrator of Samuel Beckett's *Molloy:* "And if I failed to mention this detail in its proper place, it is because you cannot mention everything in its proper place, you must choose, between the things worth mentioning and those even less so. For if you set out to mention everything you would never be done, and that's what counts, to be done, to have done. Oh I know, even when you mention only a few of the things there are, you do not get done either, I know, I know." The proof finally is in the reading. We may question the author's bases of selection and arrangement, but the question is less important than the fulfillment. If he has been properly discriminating, the signs of his control, imagination, and intelligence will be demonstrable in a unified, satisfying novel.

Mood and Tone

The subjective quality is fundamental to the ordering of fiction; it is basic to the control which makes a novel an interpretation of experience and not a journalistic report. Nevertheless, many authors remain as invisible to their audiences as they possibly can. That is, they choose to maintain a separation between the creative personality and the materials set down in the novel. No writer, of course, can obliterate himself totally from the reader's awareness. And not all writers (as will be demonstrated under *point-of-view*) insist upon invisibility. Yet there are occasions when an impression of aloofness, of distance between writer and audience, has a liberating effect on the work of art. Behind the masks of his characters, the writer may speak without fear of autobiographical inferences.

Of course, the question of whether an author effaces his personal image from the novel is purely academic, since the fact of his presence can never be doubted. But the degree to which he has divorced his private self from the public work may have a significant bearing upon our responses to the esthetic and thematic intention. As a man with a personal commitment, the author reveals his subjectivity by what he includes (and often by what he excludes) and the way in which he arranges his material. For another important source of revelation we may look to the emotions and attitudes depicted in the novel. The revelation may be direct and obvious, as with the novelist who intends to emphasize a theme that is socially or didactically important to him; or it may be implied and subtle, as when an author is deeply concerned with nuances of character. That is not to say moral and social problems cannot be treated implicitly, or character explicitly. It is all a matter of intention and achievement.

The novelist writes because he has feelings and attitudes about a subject; and these, stemming from his senses and intelligence, are directed toward his subject and his readers. Generally, in keeping with the tendency in modern fiction (although as usual there are exceptions), he permits one or more of the fictive characters to serve as his voice, while he himself remains in the wings. Our task, then, is to identify feelings and attitudes lodged in the novel and, more importantly, relate them to the total work.

First, let us consider *mood*, which shall be understood here as the author's attitude toward the subject (i.e., the event, action, scene, person, or quality) with which the narration deals. Mood is by and large a product of the author's senses, although his obligation to discriminate various kinds of mood obviously entails a certain amount of intellectual activity.

Although the mood of a novel is often persistent and cumulative, it may alternately be fragmented or variable. In other words, the feelings imparted by some novels follow generally consistent patterns, their effects intensified by the authors' absorption in ruling attitudes. On the other hand, some novels evoke mixed feelings because their authors assign differing emotional values to successive actions or to the responses of characters to them. The general emotional temper of a novel like *Pride and Prejudice* is relatively serene, despite necessary internal variations. That of *Wuthering Heights* is pervasively dark and tempestuous. The moods are altogether different, but in each novel consistency of mood coincides with consistency of narrative development.

By contrast, Dickens rings frequent changes of feeling in *David Copperfield*, from high comedy to tragic seriousness. Laughter, sentimentality, pathos, and loathing are among the emotions recalled by such familiar names as Mr. Micawber, Clara Peggotty and Barkis, Little Em'ly and Ham, Uriah Heep. Variability of mood is thus adapted to variability of character and situation. The total emotional effect of *David Copperfield* reflects an attitude toward life more complex than that expressed in either *Pride and Prejudice* or *Wuthering Heights*. Note should be taken, however, that even when feelings are mixed, they may result in the establishment of a dominant mood. This is true in the Dickens novel, which ultimately insists that all the moods be resolved into one that is thoughtful and sober. Similarly, Faulkner in *Light in August* is deeply serious, but he enhances his gravity by the bittersweet evocation of Lena Grove and Byron Bunch as well as by the astringent violence of Joe Christmas and Hightower.

In a massive novel like *Middlemarch*, George Eliot has treated

several thematic strains and several sets of characters who symbol-
ize the actions and motives within those strains. Without sacrific-
ing the unity and order of her novel, she has developed such concepts
as misdirected idealism, materialism, and religious hypocrisy, and
she has complemented each with a mood or feelings appropriate to
it. If, on a much reduced plane, we turn back to "The Bride Comes
to Yellow Sky," we discover similar instances of controlled variability. The opening scene is marked by the tenderness of the newlyweds and the mild mockery of the passengers and porter. In the second scene the mood is predominantly boisterous but modified by
anxiety in anticipation of Scratchy Wilson's rampage. Next, the
anxiety is sustained but the seriousness of the occasion is mingled
with comedy and even pathos as we discover Scratchy's adolescent
mannerisms. And finally, there is the ominous threat of the showdown, succeeded by the gravity and nobility engendered by Potter
and a counterbalance of pathos in the disappointed and confused
Scratchy. In each of the narratives just discussed, once the totality
has been realized interior differences of mood are reconciled; a unified structure dispels the impression of diversity.

Emotions are promoted most effectively when they assume identification with particular events, objects, or sensory data within the
narrative structure. Such evocation of feelings, through what T. S.
Eliot calls the "objective correlative," brings the reader into close
conjunction with the novel's emotional temper. Sometimes, however, novelists do not altogether trust this power of transference and
complement the evoked mood with a statement to explain it. Developing the isolation of Henry Fleming, Crane gives us numerous
correlatives to establish a mood of compassion on the boy's behalf.
Yet he does not always permit the external fact to carry its own interpretation, and supplies a bridge of meaning: "He lay down in
the grass. The blades pressed tenderly against his cheek. The moon
had been lighted and was hung in a tree-top. The liquid stillness
of the night enveloping him made him feel a vast pity for himself.
There was a caress in the soft winds; and the whole mood of the
darkness, he thought, was one of sympathy for himself in his dis-
tress." And though some may object to such explicit statement of
Henry's feelings, verging on the sentimental, we have been prepared

by Crane for the boy's gloom and let our sympathy for him merge with his self-pity.

Another kind of isolation, that of Stephen Dedalus in *A Portrait of the Artist as a Young Man,* evokes in the reader a mood of vital exuberance, an approximation of Stephen's free, creative spirit: "He was alone. He was unheeded, happy, and near to the wild heart of life. He was alone and young and wilful and wildhearted, alone amid a waste of wild air and brackish waters and the seaharvest of shells and tangle and veiled grey sunlight and gayclad lightclad figures of children and girls and voices childish and girlish in the air." Then he sees a girl in midstream, like a beautiful apparition, at whom he stares reverentially. "He turned away from her suddenly and set off across the strand. His cheeks were aflame; his body was aglow; his limbs were trembling. On and on and on and on he strode, far out over the sands, singing wildly to the sea, crying to greet the advent of the life that had cried to him." The mood here, though for another end, is almost as explicitly stated as that by Crane. Both authors have made specific claims upon us for emotional response, and it is a response which we make gladly and inevitably, for the respective situations are conducive to it. This "naturalness" of mood may be contrasted profitably with the stridently artificial feelings depicted by O. Henry.

Although multiple moods within a narrative structure can elicit pleasure, the single or controlling mood can be equally gratifying. The main thing is that the writer wishes to impress those created feelings upon his readers. If his symbols of communication—e.g., characters, setting, plot—are good, he will probably succeed in his goal. If, on the other hand, the symbols and their treatment have not been effective or credible, the reader is likely to reject the mood or refuse to participate in it. The fault, to be sure, may be the reader's. He may be inattentive and miss its significance, or simply be deficient in sensitivity and judgment. Or, as another possibility, he may be constitutionally poles apart from the emotional complexities depicted. For final effectiveness, there must be some kind of rapport or compatibility between writer and reader.

Mood, then, is an often subtle rendering by the author of his feelings about the subject, and he expresses them through the var-

ious activities and thoughts of the characters, situations, scenic arrangement, descriptions, and so forth. At the same time that the
author is projecting an attitude toward his subject, he may be projecting one (*tone*) toward his audience. The attitude intended by
the author toward the subject may be very close to, if not identical
with, that toward the audience; or the attitudes may be quite distinct. Hemingway, in *A Farewell to Arms*, implies his sympathetic
interest in the fate of Lieutenant Henry and Catherine Barkley.
Choosing a semblance of detachment, however, he directs toward
his subject a mood as overtly impersonal as the tone in which he
addresses his audience. Paton, on the other hand, openly enunci-
ates his profound compassion for the South African protagonists of
Cry, the Beloved Country. At the same time, his tone strongly implies censure, for he demands that his readers participate in the
guilt responsible for the natives' downtrodden condition.

Tone, like mood, is related to feeling. As is true of mood, tone
involves a generally conscious emotional commitment on the part
of the author, regardless of the overtness or reticence with which he
forwards his attitude. I. A. Richards' introductory statement about
tone (in *Practical Criticism*) is helpful. The author "chooses or arranges his words differently as his audience varies, in automatic or
deliberate *recognition of his relation to them.* The tone of his utterance reflects his awareness of this relation, his sense of how he
stands towards those he is addressing. Again the exceptional case
of dissimulation, or instances in which the speaker unwittingly reveals an attitude he is not consciously desirous of expressing, will
come to mind."

Tone is not necessarily more subtle than mood, but as a rule it is
more difficult to isolate or identify. Feeling is so much a part of the
texture of a story that we are inclined to relate its focus to the subject rather than to ourselves. There are exceptions, of course, as
when an author drops his reticence and is more concerned with direct statement than with inference. Such an exception is Frank Norris, who lets the thoughts of a character become bluntly expository.
"She was a little frightened—frightened of the vast, cruel machinery
of the city's life, and of the men who could dare it, who conquered
it. For a moment they seemed, in a sense, more terrible than the city

itself—men for whom all this crash of conflict and commerce had
no terrors. Those who could subdue it to their purposes, must they
not be themselves more terrible, more pitiless, more brutal?"

If Norris, in this passage from *The Pit,* is creating a mood centered in the impressions of Laura, he is also setting a tone which
forces upon the reader (at least, the reader of 1903) an awareness
of ruthless financial conditions that were a fact of American eco-
nomics. Not only is Norris describing a character's attitudes, he is
also assessing a public responsibility. This kind of overt address to
the reader often characterizes "naturalistic" or documentary fiction,
in which protest figures as a major element of intention.

The social anger of Ralph Ellison's *The Invisible Man,* though
stated within the narrative context by his Negro protagonist, sometimes becomes an undisguised recrimination spoken to the reader.
At one point, when the protagonist is reluctantly dancing with a white
woman, he broods: "I felt that somehow they expected me to perform even those tasks for which nothing in my experience—except
perhaps my imagination—had prepared me. Still it was nothing
new, white folks seemed always to expect you to know those things
which they'd done everything they could think of to prevent you
from knowing. The thing to do was to be prepared—as my grandfather had been when it was demanded that he quote the entire
United States Constitution as a test of his fitness to vote. He had
confounded them all by passing the test, although they still refused
him the ballot. . . ."

Nothing could be more explicit than this, and yet tone may be
achieved successfully—probably more artistically—by less obvious
means. Fictional tone has the attributes of speech, enabling one to
produce shades of meaning without always resorting to specific statement or exposition. When we speak, we are able to show by the inflection of the voice, by emphasis, by hesitation, any number of attitudes. (Joyce Cary illustrates the point thus: "If a child is told,
'Don't eat too much cake', and 'Don't torture the cat', with the
same mild emphasis, it will regard both with the same indulgence.")
In a simple phrase like "My friend," for example, we may register
respect, or mockery, or contempt for the person being addressed. The
novelist often wishes to suggest his opinion of the reader in order

that he may convince or impress him, deliberately anger him as an impulse toward action, or even express affinity and admiration. The writer who forbears the use of direct exposition of the kind evident in Norris and Ellison, needs a more subtle approach, that of literary inflection.

For this reason, tone has been called "the voice of the author as expressed by the literary style, by the texture of his prose, by the resonance of the recorded event." Texture and resonance may be interpreted as the sound qualities of the prose—the use of words that are musical or unmusical, harsh or gentle, euphonious or cacophonous. Tone as an integral part of selection and arrangement involves the treatment of the materials. Hemingway's "The Killers," though it is not presented overtly as a story of protest, imparts in the title the savage theme underlying the story. Starkly descriptive of the two assassins who ruthlessly hunt down their human quarry, "The Killers" connotes a tone of warning, fear, and condemnation. *Intruder in the Dust* conveys a social indictment, its tone urging upon the audience indignation over and protest against the intolerance accorded men like Lucas Beauchamp. The ambiguous title, furthermore, contains a tone of irony; for while it may be taken as an allusion to the hidden corpse of the murdered man, it may also be related to the unjustly accused Lucas as an intruder unwelcome to his white neighbors.

Tone and mood, when skillfully employed, act in a harmonious and frequently subtle interrelationship. *The Grapes of Wrath*, for example, expresses Steinbeck's mood of sympathy and tenderness for the Okies out of which emerges a tone of anger at the natural and man-made conditions responsible for their plight. Steinbeck achieves this duality by placing explicit emphasis on character and situation; but also, implicitly, by appealing to his reader's sense of justice. More abstractly, Herman Melville establishes a mood of fearful anticipation by depicting the search for the white whale in a cruel ocean. Concurrently, his tone is one of awe mingled with that of pessimism or fatality as he makes us aware of the cosmic force of nature and evil.

Through careful selection of details and incidents, F. Scott Fitzgerald in *The Great Gatsby* combines a mood and tone of reckless

abandon: the jazz age expressing its futility in breezy, foolish di-
alogues, a lost generation spending itself in hopeless drinking orgies.
Every story has its own mixture: the deliberately banal, domestic
dialogue of "The Fur Coat" combines a mood and tone that are
both fretful and melancholy; the protracted monologue of "Gooseberries" through its union of mood and tone challenges wasteful
striving and moral inaction. There is virtually no limit to the attitudes which may be revealed in fiction toward subject and audience; and it is these attitudes which supply emotional credibility.

Style

Just as each author injects a personal quality into his fiction
through relevant attitudes, so he distinguishes the manner of his
writing by *style*. As has already been suggested, style—the ordering of language—works closely with all the elements of fiction. For
Richards, style has its most intimate connection with tone, involving "the perfect recognition of the writer's relation to the reader in
view of what is being said and their joint feeling about it." Like
atmosphere—and as is often true of both mood and tone—creative
style is dependent on subtle effects rather than on analyses. In formal rhetoric, to be sure, style can be measured in terms of syntax,
figures of speech, imagery, and so on. It has become commonplace,
for instance, to take note of Hemingway's terse, staccato statements
or of Faulkner's elaborate, involuted language and sentence structure. These properties are interesting as rhetorical facts, but not so
interesting as the intangible effects they promote in support of their
author's intentions. The test of style is its inevitability, the apprehension by writer and reader that no other manner or quality of expression could be substituted for the occasion with comparable effect.

Style is more, much more, than contrived mannerism, if it is to be
successful. It is one more unifying condition, another way of bringing into conjunction the technical and thematic aspects of the work
of art. According to Richards, "the close co-operation of the form
with the meaning—modifying it and being modified by it in ways

that though subtle are, in general, perfectly intelligible—is the chief secret of Style." This is similar to André Gide's observation: "One gets into that bad habit of dissociating form from content, the emotion and the expression of the emotion from the thought, which ought to remain inseparable." Since stylistic effectiveness is highly dependent upon a reader's subjective response, critical judgments are often controversial. What is a good style and what is a bad one?

Obviously, there can be no operative generalization on the ideal style, apart from its inevitability or rightness in relation to the matter and emotions of fiction. When we become unduly conscious of style, we should be especially careful to examine its affinity with content. Some readers, for instance, are disturbed by complicated syntax or unusual language, such as are characteristic of Faulkner or Durrell. But before condemning, they should attempt to see what intellectual or sensuous effects are intended and what success has been achieved. If, on the other hand, a "plain style" coincides with the effects an author attempts to evoke, we should not be disappointed by the absence of glitter. When Jane Austen was once taken to task for stylistic restraint, she defended her self-imposed limitation with gentle satire. "I begin already to weigh my words and sentences more than I did, and am looking about for a sentiment, an illustration or a metaphor in every corner of the room."

The dangers of stylistic excess are apparent in the empurpled prose of Sherwood Anderson, who, by his own joyous admission, was intrigued by the "perfume" of words. Yet plainness is no more a virtue than ornateness, if it is the result of a self-conscious preoccupation. "The whole secret of a living style and the difference between it and a dead style," for Thomas Hardy, "lies in not having too much style—being in fact a little careless, or rather seeming to be, here and there." The key, of course, is in the final clause, for art always gives the impression of creative ease no matter what pains the artist endured in reaching his goal. Only an artist can give a sense of casualness in a medium that is anything but casual. What Hardy implies, indeed, is that style should never be intrusive.

Developing a similar notion, Ford Madox Ford warns: "Too startling words, however apt, *too* just images, too great displays of cleverness are apt in the long run to be as fatiguing as the most over-used words or the most jog-trot cadences." Freshness without cleverness was the goal also of Gustave Flaubert, who sought indefatigably for *le mot juste*, "the right expression, which is by the same token the only one that is at the same time possible and harmonious." And harmoniousness plus intelligibility were the stylistic aims of Anthony Trollope. To be intelligible, "language should be so pellucid that the meaning should be rendered without an effort to the reader." To be harmonious, language "must come from the practice of the ear." The writer "must so train his ear that he shall be able to weigh the rhythm of every word as it falls from the pen."

But perhaps the final word on style may be left to Joseph Conrad, who insists that "the *whole* of truth lies in the presentation; therefore the expression should be studied in the interest of veracity. This is the only morality of *art* apart from *subject*." Conrad in effect sums up what the others have written about the problem, giving to it his distinctive idealizing touch, and adding to it the proviso that even in matters of style the reader must be given an opportunity to exercise his own imagination. Without such participation the reader cannot be expected to share in the total literary experience.

Before proceeding with a detailed discussion of other elements of fiction, we should once again look for practical applications of theory. In the following story we have an opportunity to see how Thomas Wolfe has rendered his materials, producing a unified creative experience. The subsequent analysis, concerned with the whole work, must emphasize certain matters of technique already explored and anticipate those yet to come.

Only the Dead Know Brooklyn

by THOMAS WOLFE

Dere's no guy livin' dat knows Brooklyn t'roo an' t'roo, because it'd take a guy a lifetime just to find his way aroun' duh f—— town.

So like I say, I'm waitin' for my train t' come when I sees dis big guy standin' deh—dis is duh foist I eveh see of him. Well, he's lookin' wild, y'know, an' I can see dat he's had plenty, but still he's holdin' it; he talks good an' is walkin' straight enough. So den, dis big guy steps up to a little guy dat's standin' deh, an' says, "How d'yuh get t' Eighteent' Avenoo an' Sixty-sevent' Street?" he says.

"Jesus! Yuh got me, chief," duh little guy says to him. "I ain't been heah long myself. Where is duh place?" he says. "Out in duh Flatbush section somewhere?"

"Nah," duh big guy says. "It's out in Bensonhoist. But I was neveh deh befoeh. How d'yuh get deh?"

"Jesus," duh little guy says, scratchin' his head, y'know—yuh could see duh little guy didn't know his way about—"yuh got me, chief. I neveh hoid of it. Do any of youse guys know where it is?" he says to me.

"Sure," I says, "It's out in Bensonhoist. Yuh take duh Fourt' Avenoo express, get off at Fifty-nint' Street, change to a Sea Beach local deh, get off at Eighteent' Avenoo an' Sixty-toid, an' den walk down foeh blocks. Dat's all yuh got to do," I says.

"G'wan!" some wise guy dat I neveh seen befoeh pipes up. "Whatcha talkin' about?" he says—oh, he was wise, y'know. "Duh guy is crazy! I tell yuh what yuh do," he says to duh big guy. "Yuh change to duh West End line at Toity-sixt'," he tells him. "Get off at Noo Utrecht an' Sixteent' Avenoo," he says. "Walk two blocks oveh, foeh blocks up," he says, "an' you'll be right deh." Oh, a *wise* guy, y'know.

"Oh, yeah?" I says. "Who told *you* so much?" He got me sore because he was so wise about it. "How long you been livin' heah?" I says.

"All my life," he says. "I was bawn in Williamsboig," he says. "An' I can tell you t'ings about dis town you neveh hoid of," he says.

"Yeah?" I says.

"Yeah," he says.

"Well, den, you can tell me t'ings about dis town dat nobody else has eveh hoid of, either. Maybe you make it all up yoehself at night," I says, "befoeh you go to sleep—like cuttin' out papeh dolls, or somp'n."

"Oh, yeah?" he says. "You're pretty wise, ain't yuh?"

"Oh, I don't know," I says. "Duh boids ain't usin' my head for Lincoln's statue yet," I says. "But I'm wise enough to know a phony when I see one."

"Yeah?" he says. "A wise guy, huh? Well, you're so wise dat some one's goin' t'bust yuh one right on duh snoot some day," he says. "Dat's how wise *you* are."

Well, my train was comin', or I'da smacked him den and dere, but when I seen duh train was comin', all I said was, "All right, mugg! I'm sorry I can't stay to take keh of you, but I'll be seein' yuh sometime, I hope, out in duh cemetery." So den I says to duh big guy, who'd been standin' deh all duh time, "You come wit me," I says. So when we gets onto duh train I says to him, "Where yuh goin' out in Bensonhoist?" I says. "What numbeh are yuh lookin' for?" I says. *You* know—I t'ought if he told me duh address I might be able to help him out.

"Oh," he says, "I'm not lookin' for no one. I don't know no one out deh."

"Then whatcha goin' out deh for?" I says.

"Oh," duh guy says, "I'm just goin' out to see duh place," he says. "I like duh sound of duh name—Bensonhoist, y'know—so I t'ought I'd go out an' have a look at it."

"Whatcha tryin' t'hand me?" I says. "Whatcha tryin' t'do—kid me?" *You* know, I t'ought duh guy was bein' wise wit me.

"No," he says, "I'm tellin' yuh duh troot. I like to go out an' take a look at places wit nice names like dat. I like to go out an' look at all kinds of places," he says.

"How'd yuh know deh was such a place," I says, "if yuh neveh been deh befoeh?"

"Oh," he says, "I got a map."

"A *map*?" I says.

"Sure," he says, "I got a map dat tells me about all dese places. I take it wit me every time I come out heah," he says.

And Jesus! Wit dat, he pulls it out of his pocket, an' so help me, but he's *got* it—he's tellin' duh troot—a big map of duh whole f—— place with all duh different pahts mahked out. You know—Canarsie an' East Noo Yawk an' Flatbush, Bensonhoist, Sout' Brooklyn, duh Heights, Bay Ridge, Greenpernt—duh whole goddam layout, he's got it right deh on duh map.

"You been to any of dose places?" I says.

"Sure," he says, "I been to most of 'em. I was down in Red Hook just last night," he says.

"Jesus! Red Hook!" I says. "Whatcha do down deh?"

"Oh," he says, "nuttin' much. I just walked aroun'. I went into a coupla places an' had a drink," he says, "but most of the time I just walked aroun'."

"Just walked aroun'?" I says.

"Sure," he says, "just lookin' at t'ings, y'know."

"Where'd yuh go?" I asts him.

"Oh," he says, "I don't know duh name of duh place, but I could find it on my map," he says. "One time I was walkin' across some big fields where deh ain't no houses," he says, "but I could see ships oveh deh all lighted up. Dey was loadin'. So I walks across duh fields," he says, "to where duh ships are."

"Sure," I says, "I know where you was. You was down to duh Erie Basin."

"Yeah," he says, "I guess dat was it. Dey had some of dose big elevators an' cranes an' dey was loadin' ships, an' I could see some ships in drydock all lighted up, so I walks across duh fields to where dey are," he says.

"Den what did yuh do?" I says.

"Oh," he says, "nuttin' much. I came on back across duh fields after a while an' went into a coupla places an' had a drink."

"Didn't nuttin' happen while yuh was in dere?" I says.

"No," he says. "Nuttin' much. A coupla guys was drunk in one of duh places an' started a fight, but dey bounced 'em out," he says, "an' den one of duh guys stahted to come back again, but duh bartender gets his baseball bat out from under duh counteh, so duh guy goes on."

"Jesus!" I said. "Red Hook!"

"Sure," he says. "Dat's where it was, all right."

"Well, you keep outa deh," I says. "You stay away from deh."

"Why?" he says. "What's wrong wit it?"

"Oh," I says, "it's a good place to stay away from, dat's all. It's a good place to keep out of."

"Why?" he says. "Why is it?"

Jesus! Whatcha gonna do wit a guy as dumb as dat? I saw it wasn't no use to try to tell him nuttin', he wouldn't know what I was talkin' about, so I just says to him, "Oh, nuttin'. Yuh might get lost down deh, dat's all."

"Lost?" he says. "No, I wouldn't get lost. I got a map," he says. A map! Red Hook! Jesus!

So den duh guy begins to ast me all kinds of nutty questions: how big was Brooklyn an' could I find my way aroun' in it, an' how long would it take a guy to know duh place.

"Listen!" I says. "You get dat idea outa yoeh head right now," I says. "You ain't neveh gonna get to know Brooklyn," I says. "Not in a hunderd yeahs. I been livin' heah all my life," I says, "an' I don't even know all deh is to know about it, so how do you expect to know duh town," I says, "when you don't even live heah?"

"Yes," he says, "but I got a map to help me find my way about."

"Map or no map," I says, "yuh ain't gonna get to know Brooklyn wit no map," I says.

"Can you swim?" he says, just like dat. Jesus! By dat time, y'know, I begun to see dat duh guy was some kind of nut. He'd had plenty to drink, of course, but he had dat crazy look in his eye I didn't like. "Can you swim?" he says.

"Sure," I says, "Can't you?"

"No," he says. "Not more'n a stroke or two. I neveh loined good."

"Well, it's easy," I says. "All yuh need is a little confidence. Duh way I loined, me older bruddeh pitched me off duh dock one day when I was eight yeahs old, cloes an' all. 'You'll swim,' he says. 'You'll swim all right—or drown.' An', believe me, I *swam!* When yuh know yuh got to, you'll do it. Duh only t'ing yuh need is con-

fidence. An' once you've loined," I says, "you've got nuttin' else
to worry about. You'll neveh forget it. It's somp'n dat stays wit
yuh as long as yuh live."

"Can yuh swim good?" he says.

"Like a fish," I tells him. "I'm a regulah fish in duh wateh," I
says. "I loined to swim right off duh docks wit all duh oddeh kids,"
I says.

"What would you do if yuh saw a man drownin'?" duh guy says.

"Do? Why, I'd jump in an' pull him out," I says. "Dat's what
I'd do."

"Did yuh eveh see a man drown?" he says.

"Sure," I says. "I see two guys—bot' times at Coney Island.
Dey got out too far, an' neider one could swim. Dey drowned befoeh
any one could get to 'em."

"What becomes of people after dey've drowned out heah?" he
says.

"Drowned out where?" I says.

"Out heah in Brooklyn."

"I don't know whatcha mean," I says. "Neveh hoid of no one
drownin' heah in Brooklyn, unless you mean a swimmin' pool. Yuh
can't drown in Brooklyn," I says. "Yuh gotta drown somewhere
else—in duh ocean, where dere's wateh."

"Drownin'," duh guy says, lookin' at his map. "Drownin'."
Jesus! I could see by den he was some kind of nut, he had dat
crazy expression in his eyes when he looked at you, an' I didn't
know what he might do. So we was comin' to a station, an' it wasn't
my stop, but I got off anyway, an' waited for duh next train.

"Well, so long, chief," I says. "Take it easy, now."

"Drownin'," duh guy says, lookin' at his map. "Drownin'."

Jesus! I've t'ought about day guy a t'ousand times since den
an' wondered what eveh happened to 'm goin' out to look at Bensonhoist because he liked duh name! Walkin' aroun' t'roo Red Hook
by himself at night an' lookin' at his map! How many people did
I see get drowned out heah in Brooklyn! How long would it take a
guy wit a good map to know all deh was to know about Brooklyn!

Jesus! What a nut *he* was! I wondeh what eveh happened to
'im, anyway! I wondeh if some one knocked him on duh head, or if

he's still wanderin' aroun' in duh subway in duh middle of duh night wit his little map! Duh poor guy! Say, I've got to laugh, at dat, when I t'ink about him! Maybe he's found out by now dat he'll neveh live long enough to know duh whole of Brooklyn. It'd take a guy a lifetime to know Brooklyn t'roo an' t'roo. An' even den, yuh wouldn't know it all.

Critical Commentary on *Only the Dead Know Brooklyn*

Until the concluding paragraphs, the story has what might be taken for a clear enough literal meaning. That is, we read a rather amusing account of an experience in Brooklyn, a well-tried subject. But the literal, we discover, does not carry us very far. What does simple paraphrase reveal? A stranger in Brooklyn looking for a location asks some natives for directions. None can agree on the location or a way of getting there, and they quarrel among themselves. Ironically, although they have lived in Brooklyn all their lives and pride themselves on their familiarity with the city, they do not have this particular information.

It is then that the truculent first-person narrator takes over, tries to guide the stranger and fails. But at the same time he has the irrepressible curiosity of the legendary Brooklynite, and pumps the stranger to discover his motives. The narrator learns—to his intense surprise—that the unnamed stranger habitually wanders around Brooklyn with a map, looking for places that have pleasant-sounding names. Suddenly, without forewarning, the stranger asks the narrator (also unnamed) whether he can swim, and whether he has ever seen a drowning. The story ends on this puzzling note and the narrator, with justification, considers the incident one of some lunacy. For such peculiar things simply do not happen in Brooklyn.

Before we consider the actual meaning, point, or significance of the story, let us look at the fundamental details of technique.

MOOD. Although we may choose to identify Wolfe with the stranger, the author at no time exposes his private personality. Rather, he permits two unidentified characters to carry the entire emotional and intellectual burden. The feeling of the story thus becomes fairly complex, even ambivalent. The stranger evokes a mood of wistfulness and sympathy. We can appreciate the esthetic hunger which drives him. Simultaneously, though we respect his yearning, we wonder whether the discovery is ever as rich as the anticipation. These are emotional details implied in the dialogue between protagonist and antagonist. The antithesis of the stranger is the narrator—commonplace, literal, irascible, and yet kindly. He intensifies a feeling of futility because of his banal repudiation of the search for beauty. The mood, then, combines sadness and frustration with provincial humor and unresolved optimism for the stranger's success.

TONE. By subtle means the author is able to assert his attitude toward the reader. First he warns us in the title that only the dead know Brooklyn. Then he draws attention to normal impatience with idealistic, impractical quests such as the stranger's. Consequently, Wolfe implies the confusion and crudity of the vast area in which the search takes place. Toward this end he relies upon the aimless arguments of the anonymous speakers, who are like disembodied voices representative of ordinary mankind. Contrasting with this disorder is the map to which the stranger refers throughout the story. Presumably a symbol of order and stability, this manmade device is hopelessly misleading. Wolfe appears to say that the individual really has nothing material to guide him in his groping for values; only innate desire can direct him toward knowledge and beauty, which cannot be charted on a map: note the random (if esthetically motivated) manner in which the stranger selects the places he will visit.

Looking for an ultimate truth which he cannot readily isolate, he nevertheless persists. Each new place that he visits may provide him with the insight he seeks, so he must continue to roam about. Indeed, to cease striving, to endure the atrophy of the sense of wonder and inquiry—as the narrator has done—is to perish. Once the stranger hits upon the notion of drowning, it becomes a disturbing metaphor to connote human failure. The word "drowning" offers a significant clue to the tone of the story, because as a form of suffocation drowning can be incorporeal as well as physical. The literal-minded narrator responds to the stranger as though he were talking about physical death. But the latter is not concerned here with physical death, only with that other death, the wasting away of the spirit. Although the stranger's attitude must be inferred, the inference follows logically from his consistent inattention to mundane matters. While the narrator returns to his world of actuality, the stranger pursues his ineffable search. In Brooklyn, where physical drowning is an impractical feat, the stranger consults his map and contemplates another kind of smothering. From his depiction of these men at cross-purposes, Wolfe has established tone in a twofold way: (1) to show us the aimlessness and inner bankruptcy of ordinary life; (2) to admonish and warn us against surrendering to spiritual and esthetic indifference.

Tone and mood are closely bound in with *theme*. The search for order, beauty, and individuality, it is suggested, may indeed be fruitless but must never be abandoned. Striving for positive values, one must also contend with ugliness and ignorance, for the good and the bad coexist. Yet that there can be no guarantee of success is implied in the ironical title. The dead are those who, like the narrator, have physically survived the material confusion and stifling effects of existence. Their survival, however, has depended upon an unquestioning attitude, one that is antithetical to the ultimate truth sought by the stranger. If people like the narrator are alive physically, the stranger's questions appear to disclose, they are dead spiritually. They know Brooklyn—which is life—only on the confused surface, and fragmentarily at that. The stranger, therefore, is left with a riddle of the disparity between material appearance and its hidden meaning. His own resolution of the riddle is left unstated, but we may assume that he will continue his search for answers.

Against the very real backdrop of Brooklyn, the *atmosphere* is paradoxically hazy and unrealistic. It emerges as a pervasive feeling of futility and impersonality—possibly an overwhelming challenge to individualism. Wolfe withholds names from his characters, who—as in *allegory*—are representative of society, of everyman. The *conflict* is not between flesh-and-blood people but between concepts: the restless individual search for the bluebird and the passivity of acceptance. The struggle is one between a broad idea of absorptive materialism and threatened ideals. The surface humor of the dialect turns to bitter realization through our awareness of the complete absence of humor in the situation. There is, indeed, a sense of tragedy, enlarged by the blindness of the narrator to his own loss of individuality.

Except for superficial details, everything in this story is implicit. Wolfe does not tell us through any direct means the exact nature of the problem with which he is concerned. Nor does he develop his characters explicitly. Everything must come out through dialogue or through the rational process of the narrator's puzzlement. Only by inference do we discover Wolfe's allegorical intention of representing Brooklyn as modern confused society which suffocates individuality. By inference also we recognize that for most people this state of suffocation is acceptable, while those who resist are stigmatized as outsiders and eccentrics.

6

The Narrator's Focus

Point-of-View

AS a critical term descriptive of the author's means of observing his subject, *point-of-view* has a well-established identification with narrative structure.* Point-of-view refers to the mind through which the author has chosen to present his story, and it is synonymous with "focus of narration," "angle of vision," or (to borrow the Jamesian phrase) "central intelligence." Having decided upon the narrator who will serve most credibly as his fictional voice, the author must determine the spatial placement of his narrator in the structure. That is, where in the story may he stand to best advantage for observing characters and actions, and for making assessments of what he has observed? The vantage points available for the author's choice are numerous, but in general they may be reduced to either external or internal positions. Whoever is responsible for telling the story must be given a position from which he can most suitably convey the author's aims. Whether the narrator is to be placed somewhere near the outer limits of the compositional framework or at some point directly within it depends, then, upon the extensiveness or intensiveness of the novel's treatment.

OMNISCIENT POINT-OF-VIEW. The most widely embracing external point-of-view is that of omniscience. In principle, every author is

---

* Point of-view has an alternative association with states of mind, opinions, or attitudes. It is suggested that since point-of-view in this book refers only to the narrative source of observation, such expressions as "ironical point-of-view," "detached point-of-view," "sympathetic point-of-view," "hedonistic point-of-view" be avoided in favor of "ironical theme," "detached tone," etc.

omniscient, for he has complete knowledge of everything that goes on within the story, within the minds of his characters, of the events preceding the central action, motivation, and so forth. Critically, however, a distinction is made between the point-of-view (reserved for later discussion) used by the author to disguise signs of his control, and that used by him as an exercise of his godlike presence. When a novelist chooses this latter, omniscient point-of-view, he in effect speaks in his own voice as well as in that of his characters. Not only does he describe all actions and thoughts, but he also offers commentaries upon them, very much as an editorial writer might pass judgments on the day's happenings. Thus, Henry Fielding frequently interrupts the progress of an incident to assert his own moral or comic interpretations. The intrusion may be a brief one of a few sentences or paragraphs. Or it may consist of an entire chapter on a philosophical or critical topic that has no visible relevance to the narration. Fielding is jealous of his identity and—to the sometimes warranted annoyance of modern readers—he is always present, mocking, goading, deriding, admiring.

William Thackeray, who inherited Fielding's distaste for anonymity, introduces himself in *Vanity Fair* as "the Manager of the Performance." He forwards himself as a manipulator of fictional characters, "proud to think that his Puppets have given satisfaction to the very best company in this empire." His intrusions, like Fielding's, are often textural asides which indicate his restless curiosity in what is going on: " 'Thank you, dear Joseph,' said Amelia, quite ready to kiss her brother, if he were so minded. (And I think for a kiss from such a dear creature as Amelia, I would purchase all Mr. Lee's conservatories out of hand.)" Or he goes to greater, more obvious extremes of deliberate officiousness: ". . . But my kind reader will please to remember that this history has 'Vanity Fair' for a title, and that Vanity Fair is a very vain, wicked, foolish place, full of all sorts of humbugs and falsenesses and pretensions. And while the moralist, who is holding forth on the cover (an accurate portrait of your humble servant), professes to wear neither gown nor bands, but only the very same long-eared livery in which his congregation is arrayed: yet, look you, one is bound to speak the truth as far as one knows it, whether one mounts a cap and bells or a shovel-hat; and a deal of disagreeable matter must come out in the course of such an undertaking."

While the effect of such a passage—both comic and didactic—is consistent with the plan of the entire novel, many critics object to the arbitrary disruption. An author's opinions, they would argue, must be assimilated within the narrative composition. George Eliot, thus, practices a form of omniscience but seldom fences off the author from the characters as Thackeray does. Consider this quotation from *Middlemarch:* "Young Ladislaw did not pay that visit to which Mr. Brooke had invited him, and only six days afterwards Mr. Casaubon mentioned that his young relative had started for the Continent, seeming by this cold vagueness to waive inquiry. Indeed, Will had declined to fix on any more precise destination than the entire area of Europe. Genius, he held, is necessarily intolerant of fetters: on the one hand it must have the utmost play for its spontaneity; on the other hand, it may confidently await those messages from the universe which summon it to its peculiar work, only placing itself in an attitude of receptivity toward all sublime chances. The attitudes of receptivity are various, and Will had sincerely tried many of them." George Eliot partially conceals her omniscience by standing behind the characters, but we know she is present. The italicized words, for example, although they are relevant to the narration, express the author's personal knowledge and insights: ". . . *seeming* by this *cold* vagueness to waive inquiry. . . . *The attitudes of receptivity* are various, and Will had *sincerely* tried many of them."

The omniscient point-of-view has the advantage of the writer's authority, confirmed by his wide-ranging vision and intelligence. For writers like Fielding and Thackeray, or Theodore Dreiser, whose aims are both extensive and didactic, a form of direct address to the reader can be valuable. They wish at almost every moment to keep their stories explicit as to situation and meaning. On the other hand, their omniscient techniques impose seriously on the reader's imaginative participation. As E. M. Forster remarks, "Intimacy is gained but at the expense of illusion and nobility. It is like standing a man a drink so that he may not criticize your opinions. . . . To take your reader into your confidence about the universe is a dangerous thing." Parenthetically, it may be noted that if in *Howard's End* Forster is not precisely the reader's confidant, he is certainly his tutor, his self-identified "commentator."

THIRD-PERSON POINT-OF-VIEW. Omniscience is no longer a fashionable narrative technique, but the need for a "central intelligence," a superior creative mind to unify the literary experience has never ceased to be important. Such an intelligence, as described by R. P. Blackmur, "served a dual purpose, with many modifications and exchanges among its branches. It made a compositional centre for art such as life never saw. If it could be created at all, then it presided over everything else, and would compel the story to be nothing but the story of what that intelligence felt about what happened." This is the technique favored by Henry James and other great novelists of the later nineteenth century. Basically, it directs focus upon a main character through whose presence, actions, and mind we are made to see and understand.

Unlike the device of omniscience, this one does away with overt awareness of the novelist. If he cannot always, as Stephen Dedalus would have it, refine himself out of existence—that is, achieve total self-effacement—he can at least stand well out of view. Whatever is said, done, or thought is conveyed to the reader dramatically, without visible authorial interference. And yet, though he may attend primarily to a single character, the author is still at liberty to narrate and describe *all* the characters, actions, and their consequences. By divorcing his directly felt presence from the story, he reduces the expository implications of omniscience and makes his authority implied rather than specific and obvious. At the same time, assuming the position of observer, he creates an illusion of objectivity. The author reports to us what "Mme. Bovary said," or what "Henry Fleming thought," or what such and such a person did. Following this kind of point-of-view, the author invites the reader to a full exercise of his own mental powers and a close share in the story. This external point-of-view, furthermore, is immediate and yet without the bias of the "I," whether a first-person or an omniscient narrator.

The line between the omniscient and the third-person point-of-view may be hazy, especially when the author is reluctant to detach himself and let the story speak for itself. Thus, William Dean Howells relates *The Rise of Silas Lapham* in an ostensibly third-person form of address. Yet the book is characterized by such explicit descriptions as this: "Simple, clear, bold, and straightforward in mind and action, Colonel Silas Lapham, with a prompt comprehensiveness and a never-failing business sagacity, is, in the best sense of that much-abused term, one of nature's noblemen, to the last inch of his five eleven and a half. His life affords an example of single-minded application and unwavering perseverance which our young men would do well to emulate. . . ." Howells plainly has not quite made up his mind about his relation to his story and his readers, and consequently has not made an effective bridge between omniscience and third person.

FIRST-PERSON POINT-OF-VIEW. The third-person point-of-view, a versatile source of externalized observation by the narrator, is capable of surprising depth. Certain fictional occasions, however, require the even deeper focus of an interior observation post. Frequently, by utilizing a first-person form of address to their readers, authors achieve a semblance of autobiographical or psychological veracity. When the narrator (not to be confused with the author) speaks in his own voice, the "I" can establish an exceptionally intimate bond with the audience. The angle of vision is necessarily very restrictive and subjective, for the narrator can report no more than falls within the limits of his experience, and we expect him to be affected in his communication by personal bias. These shortcomings may be offset, however, by the intimacy of his revelations and the authority of his self-knowledge. Huckleberry Finn affords an excellent instance of a main character who tells his own story:

> The widow she cried over me, and called me a poor lost lamb, and she called me by a lot of other names, too, but she never meant no harm by it. She put me in them new clothes again, and I couldn't do nothing but sweat and sweat, and feel all cramped up. Well, then, the old thing commenced again. The widow rung a bell for supper, and you had to come to time. When you got to the table you couldn't go right to eating, but you had to wait for the widow to tuck down her head and grumble a little over the victuals, though there warn't really anything the matter with them—that is, nothing only everything was cooked by itself. In a barrel of odds and ends it is different; things get mixed up, and the juice kind of swaps around, and the things go better.

An adolescent boy telling his own story establishes a close union with his audience, for he presents a more credible vision of his own universe than would an adult attempting to *re*capture childhood experiences. This, at any rate, is true in *The Adventures of Huckleberry Finn* because Mark Twain had a genius for reproducing the semi-literate humor and sensitivity of his young protagonist without visible adult intervention. We are thus in direct communion with the boy, sympathizing with his rebellion against the restraining civilities of the Widow Douglas and Miss Watson. By an interesting reversal, effected to a large extent by the interior point-of-view, adults are seen through a boy's eyes rather than the other way around. This fictional approach to childhood is infrequently employed for the obvious reason that not many adults have the ability to create the necessary illusion.*

A more common usage of first-person narration is the revelation by an adult of his own experiences, as in Ralph Ellison's *The Invisible Man*, or in *A Farewell to Arms*. A paragraph from the latter may be suggestive:

> It was dusk when the priest came. They had brought the soup and afterward taken away the bowls and I was lying looking at the row of beds and out the window at the tree-top that moved a little in the evening breeze. The breeze came in through the window and it was cooler with the evening. The flies were on the ceiling now and on the electric light bulbs that hung on wires. The lights were only turned on when someone was brought in at night or when something was being done. It made me feel very young to have the dark come after the dusk and then remain. It was like being put to bed after early supper. The orderly came down between the beds and stopped. Some one was with him. It was the priest. He stood there small, brown-faced and embarrassed.

A variation on the first-person point-of-view is achieved by the *epistolary* form. That is, the composition is created entirely—or nearly so—out of letters exchanged between a principal character and a group of correspondents. This device was made famous by Samuel Richardson's *Pamela*, and it has been adopted by numerous writers, among them, Tobias Smollett (*Humphry Clinker*),

* A popular and interesting exception is J. D. Salinger, author of *Catcher in the Rye*.

Fanny Burney (*Evelina*), John P. Marquand (*The Late George Apley*), and Thornton Wilder (*The Ides of March*). Again, this has the advantage of intimacy and authority. It has the further advantage of expanding the limits of observable experience, for several correspondents may reveal details, individual traits, and diversity of attitude from the "I" view without necessarily diminishing the centrality of the dominant character (although there may be deliberate exceptions, as in *Humphry Clinker*). The disadvantage of the letter technique is a reduction in dramatic force and narrative progression. Letters tend to be chatty or informative—even in earlier, letter-writing ages—and only the unusually gifted writer can make us believe that their scribblers (e.g., naive girls like Pamela and Evelina) have such literary powers that they can handle all the details of a unified artistic composition.

Another, more significant, variation is that which may be called the *first-person observer* point-of-view. This is effected by a narrator who has the responsibility for relating the story of a character other than himself. He is able to do this because he has been an observer, has received reports from others who have been observers, or (perhaps in combination with observation and hearsay) has been a participant. In any event, this speaker has access to first-hand knowledge which gives his eye-witness report credibility and an air of authenticity. Thus, we feel a certain confidence in the immediacy of his tale. At the same time, we feel that since he is not the major participant, his view of the entire situation—though somewhat more distant than that of a principal character telling his own story— may be more comprehensive. He must be a good storyteller, of course, capable of evoking mood and suspense. Because of his proximity to the main character or the events, he is usually less detached than a third-person narrator might be; yet, he is not so emotionally involved (as a rule) as the principal. The first-person observer consequently supplies an impression that bespeaks close familiarity but is sometimes moderately objective.

An anonymous townsman in Faulkner's "A Rose for Emily" serves merely as the witness who reports the gothic horror. His presence is barely detected. On the other hand, Ring Lardner's voluble and callous barber in "Haircut" is a prime example of the uncommitted but ever-present narrator. His authority as spokesman depends essentially on what he has seen and heard. Unlike the narrator in "Only the Dead Know Brooklyn," the barber is not a participant. Despite a role far more complex than those fashioned by Faulkner, Lardner, and Wolfe, Conrad's Marlow in *Lord Jim* is still a first-person observer and narrator. Although he is acquainted with Jim, he like the barber must depend largely on reports of others. His personal knowledge of the tragedy is too limited for reliability, and so he must piece together the ambiguous evidence from numerous sources. Thus, he must provide an expository background and then, in the course of his lengthy narration, quote the observations and opinions of various people, each of whom is responsible for a fragmented view. As observer and recorder, Marlow must assimilate this diversity of voices and produce a coherent, articulate account. The technical procedure is difficult and complicated, for the center of interest—Jim—is examined from a point-of-view that is multiple yet paradoxically intimate.

Another kind of complexity is apparent in Emily Brontë's *Wuthering Heights*. With Lockwood and Nelly Dean sharing responsibility for telling the story of Catherine and Heathcliff, the novel provides a double focus which has been justified by V. S. Pritchett. ". . . Mr. Lockwood is a condescending prig, a passive on-looker, will-less and incapable of love altogether. . . . People as violent as the protagonists, a story as strong and outlandish, needs the double focus. The triumph is Nelly, but the story cannot be left to her; she is too greatly implicated. She is the shrewd, plain Yorkshire stuff, but as an eavesdropper, nurse, messenger, and self-appointed spy, she is too much a character to be trusted with an absolute narration; as well ask the nurse in *Romeo and Juliet* to tell the story of the play." In addition to the insights provided by this dualistic point-of-view, Emily Brontë at one time resorts to the epistolary technique for a fresh attitude, having Isabella Linton write a long descriptive letter to her brother.

Although such multiplicity in the first-person (to say nothing of the third-person) is not rare, most novelists prefer the greater, more credible intensity afforded by the single narrator, such as Nick Carraway of F. Scott Fitzgerald's *The Great Gatsby*. To stake out his

claim as narrator, Nick takes charge at the very outset. After a rather
laborious passage in which he states his inclination "to reserve all
judgments" and admits his snobbishness, he goes on:

> And, after boasting this way of my tolerance, I come to the admis-
> sion that it has a limit. Conduct may be founded on the hard rock or the
> wet marshes, but after a certain point I don't care what it's founded
> on. When I came back from the East last autumn I felt that I wanted the
> world to be in uniform and at a sort of moral attention forever; I
> wanted no more riotous excursions with privileged glimpses into the
> human heart. Only Gatsby, the man who gives his name to this book,
> was exempt from my reaction—Gatsby, who represented everything for
> which I have an unaffected scorn. . . .

Thus Nick identifies the beginning of his strange fellowship
with Jay Gatsby. Throughout the story, we see Gatsby exclusively
through Nick's eyes. And though Nick is an important character,
about whom we learn almost as much as we do about Gatsby, we
are never permitted to forget that Gatsby is central. Because the
narrator assumes a prominent position in the novel and in Gatsby's
social orbit, we have no difficulty accepting his authority as the author's spokesman. In this instance, the voice of the first-person observer is unusually suitable. Nick's presence is as natural as that of
the author, and he affords the credibility of an eye-witness. To understand Gatsby as Fitzgerald wishes us to do, we must have constant access to the close-up; and this Nick provides.

Similarly, Robert Penn Warren is intent upon a dramatic, virtually
microscopic examination of the political boss Willie Stark. Consequently, he has created for *All the King's Men* an intelligent, keenly
sensitive man, Jack Burden, who is thrust into Willie's alien world.
His experiences then radiating from Willie's, he tells two stories
really, his and Willie's. Jack is less the ubiquitous observer than
Nick; nevertheless, we depend on his vision for our understanding
of Willie.

Whatever point-of-view a novelist adopts, the only demand we
may make of him is that it be appropriate for control, effect, and
meaning. And this is a great deal. Point-of-view is one of the most
important ordering devices at the author's disposal, bearing a large
responsibility for direction of plot, clarification of character, estab-

lishment of mood, tone, and theme. While consistency of point-of-view is generally desirable because of its greater manageability, consistency—despite the cavils of many modern critics—is not an arbitrary imperative. A shifting point-of-view, far from being a literary sin, may under appropriate circumstances be a virtue. For example, the major characters in *Point Counter Point* are diversified, but they have a corporate responsibility for furthering the novel's total intention. Each requires the author's full and searching scrutiny. By fixing the point-of-view firmly on successive characters, Huxley assures their prominence and thematic correspondences in the narrative structure. In *Lord Jim*, contrarily, the single character who absorbs our attention is presented through a series of fragmented observations. The shifting point-of-view is a collage which, despite Marlow's unifying presence, fails to give a really satisfying impression of Jim as a whole character. Conrad's overly ingenious point-of-view threatens to make a *tour de force* of innately grave art.

The problems incident to shifts in narrative focus are also apt to be vexing in a massive novel like Dickens' *Bleak House*. Here the author does not change within a single type of point-of-view. Rather, he lets the novel's protagonist, Esther Summerson, tell her story in the first-person, and he also speaks in the voice of the author, omnisciently and third-person. There have been critical objections to this prodigality, but also praise. Despite his opinion that *Bleak House* appears to be structurally unruly because of shifting points-of-view, Forster feels that Dickens has successfully related them to his scheme. While it is true that we may be disconcerted by the prescience and knowledge evinced by the naive girl, we are obliged to take notice of the balance provided by the author's voice. Like Forster, Morton Dauwen Zabel is well aware of the strains imposed on Dickens' ingenuity by the scope of his novel. Agreeing that the mixture of points-of-view has faults, he too finds artistic justification for the unusual technique. By alternating two narratives—that is, Esther's and his own—Dickens has brought exceptional insight and sympathy to his subject, and has enriched its moral and narrative substance. The "complication of his form," according to Zabel, "supports the complication and depth of his drama and intelligence."

The structure and point-of-view of *Bleak House* are incidental here to the larger issues of structure and point-of-view in general. Dickens' novel, however, serves as an excellent illustration of the pains novelists take to realize their intentions through technique. As has been demonstrated repeatedly, arbitrary caveats and rules are seldom binding upon the creative imagination. They may offer a guide-line or a general way of procedure, but ultimately creative instinct and judgment will dictate the proper modifications. The critic's duty to weigh regulations against creative necessity is one of the most demanding and interesting aspects of his task.

Stream-of-Consciousness

In the discussion of plot we had occasion to introduce *stream-of-consciousness* or interior monologue as a device for representing actions and events. What was said there merely touches on a subject whose scientific and quasi-scientific origins, as well as its great diversity of literary use, make it too massive for much more than allusive treatment in a book of this kind. We should note by way of afterword, at least, that stream-of-consciousness may have a profound bearing upon characterization and point-of-view. The most exploratory of all fictional states of mind, it is also the most intimate. Conventional methods of organization and control become inadequate, for the author must place the entire burden of coherence and direction upon a character's flow of memory and subconscious or even unconscious reflection.

Stream-of-consciousness has an affinity with point-of-view or, indeed it may *be* the point-of-view. That is, the psychological process may dominate the angle of vision from which we are made to see the story. This ultimate form of interior address may be used partially, in conjunction with a point-of-view that operates from the conscious and material plane of existence, as in *A Portrait of the Artist as a Young Man*. Or it may be used wholly, as in *Ulysses*, at a level of communication that is below the conscious. However it is used, the author evinces his abiding concern with the mind that projects the story. He faces the extremely complex task of bringing compositional order out of a phenomenon which is essentially un-ordered or detached from rational control. His purpose is to represent the flux of thoughts and emotions which succeed each other in a random rather than logical manner. And yet, while imparting the ir-rational nature of the inner, pre-speech condition, he must still set bounds about his structure. Furthermore, he must sacrifice his own conscious personality—sometimes to the point of total obliteration.

Virginia Woolf, in *To the Lighthouse,* comes close to making this artistic sacrifice, although she does not vanish entirely. Rather, she effects a fine balance between external reality and the unspoken mental images set free by it. During a mundane conversation about a lost brooch, Paul Rayley says, "I'm going to find it . . . I'm get-ting up early." Lily Briscoe's reaction is a dualism of thought and speech, with the author offering sparse clues to help the reader dis-tinguish between inner and outer reality:

> Lily wanted to protest violently and outrageously her desire to help him, envisaging how in the dawn on the beach she would be the one to pounce on the brooch half-hidden by some stone, and thus herself be included among the sailors and adventurers. But what did he reply to her offer? *She actually said with an emotion that she seldom let appear* [italics are mine], "Let me come with you," and he laughed. He meant yes or no—either perhaps. But it was not his meaning—it was the odd chuckle he gave, as if he had said, Throw yourself over the cliff if you like, I don't care. He turned on her cheek the heat of love, its horror, its cruelty, its unscrupulosity. It scorched her, and Lily, *looking at Minta, being charming to Mr. Ramsay at the other end of the table,* flinched for her exposed to these fangs, and was thankful. For at any rate, *she said to herself,* catching sight of the salt cellar on the pattern, she need not marry, thank Heaven: she need not undergo that degradation. She was saved from that dilution. She would move the tree rather more to the middle.

The subtle movement between thought and narrative fact is again illustrated in *The Bear,* by William Faulkner. The action of the story is more detailed and explicit than that of *To the Lighthouse.* Con-cerned with a crucial experience in the life of a young boy, *The Bear* is related in the third-person and focused on the boy. Like Mrs. Woolf, Faulkner creates an interfusion of circumstance and reflection, although the distinction is more emphatic, more visibly controlled by the author for dramatic effect. As an instance, a scene is concluded realistically, thus:

> "He's smart," Sam said. "Too smart." He looked down at the hound, trembling faintly and steadily against the boy's knee. From a raked shoulder a few drops of fresh blood oozed and clung. "Too big. We ain't got the dog yet. But maybe someday. Maybe not next time. But someday."

Then Faulkner leaves a space and carries us directly into the boy's reflective flow:

> *So I must see him,* he thought. *I must look at him.* Otherwise, it seemed to him that it would go on like this forever, as it had gone on with his father and Major de Spain, who was older than his father, and even with old General Compson, who had been old enough to be a brigade commander in 1865. Otherwise, it would go on so forever, next time and next time, after and after and after. It seemed to him that he could never see the two of them, himself and the bear, shadowy in the limbo from which time emerged, becoming time; the old bear absolved of mortality and himself partaking, sharing a little of it, enough of it. And he knew now what he had smelled in the huddled dogs and tasted in his saliva. He recognized fear. *So I will have to see him,* he thought, without dread or hope. *I will have to look at him.*

Both passages descriptive of the inner state are vibrantly personal, each one an exposure of a character's private identity. It is as though Mrs. Woolf and Faulkner opened windows that let us look into normally sealed recesses and then share sensations and attitudes with the principals. Nevertheless, the guiding hand of each author is perceptible, if only dimly. Sometimes an author removes even the trace of his creative agency and lets everything—action and thought—emerge without transition from author to reader. This is the achievement of Joyce in *Ulysses*. See how action flows into thought in a few paragraphs from "Hades," the description of Paddy Dignam's funeral:

> The high railings of Prospects rippled past their gaze. Dark poplars, rare white forms. Forms more frequent, white shapes thronged amid the trees, white forms and fragments streaming by mutely, sustaining vain gestures on the air.
> The felly harshed against the curbstone: stopped. Martin Cunningham put out his arm and, wrenching back the handle, shoved the door open with his knee. He stepped out. Mr Power and Mr Dedalus followed.

Change that soap now. Mr Bloom's hand unbuttoned his hip pocket swiftly and transferred the paperstuck soap to his inner handkerchief pocket. He stepped out of the carriage, replacing the newspaper his other hand still held.

Paltry funeral: coach and three carriages. It's all the same. Pall-bearers, gold reins, requiem mass, firing a volley. Pomp of death. Beyond the hind carriage a hawker stood by his barrow of cakes and fruit. Simnel cakes those are, stuck together: cakes for the dead. Dog-biscuits. Who ate them? Mourners coming out.

The shifts from outer event to inner thought occur so swiftly and inevitably that we have the impression of being controlled exclusively by Mr. Bloom's sensibility and observation. There is no authorial direction—"he said" or "he reflected"—only the passage from detail to inner recognition and back again. We see with Mr. Bloom's eyes.

Then look at one more paragraph, this from *A Portrait of the Artist as a Young Man:*

Disheartened, he [Stephen Dedalus] raised his eyes towards the slow-drifting clouds, dappled and seaborne. They were voyaging across the deserts of the sky, a host of nomads on the march, voyaging high over Ireland, westward bound. The Europe they had come from lay out there beyond the Irish Sea, Europe of strange tongues and valleyed and wood-begirt and citadelled and of entrenched and marshalled races. He heard a confused music within him as of memories and names which he was almost conscious of but could not capture even for an instant; then the music seemed to recede, to recede, to recede: and from each receding trail of nebulous music there fell always one long-drawn calling note, piercing like a star the dusk of silence. Again! Again! Again! A voice from beyond the world was calling.

Here Joyce gives some signs of his presence. It is an author's opinion that the boy is "disheartened," not Stephen's own description of his inner condition. And it is the author who says *"He heard a confused music within him as of memories. . . ."* But the dominant quality is of stream-of-consciousness emanating from Stephen. It is Stephen's vision of which we are aware. From his physical view of the clouds, his mind creates an image, drifts toward their European source, and produces a succession of thoughts separate from his physical surroundings. The process is that of associationism (a frequently employed device from the time of Locke and Sterne), in which an object or event initiates a stream of random, only seemingly unrelated impressions. Stephen is caught between his imagination and reality when he hears "A voice from beyond the world . . ." But the voice is that of his friends:

"——Hello, Stephanos!

"——Here comes The Dedalus!"

And he is reluctantly brought back to the tangible moment of fact, the magic disrupted.

The Garden-Party

by KATHERINE MANSFIELD

And after all the weather was ideal. They could not have had a more perfect day for a garden-party if they had ordered it. Windless, warm, the sky without a cloud. Only the blue was veiled with a haze of light gold, as it is sometimes in early summer. The gardener had been up since dawn, mowing the lawns and sweeping them, until the grass and the dark flat rosettes where the daisy plants had been seemed to shine. As for the roses, you could not help feeling they understood that roses are the only flowers that impress people at garden-parties; the only flowers that everybody is certain of knowing. Hundreds, yes, literally hundreds, had come out in a single night; the green bushes bowed down as though they had been visited by archangels.

Breakfast was not yet over before the men came to put up the marquee.

"Where do you want the marquee put, mother?"

"My dear child, it's no use asking me. I'm determined to leave everything to you children this year. Forget I am your mother. Treat me as an honoured guest."

But Meg could not possibly go and supervise the men. She had washed her hair before breakfast, and she sat drinking her coffee in a green turban, with a dark wet curl stamped on each cheek. Jose, the butterfly, always came down in a silk petticoat and a kimono jacket.

"You'll have to go, Laura; you're the artistic one."

Away Laura flew, still holding her piece of bread-and-butter. It's so delicious to have an excuse for eating out of doors, and besides, she loved having to arrange things; she always felt she could do it so much better than anybody else.

Four men in their shirt-sleeves stood grouped together on the garden path. They carried staves covered with rolls of canvas, and they had big tool-bags slung on their backs. They looked impressive. Laura wished now that she had not got the bread-and-butter, but there was nowhere to put it, and she couldn't possibly throw it away. She blushed and tried to look severe and even a little bit short-sighted as she came up to them.

"Good morning," she said, copying her mother's voice. But that sounded so fearfully affected that she was ashamed, and stammered like a little girl, "Oh—er—have you come—is it about the marquee?"

"That's right, miss," said the tallest of the men, a lanky, freckled fellow, and he shifted his tool-bag, knocked back his straw hat and smiled down at her. "That's about it."

His smile was so easy, so friendly that Laura recovered. What nice eyes he had, small, but such a dark blue! And now she looked at the others, they were smiling too. "Cheer up, we won't bite," their smile seemed to say. How very nice workmen were! And what a beautiful morning! She mustn't mention the morning; she must be business-like. The marquee.

"Well, what about the lily-lawn? Would that do?"

And she pointed to the lily-lawn with the hand that didn't hold the bread-and-butter. They turned, they stared in the direction. A little fat chap thrust out his under-lip, and the tall fellow frowned.

"I don't fancy it," said he. "Not conspicuous enough. You see, with a thing like a marquee," and he turned to Laura in his easy way, "you want to put it somewhere where it'll give you a bang slap in the eye, if you follow me."

Laura's upbringing made her wonder for a moment whether it was quite respectful of a workman to talk to her of bangs slap in the eye. But she did quite follow him.

"A corner of the tennis-court," she suggested. "But the band's going to be in one corner."

"H'm, going to have a band, are you?" said another of the workmen. He was pale. He had a haggard look as his dark eyes scanned the tennis-court. What was he thinking?

"Only a very small band," said Laura gently. Perhaps he wouldn't mind so much if the band was quite small. But the tall fellow interrupted.

"Look here, miss, that's the place. Against those trees. Over there. That'll do fine."

Against the karakas. Then the karaka-trees would be hidden. And they were so lovely, with their broad, gleaming leaves, and their clusters of yellow fruit. They were like trees you imagined growing on a desert island, proud, solitary, lifting their leaves and fruits to the sun in a kind of silent splendour. Must they be hidden by a marquee?

They must. Already the men had shouldered their staves and were making for the place. Only the tall fellow was left. He bent down, pinched a sprig of lavender, put his thumb and forefinger to his nose and snuffed up the smell. When Laura saw that gesture she forgot all about the karakas in her wonder at him caring for things like that —caring for the smell of lavender. How many men that she knew would have done such a thing? Oh, how extraordinarily nice workmen were, she thought. Why couldn't she have workmen for friends rather than the silly boys she danced with and who came to Sunday night supper? She would get on much better with men like these.

It's all the fault, she decided, as the tall fellow drew something on the back of an envelope, something that was to be looped up or left to hang, of these absurd class distinctions. Well, for her part, she didn't feel them. Not a bit, not an atom. . . . And now there came the chock-chock of wooden hammers. Some one whistled, some one sang out, "Are you right there, matey?" "Matey!" The friendliness of it, the—the——Just to prove how happy she was, just to show the tall fellow how at home she felt, and how she despised stupid conventions, Laura took a big bite of her bread-and-butter as she stared at the little drawing. She felt just like a work-girl.

"Laura, Laura, where are you? Telephone, Laura!" a voice cried from the house.

"Coming!" Away she skimmed, over the lawn, up the path, up

the steps, across the veranda, and into the porch. In the hall her father and Laurie were brushing their hats ready to go to the office.

"I say, Laura," said Laurie very fast, "you might just give a squiz at my coat before this afternoon. See if it wants pressing."

"I will," said she. Suddenly she couldn't stop herself. She ran at Laurie and gave him a small, quick squeeze. "Oh, I do love parties, don't you?" gasped Laura.

"Ra-ther," said Laurie's warm, boyish voice, and he squeezed his sister too, and gave her a gentle push. "Dash off to the telephone, old girl."

The telephone. "Yes, yes; oh yes. Kitty? Good morning, dear. Come to lunch? Do, dear. Delighted of course. It will only be a very scratch meal—just the sandwich crusts and broken meringue-shells and what's left over. Yes, isn't it a perfect morning? Your white? Oh, I certainly should. One moment—hold the line. Mother's calling." And Laura sat back. "What, mother? Can't hear."

Mrs. Sheridan's voice floated down the stairs. "Tell her to wear that sweet hat she had on last Sunday."

"Mother says you're to wear that *sweet* hat you had on last Sunday. Good. One o'clock. Bye-bye."

Laura put back the receiver, flung her arms over her head, took a deep breath, stretched and let them fall. "Huh," she sighed, and the moment after the sigh she sat up quickly. She was still, listening. All the doors in the house seemed to be open. The house was alive with soft, quick steps and running voices. The green baize door that led to the kitchen regions swung open and shut with a muffled thud. And now there came a long, chuckling absurd sound. It was the heavy piano being moved on its stiff castors. But the air! If you stopped to notice, was the air always like this? Little faint winds were playing chase, in at the tops of the windows, out at the doors. And there were two tiny spots of sun, one on the inkpot, one on a silver photograph frame, playing too. Darling little spots. Especially the one on the inkpot lid. It was quite warm. A warm little silver star. She could have kissed it.

The front door bell pealed, and there sounded the rustle of Sadie's print skirt on the stairs. A man's voice murmured; Sadie answered, careless, "I'm sure I don't know. Wait. I'll ask Mrs. Sheridan."

"What is it, Sadie?" Laura came into the hall.

"It's the florist, Miss Laura."

It was, indeed. There, just inside the door, stood a wide, shallow tray full of pots of pink lilies. No other kind. Nothing but lilies—canna lilies, big pink flowers, wide open, radiant, almost frighteningly alive on bright crimson stems.

"Oh-oh, Sadie!" said Laura, and the sound was like a little moan. She crouched down as if to warm herself at that blaze of lilies; she felt they were in her fingers, on her lips, growing in her breast.

"It's some mistake," she said faintly. "Nobody ever ordered so many. Sadie, go and find mother."

But at that moment Mrs. Sheridan joined them.

"It's quite right," she said calmly. "Yes, I ordered them. Aren't they lovely?" She pressed Laura's arm. "I was passing the shop yesterday, and I saw them in the window. And I suddenly thought for once in my life I shall have enough canna lilies. The garden-party will be a good excuse."

"But I thought you said you didn't mean to interfere," said Laura. Sadie had gone. The florist's man was still outside at his van. She put her arm round her mother's neck and gently, very gently, she bit her mother's ear.

"My darling child, you wouldn't like a logical mother, would you? Don't do that. Here's the man."

He carried more lilies still, another whole tray.

"Bank them up, just inside the door, on both sides of the porch, please," said Mrs. Sheridan. "Don't you agree, Laura?"

"Oh, I *do*, mother."

In the drawing-room Meg, Jose and good little Hans had at last succeeded in moving the piano.

"Now, if we put this chesterfield against the wall and move everything out of the room except the chairs, don't you think?"

"Quite."

"Hans, move these tables into the smoking-room, and bring a sweeper to take these marks off the carpet and—one moment, Hans——" Jose loved giving orders to the servants, and they loved obeying her. She always made them feel they were taking part in some drama. "Tell mother and Miss Laura to come here at once."

"Very good, Miss Jose."

She turned to Meg. "I want to hear what the piano sounds like, just in case I'm asked to sing this afternoon. Let's try over 'This Life is Weary.'"

Pom! Ta-ta-ta *Tee*-ta! The piano burst out so passionately that Jose's face changed. She clasped her hands. She looked mournfully and enigmatically at her mother and Laura as they came in.

> This Life is *Wee*-ary,
> A Tear—a Sigh.
> A Love that *Chan*-ges,
>   This Life is *Wee*-ary,
> A Tear—a Sigh.
> A Love that *Chan*-ges,
> And then . . . Good-bye!

But at the word "Good-bye," and although the piano sounded more desperate than ever, her face broke into a brilliant, dreadfully unsympathetic smile.

"Aren't I in good voice, mummy?" she beamed.

> This Life is *Wee*-ary,
> Hope comes to Die.
> A Dream—a *Wa*-kening.

But now Sadie interrupted them. "What is it, Sadie?"

"If you please, m'm, cook says have you got the flags for the sand-wiches?"

"The flags for the sandwiches, Sadie?" echoed Mrs. Sheridan dreamily. And the children knew by her face that she hadn't got them. "Let me see." And she said to Sadie firmly, "Tell cook I'll let her have them in ten minutes."

Sadie went.

"Now, Laura," said her mother quickly. "Come with me into the smoking-room. I've got the names somewhere on the back of an envelope. You'll have to write them out for me. Meg, go upstairs this minute and take that wet thing off your head. Jose, run and finish dressing this instant. Do you hear me, children, or shall I have to tell your father when he comes home to-night? And—and, Jose, pacify cook if you do go into the kitchen, will you? I'm terrified of her this morning."

The envelope was found at last behind the dining-room clock, though how it had got there Mrs. Sheridan could not imagine.

"One of you children must have stolen it out of my bag, because I remember vividly—cream cheese and lemon-curd. Have you done that?"

"Yes."

"Egg and——" Mrs. Sheridan held the envelope away from her. "It looks like mice. It can't be mice, can it?"

"Olive, pet," said Laura, looking over her shoulder.

"Yes, of course, olive. What a horrible combination it sounds. Egg and olive."

They were finished at last, and Laura took them off to the kitchen. She found Jose there pacifying the cook, who did not look at all terrifying.

"I have never seen such exquisite sandwiches," said Jose's rapturous voice. "How many kinds did you say there were, cook? Fifteen?"

"Fifteen, Miss Jose."

"Well, cook, I congratulate you."

Cook swept up crusts with the long sandwich knife, and smiled broadly.

"Godber's has come," announced Sadie, issuing out of the pantry. She had seen the man pass the window.

That meant the cream puffs had come. Godber's were famous for their cream puffs. Nobody ever thought of making them at home.

"Bring them in and put them on the table, my girl," ordered cook.

Sadie brought them in and went back to the door. Of course Laura and Jose were far too grown-up to really care about such things. All the same, they couldn't help agreeing that the puffs looked very attractive. Very. Cook began arranging them, shaking off the extra icing sugar.

"Don't they carry one back to all one's parties?" said Laura.

"I suppose they do," said practical Jose, who never liked to be carried back. "They look beautifully light and feathery, I must say."

"Have one each, my dears," said cook in her comfortable voice. "Yer ma won't know."

Oh, impossible. Fancy cream puffs so soon after breakfast. The very idea made one shudder. All the same, two minutes later Jose and Laura were licking their fingers with that absorbed inward look that only comes from whipped cream.

"Let's go into the garden, out by the back way," suggested Laura. "I want to see how the men are getting on with the marquee. They're such awfully nice men."

But the back door was blocked by cook, Sadie, Godber's man and Hans.

Something had happened.

"Tuk-tuk-tuk," chucked cook like an agitated hen. Sadie had her hand clapped to her cheek as though she had toothache. Hans's face was screwed up in the effort to understand. Only Godber's man seemed to be enjoying himself; it was his story.

"What's the matter? What's happened?"

"There's been a horrible accident," said Cook. "A man killed."

"A man killed! Where? How? When?"

But Godber's man wasn't going to have his story snatched from under his very nose.

"Know those little cottages just below here, miss?" Know them? Of course, she knew them. "Well, there's a young chap living there, name of Scott, a carter. His horse shied at a traction-engine, corner of Hawke Street this morning, and he was thrown out on the back of his head. Killed."

"Dead!" Laura stared at Godber's man.

"Dead when they picked him up," said Godber's man with relish. "They were taking the body home as I come up here." And he said to the cook, "He's left a wife and five little ones."

"Jose, come here." Laura caught hold of her sister's sleeve and dragged her through the kitchen to the other side of the green baize door. There she paused and leaned against it. "Jose!" she said, horrified, "however are we going to stop everything?"

"Stop everything, Laura!" cried Jose in astonishment. "What do you mean?"

"Stop the garden-party, of course." Why did Jose pretend?

But Jose was still more amazed. "Stop the garden-party? My dear

Laura, don't be so absurd. Of course we can't do anything of the kind. Nobody expects us to. Don't be so extravagant."

"But we can't possibly have a garden-party with a man dead just outside the front gate."

That really was extravagant, for the little cottages were in a lane to themselves at the very bottom of a steep rise that led up to the house. A broad road ran between. True, they were far too near. They were the greatest possible eyesore, and they had no right to be in that neighbourhood at all. They were little mean dwellings painted a chocolate brown. In the garden patches there was nothing but cabbage stalks, sick hens and tomato cans. The very smoke coming out of their chimneys was poverty-stricken. Little rags and shreds of smoke, so unlike the great silvery plumes that uncurled from the Sheridans' chimneys. Washerwomen lived in the lane and sweeps and a cobbler, and a man whose house-front was studded all over with minute bird-cages. Children swarmed. When the Sheridans were little they were forbidden to set foot there because of the revolting language and of what they might catch. But since they were grown up, Laura and Laurie on their prowls sometimes walked through. It was disgusting and sordid. They came out with a shudder. But still one must go everywhere; one must see everything. So through they went.

"And just think of what the band would sound like to that poor woman," said Laura.

"Oh, Laura!" Jose began to be seriously annoyed. "If you're going to stop a band playing every time some one has an accident, you'll lead a very strenuous life. I'm every bit as sorry about it as you. I feel just as sympathetic." Her eyes hardened. She looked at her sister just as she used to when they were little and fighting together. "You won't bring a drunken workman back to life by being sentimental," she said softly.

"Drunk! Who said he was drunk?" Laura turned furiously on Jose. She said, just as they had used to say on those occasions, "I'm going straight up to tell mother."

"Do, dear," cooed Jose.

"Mother, can I come into your room?" Laura turned the big glass door-knob.

"Of course, child. Why, what's the matter? What's given you such a colour?" And Mrs. Sheridan turned round from her dressing-table. She was trying on a new hat.

"Mother, a man's been killed," began Laura.

"*Not* in the garden?" interrupted her mother.

"No, no!"

"Oh, what a fright you gave me!" Mrs. Sheridan sighed with relief, and took off the big hat and held it on her knees.

"But listen, mother," said Laura. Breathless, half-choking, she told the dreadful story. "Of course, we can't have our party, can we?" she pleaded. "The band and everybody arriving. They'd hear us, mother; they're nearly neighbours!"

To Laura's astonishment her mother behaved just like Jose; it was harder to bear because she seemed amused. She refused to take Laura seriously.

"But, my dear child, use your common sense. It's only by accident we've heard of it. If some one had died there normally—and I can't understand how they keep alive in those poky little holes—we should still be having our party, shouldn't we?"

Laura had to say "yes" to that, but she felt it was all wrong. She sat down on her mother's sofa and pinched the cushion frill.

"Mother, isn't it really terribly heartless of us?" she asked.

"Darling!" Mrs. Sheridan got up and came over to her, carrying the hat. Before Laura could stop her she had popped it on. "My child!" said her mother, "the hat is yours. It's made for you. It's much too young for me. I have never seen you look such a picture. Look at yourself!" And she held up her hand-mirror.

"But, mother," Laura began again. She couldn't look at herself; she turned aside.

This time Mrs. Sheridan lost patience just as Jose had done.

"You are being very absurd, Laura," she said coldly. "People like that don't expect sacrifices from us. And it's not very sympathetic to spoil everybody's enjoyment as you're doing now."

"I don't understand," said Laura, and she walked quickly out of the room into her own bedroom. There, quite by chance, the first thing she saw was this charming girl in the mirror, in her black hat trimmed with gold daisies, and a long black velvet ribbon. Never had she imagined she could look like that. Is mother right? she thought. And now she hoped her mother was right. Am I being extravagant? Perhaps it was extravagant. Just for a moment she had another glimpse of that poor woman and those little children, and the body being carried into the house. But it all seemed blurred, unreal, like a picture in the newspaper. I'll remember it again after the party's over, she decided. And somehow that seemed quite the best plan. . . .

Lunch was over by half-past one. By half-past two they were all ready for the fray. The green-coated band had arrived and was established in a corner of the tennis-court.

"My dear!" trilled Kitty Maitland, "aren't they too like frogs for words? You ought to have arranged them round the pond with the conductor in the middle on a leaf."

Laurie arrived and hailed them on his way to dress. At the sight of him Laura remembered the accident again. She wanted to tell him. If Laurie agreed with the others, then it was bound to be all right. And she followed him into the hall.

"Laurie!"

"Hallo!" He was half-way upstairs, but when he turned round and saw Laura he suddenly puffed out his cheeks and goggled his eyes at her. "My word, Laura! You do look stunning," said Laurie. "What an absolutely topping hat!"

Laura said faintly "Is it?" and smiled up at Laurie, and didn't tell him after all.

Soon after that people began coming in streams. The band struck up; the hired waiters ran from the house to the marquee. Wherever you looked there were couples strolling, bending to the flowers, greeting, moving on over the lawn. They were like bright birds that had alighted in the Sheridans' garden for this one afternoon, on their way to—where? Ah, what happiness it is to be with people who all are happy, to press hands, press cheeks, smile into eyes.

"Darling Laura, how well you look!"

"What a becoming hat, child!"

"Laura, you look quite Spanish. I've never seen you look so striking."

And Laura, glowing, answered softly, "Have you had tea? Won't

you have an ice? The passion-fruit ices really are rather special."
She ran to her father and begged him. "Daddy darling, can't the
band have something to drink?"

And the perfect afternoon slowly ripened, slowly faded, slowly its
petals closed.

"Never a more delightful garden-party . . ." "The greatest success . . ." "Quite the most . . ."

Laura helped her mother with the good-byes. They stood side by
side in the porch till it was all over.

"All over, all over, thank heaven," said Mrs. Sheridan. "Round
up the others, Laura. Let's go and have some fresh coffee. I'm ex-
hausted. Yes, it's been very successful. But oh, these parties, these
parties! Why will you children insist on giving parties!" And they
all of them sat down in the deserted marquee.

"Have a sandwich, daddy dear. I wrote the flag."

"Thanks." Mr. Sheridan took a bite and the sandwich was gone.
He took another. "I suppose you didn't hear of a beastly accident
that happened to-day?" he said.

"My dear," said Mrs. Sheridan, holding up her hand, "we did. It
nearly ruined the party. Laura insisted we should put it off."

"Oh, mother!" Laura didn't want to be teased about it.

"It was a horrible affair all the same," said Mr. Sheridan. "The
chap was married too. Lived just below in the lane, and leaves a
wife and half a dozen kiddies, so they say."

An awkward little silence fell. Mrs. Sheridan fidgeted with her
cup. Really, it was very tactless of father . . .

Suddenly she looked up. There on the table were all those sand-
wiches, cakes, puffs, all uneaten, all going to be wasted. She had one
of her brilliant ideas.

"I know," she said. "Let's make up a basket. Let's send that poor
creature some of this perfectly good food. At any rate, it will be the
greatest treat for the children. Don't you agree? And she's sure to
have neighbours calling in and so on. What a point to have it all
ready prepared. Laura!" She jumped up. "Get me the big basket out
of the stairs cupboard."

"But, mother, do you really think it's a good idea?" said Laura.

Again, how curious, she seemed to be different from them all. To take scraps from their party. Would the poor woman really like that?

"Of course! What's the matter with you to-day? An hour or two ago you were insisting on us being sympathetic, and now——"

Oh, well! Laura ran for the basket. It was filled, it was heaped by her mother.

"Take it yourself, darling," said she. "Run down just as you are. No, wait, take the arum lilies too. People of that class are so impressed by arum lilies."

"The stems will ruin her lace frock," said practical Jose.

So they would. Just in time. "Only the basket, then. And, Laura!" —her mother followed her out of the marquee—"don't on any account——"

"What, mother?"

No, better not put such ideas into the child's head! "Nothing! Run along."

It was just growing dusky as Laura shut their garden gates. A big dog ran by like a shadow. The road gleamed white, and down below in the hollow the little cottages were in deep shade. How quiet it seemed after the afternoon. Here she was going down the hill to somewhere where a man lay dead, and she couldn't realize it. Why couldn't she? She stopped a minute. And it seemed to her that kisses, voices, tinkling spoons, laughter, the smell of crushed grass were somehow inside her. She had no room for anything else. How strange! She looked up at the pale sky, and all she thought was, "Yes, it was the most successful party."

Now the broad road was crossed. The lane began, smoky and dark. Women in shawls and men's tweed caps hurried by. Men hung over the palings; the children played in the doorways. A low hum came from the mean little cottages. In some of them there was a flicker of light, and a shadow, crab-like, moved across the window. Laura bent her head and hurried on. She wished now she had put on a coat. How her frock shone! And the big hat with the velvet streamer—if only it was another hat! Were the people looking at her? They must be. It was a mistake to have come; she knew all along it was a mistake. Should she go back even now?

No, too late. This was the house. It must be. A dark knot of people stood outside. Beside the gate an old, old woman with a crutch sat in a chair, watching. She had her feet on a newspaper. The voices stopped as Laura drew near. The group parted. It was as though she was expected, as though they had known she was coming here.

Laura was terribly nervous. Tossing the velvet ribbon over her shoulder, she said to a woman standing by, "Is this Mrs. Scott's house?" and the woman, smiling queerly, said, "It is, my lass."

Oh, to be away from this! She actually said, "Help me, God," as she walked up the tiny path and knocked. To be away from those staring eyes, or to be covered up in anything, one of those women's shawls even. I'll just leave the basket and go, she decided. I shan't even wait for it to be emptied.

Then the door opened. A little woman in black showed in the gloom.

Laura said, "Are you Mrs. Scott?" But to her horror the woman answered, "Walk in please, miss," and she was shut in the passage.

"No," said Laura, "I don't want to come in. I only want to leave this basket. Mother sent——"

The little woman in the gloomy passage seemed not to have heard her. "Step this way, please, miss," she said in an oily voice, and Laura followed her.

She found herself in a wretched little low kitchen, lighted by a smoky lamp. There was a woman sitting before the fire.

"Em," said the little creature who had let her in. "Em! It's a young lady." She turned to Laura. She said meaningly, "I'm 'er sister, Miss. You'll excuse 'er, won't you?"

"Oh, but of course!" said Laura. "Please, please don't disturb her. I—I only want to leave——"

But at that moment the woman at the fire turned round. Her face, puffed up, red, with swollen eyes and swollen lips, looked terrible. She seemed as though she couldn't understand why Laura was there. What did it mean? Why was this stranger standing in the kitchen with a basket? What was it all about? And the poor face puckered up again.

"All right, my dear," said the other. "I'll thenk the young lady."

And again she began, "You'll excuse her, miss, I'm sure," and her face, swollen too, tried an oily smile.

Laura only wanted to get out, to get away. She was back in the passage. The door opened. She walked straight through into the bedroom, where the dead man was lying.

"You'd like a look at 'im, wouldn't you?" said Em's sister, and she brushed past Laura over to the bed. "Don't be afraid, my lass,—" and now her voice sounded fond and sly, and fondly she drew down the sheet—" 'e looks a picture. There's nothing to show. Come along, my dear."

Laura came.

There lay a young man, fast asleep—sleeping so soundly, so deeply, that he was far, far away from them both. Oh, so remote, so peaceful. He was dreaming. Never wake him up again. His head was sunk in the pillow, his eyes were closed; they were blind under the closed eyelids. He was given up to his dream. What did garden-parties and baskets and lace frocks matter to him? He was far from all those things. He was wonderful, beautiful. While they were laughing and while the band was playing, this marvel had come to the lane. Happy . . . happy. . . . All is well, said that sleeping face. This is just as it should be. I am content.

But all the same you had to cry, and she couldn't go out of the room without saying something to him. Laura gave a loud childish sob.

"Forgive my hat," she said.

And this time she didn't wait for Em's sister. She found her way out of the door, down the path, past all those dark people. At the corner of the lane she met Laurie.

He stepped out of the shadow. "Is that you, Laura?"

"Yes."

"Mother was getting anxious. Was it all right?"

"Yes, quite. Oh, Laurie!" She took his arm, she pressed up against him.

"I say, you're not crying, are you?" asked her brother.

Laura shook her head. She was.

Laurie put his arm round her shoulder. "Don't cry," he said in his warm, loving voice. "Was it awful?"

"No," sobbed Laura. "It was simply marvelous. But, Laurie——"

She stopped, she looked at her brother. "Isn't life," she stammered, "isn't life——" But what life was she couldn't explain. No matter. He quite understood.

"*Isn't* it, darling?" said Laurie.

Critical Commentary on *The Garden Party*

The unobtrusively controlled point-of-view affords insight into several characters, each of whom is peripheral to Laura Sheridan. Concomitantly, their reactions to a single situation, conflicting with hers, help to amplify the reader's awareness of her discovery of the end of childhood. By avoiding an absolute focus on Laura, Katherine Mansfield has created a balanced structure, that is, a composition in which normal human experience is seen from a variety of angles. In a few hours Laura has moved from pampered, adolescent innocence to the brink of maturity, but is reluctant to accept her responsibility and is still too inexperienced to articulate her intuition of the mystery. " 'Isn't life,' she stammered, 'isn't life——' But what life was she couldn't explain."

For Laura knowledge of death is the beginning of perception. If she is appalled by the indifference of her mother and Jose, she is equally alienated by the personal grief of the mourners. That she will learn in time, we are confident. For the moment, however, she resists the transition to the world of decay and change. Now she is old enough to reject "the garden-parties and baskets and lace frocks" so trivial and so dear to her mother and Jose, and even—until recently—to herself. "Yes," she had thought on the way to the dead man's cottage, "it was the most successful party." But when she sees death for the first time, she is enchanted by a tranquillity that she intuits is not a part of mortality. "While they were laughing and while the band was playing, this marvel had come to the lane. Happy . . . Happy. . . . All is well, said that sleeping face. This is just as it should be, I am content." The child envies death as a happy, esthetic state which is a contradiction of the reality she tries to communicate to her sympathetic brother.

The comfortable, aristocratic environment in which she has been reared is conducive to this attitude. All her short life she has been brought up to expect ease, love, and kindness. Shielded from the discord and commonness of the outside world, she unconsciously resists disquieting frictions. Sunnily imaginative—"the artistic one" of the family—she is buoyant, receptive to gentleness and beauty. The four workmen, thus, are alien to her kind of life; but she—even knowing they are not of her class—is taken by their easy, pleasant manner with her. She is pleased to discover "How very nice workmen were!" And the tall fellow's gesture with the sprig of lavender fills her with happiness.

The death of the man in the lane disrupts her festive mood, but only temporarily. After all, as she must admit to herself, the death really has nothing to do with her, and the lane "was disgusting and sordid." Yet, she senses the impropriety of going through with the party, and cannot understand her mother's loss of patience. The mood does not last however, and when her mother suggests that she carry down a basket of party food, she can be quite impersonal. "Oh, well! Laura ran for the basket." It's all part of her acceptance that "one must go everywhere; one must see everything." She thinks not of her somber mission but of the success of the party.

The reality of the occasion is forced upon her only when she comes to the house of mourning, "the dark knot of people" contrasting with the gaiety of the afternoon. Here there is no friendliness, as with the workmen, only the ugliness of grief and formal mourning. Furthermore, it is now she who is in an alien atmosphere. Unable to bear the intrusion of ugliness and disquiet into her ordered, serene life, she thinks of escape. The illusion of order, ironically, is restored when she sees the peacefulness of death. Ardently she yearns for permanent happiness and content, becoming aware for the first time that the world can never offer more than transient satisfactions.

The point-of-view, then, is essentially Laura's, and whatever meaning and mood the story has are related to her initiation into a life of judgment and conscious values. That she wishes desperately to cling to the illusion of unformed childhood is the distinguishing trait of her personality, even though with the real beginning of experience her illusions are already paling. Of all the characters, only her brother Laurie appears to share her sense of loss. The others—adults and children alike—for the most part represent the life of selfish pleasure or of hard reality.

From time to time, therefore, the point-of-view shifts to reveal experience in a mold other than Laura's. The introductory point-of-view is general, the author lending her eyes to the entire scene and, consequently, evoking a gay mood that is to be repudiated by the news of the man's death and the events leading to the conclusion. Once Laura is introduced, her dominating point-of-view is measured by that of characters who reflect two aspects of normal human experience: adolescent and adult. Of the former, Jose is the most significant because her contrast to Laura is so marked. Laurie offers affection but beyond that remains in his sister's shadow. Meg and Hans are narrative props. But Jose, impatient with her sister's sensitivity, is a miniature of the mother, intent on unreasoning pleasure. Her song—"This Life is Weary"—a parody of Laura's feeling, is symbolic of a wholehearted acceptance of her mother's values. "But at the word 'Good-bye' . . . her face broke into a brilliant, dreadfully unsympathetic smile."

The adults fall into two classes: those of social eminence, represented by Mrs. Sheridan; and those of inferior station. Mrs. Sheridan reveals herself as a fond parent but as an utterly selfish human being. Her values are isolated from genuine compassion or charity that do not touch directly upon her family. She resents any disruption of her family's serenity. When Mr. Sheridan reported the "beastly accident," she "fidgeted with her cup. Really, it was very tactless of father . . ." She is good to the lower classes, but she insists upon observing the class distinctions which Laura comes to think "absurd."

Those of the working class are as remote in their private lives from the Sheridans as the Sheridans are from them. Thus, they are condescendingly polite to Laura and fastidiously aloof. Yet they are essential to the beginnings of Laura's discovery, for their presence enlarges her attitude toward humanity. From the workmen she learns that even the lower classes are capable of sensitivity, of "caring for things like . . . the smell of lavender." And she also learns to deprecate "these absurd class distinctions." But from the mourners she learns that their society is just as closed as hers, that they tolerate her even as in a sense the kind workmen tolerate her.

Out of these varying points-of-view, then, Laura emerges as an interesting, maturing human being. Her transition from gay childhood is not yet complete, to be sure, but the foundation has been laid. We know that she has limitations and illusions, of course; and we also know that she can never again give herself entirely to the selfishness encouraged by her mother and indulged by Jose. Nor, for that matter, do we expect her to live indefinitely in her illusion. Her anguished observation to Laurie is at least an intimation that she is about to face life, with all its disappointments. Centering our gaze on Laura but glancing at times toward the others, we absorb with her varying degrees of emotion: acute pleasure, anger, disappointment, sympathy, grief. In short, we derive from her experiences the mutations of feeling which are a part of growing up.

The Meaning of Fiction

CHAPTER 7

Content and Purpose

Theme and Intention

IN THE preceding chapters we have emphasized such interrelated qualities of fiction as structure, order, and emotion. Now we turn to intellectual content as another quality which contributes to the whole fictional experience. Like everyone who has thought earnestly about experience, the novelist has probably formed opinions regarding the universe and the people who tenant it. Questions of good and evil, human relationships and aspirations, and any number of others constantly provoke speculation or judgment. Every mature writer is a philosopher of a kind, having some interpretation or criticism of life to impart. This becomes the intellectual stratum in fiction, the controlling or underlying concept, which we call *theme*. Simply defined, theme is the abstract statement of the novel's dominant idea, moral lesson, interpretation, or criticism of event and reality.

Even without subscribing to a formal code of ideas, any dedicated novelist brings to his work a set of attitudes which express his personal philosophical convictions. But many writers, indeed, have incorporated formal philosophical theories into their fiction: to name a few, Huxley is influenced by Eastern thought, Farrell by Marxism, and Steinbeck by Darwinism. With or without methodized philosophical indoctrination, however, writers in every age are strongly affected by contemporary currents of thought. These may be rationalism, humanism, existentialism, and the like. In any event, ideas are assimilated until they become the novelist's own and are expressed thematically in his writings. At the same time, philosophy in fiction—whether derivative or original—is related to the emo-

tional complexes projected in the work of art. Consequently, feeling
and thought must be considered together, as parts of a common experience. Both of these components—intellectual and emotional—
win expression in character, plot, and setting.

Too often this dualism is ignored and judgments are based upon
theme alone. Such a practice emerges from a fallacious assumption
that fiction, to be worthwhile, must be morally edifying. Inevitably, this attitude leads to a search for "messages" and "good"
themes, as well as a misguided insistence upon clarity and emphasis
of salutary meaning, which is to say, meaning acceptable to the
reader. Naturally, when an underlying idea is compatible with our
own view of life, we are likely to flatter the author for having such
good sense. The worth of a novel, however, is not to be determined
by its proximity to a reader's attitudes, for differences of opinion
must be allowed. Furthermore, we must at all costs resist the temptation to judge art exclusively on the basis of idea or theme, which
is generally at most but one half of artistic purpose.

The theme of the story—whether or not it coincides with ideas
cherished by the reader—is valuable only as long as it is considered
in relation to the artistic totality. Just as technique cannot provide
the sole criterion for analyzing and evaluating a novel, so theme cannot stand alone. If it is a message that we want or a "good" theme,
we may turn more profitably to a collection of essays or attend to a
pulpit sermon. Dogmatic celebration of didactic and moralizing
tendencies in a novel would by itself be a serious distortion of fictional purpose. An author may use a narrative disguise for conveying homilies, but we ought to avoid confusing homily with fiction.
Thus, a mature reader understands well enough that Aesop in any
one of his fables is mainly concerned with the moral rather than the
narrative line. The account which follows (from a version printed
by William Caxton in 1484) is characteristic:

The Thyrdde Fable is of the Foxe and of the Gote

He which is wyse and sage ought fyrst to loke and behold the ende/
or he begynneth the werke or dede/ as hyer appiereth by this fable/ Of

a foxe & of a gote/ that sometyme descended and wente doune in to a depe welle/ for to drynke. And Whanne they had wel dronke/ by cause that thei coude not come vpward ageyne/ the Foxe sayd to the gote in this maner/ my frend yf thow wylt helpe me/ we shall sone been bothe out of this welle/ For yf thow wylt sette thy two feet ageynste the walle/ I shal wel lepe vpon the/ & vpon thy hornes And thenne I shal lepe oute of this welle/

And whanne I shalle be oute of hit/ thou shalt take me by the handes/ and I shal plucke and drawe the oute of the welle/ And at this request the gote/ accorded and ansuerd/ I wylle wel/ And thene the gote lyfte vp his feet ageynst the walle/ and the foxe dyd so moche by his malyce that he got out of the welle/ Ane whan he was oute/ he began to loke on the gote/ whiche was within the welle/ & thenne/ the gote sayd to hym/ help me now as thow hast promysed/ And thene/ the foxe beganne to lawhe and to scorne hym and sayd to hym/ O mayster goote/ yf thow haddest be well wyse with thy fayre berde/ or euer thow haddest entryd in to the welle/ thow sholdest fyrst haue taken hede/ how thow sholdest haue comen oute of hit ageyne/

And therfore he whiche is wyse/ yf he wysely wylle gouerne hym self/ ought to take euer good hede to the ende of his werke

The fable was once a popular form of fictional discourse in which animals or supernatural beings, given human attributes and attitudes, underwent experiences intended to convey a lesson. In the present instance, attention is held by a rudimentary story consisting of action, characters, dialogue, and setting. But these merely constitute a vehicle for the moral which begins and ends the fable: "He whiche is wyse and sage ought fyrst to loke and behold the ende/ or he begynneth the werke or dede/ as hyer appiereth by this fable/ . . . . And therfore he whiche is wyse/ yf he wysely wylle gouerne hym self/ ought to take euer good hede to the ende of his werke."

The modern fable which follows, by James Thurber, is adapted to precisely the same procedure and is directed likewise to a moralistic end. Thurber's attitude is overtly satiric and more sophisticated than Aesop's. Yet his concluding moral, a deliberate inversion of a cliché, merits serious ethical consideration. In both Aesop and Thurber, it will be observed, the moral theme is the most important element.

The Glass in the Field*

by JAMES THURBER

A short time ago some builders, working on a studio in Connecticut, left a huge square of plate glass standing upright in a field one day. A goldfinch flying swiftly across the field struck the glass and was knocked cold. When he came to he hastened to his club, where an attendant bandaged his head and gave him a stiff drink. "What the hell happened?" asked a sea gull. "I was flying across a meadow when all of a sudden the air crystallized on me," said the goldfinch. The sea gull and a hawk and an eagle all laughed heartily. A swallow listened gravely. "For fifteen years, fledgling and bird, I've flown this country," said the eagle, "and I assure you there is no such thing as air crystallizing. Water, yes; air, no." "You were probably struck by a hailstone," the hawk told the goldfinch. "Or he may have had a stroke," said the sea gull. "What do you think, swallow?" "Why, I—I think maybe the air crystallized on him," said the swallow. The large birds laughed so loudly that the goldfinch became annoyed and bet them each a dozen worms that they couldn't follow the course he had flown across the field without encountering the hardened atmosphere. They all took his bet; the swallow went along to watch. The sea gull, the eagle, and the hawk decided to fly together over the route the goldfinch indicated. "You come, too," they said to the swallow. "I—I—well, no," said the swallow. "I don't think I will." So the three large birds took off together and they hit the glass together and they were all knocked cold.

Moral: *He who hesitates is sometimes saved.*

Each fable, especially Thurber's, tells an agreeably entertaining story, but for such an obviously moralistic purpose that the function overshadows the narrative. Neither is likely to be mistaken for a short story, and we are pleased to accept the domination of theme. When, however, we understand that we are dealing with fiction of a more or less conventional kind, we expect theme to be implied rather than stated, and contributory rather than all-important. To illustrate the point, let us paraphrase a contemporary novel and indicate how an important theme may engage us and yet not distract attention from the totality.

Nathanael West in *Miss Lonelyhearts* tells the story of a reporter who writes a newspaper's agony column. All the tragedy, sorrow, and sordidness of contemporary living are revealed in the illiterate letters that come to his desk for advice. Unable to remain objective about them, as his editor Shrike can be, Miss Lonelyhearts treats these problems until they become unbearable to him. They are unbearable because he does not have the soul of a Christ and cannot help his petitioners. Lacking this exemplary quality and torn by his sub-jectivism, he sinks lower and lower until he is destroyed by the hus-band of a woman who had sought his advice.

Turning from this bare statement of what occurs in the novel to its meaning, we find an abstract principle that can be summed up thematically like this: it is impossible to identify yourself com-passionately with others unless you are capable of making a perfect sacrifice for them, as Christ did. To want to help and not be able to do so for want of this spirituality is the tragedy of Miss Lonely-hearts. There is an implication, however, that in being destroyed by those he wished to assist he does achieve a kind of sanctity. At least, what he does is better than cynicism and disinterest, even if his destruction results.

To state subject and theme in this way of course precludes en-joyment of the half-real atmosphere, of the symbolic and allegori-cal motif, and of the fearsome mood of the novel. Nevertheless, it may suggest the interworking of theme with the other fictional in-gredients. The reader interested in *Miss Lonelyhearts* might also turn to *The Day of the Locust* for a view of West's consistency of theme. Here, again in a symbolic and allegorical framework, the au-thor treats the frenzied, amoral life of Hollywood. Thematically, very much as in *Miss Lonelyhearts*, he deplores the rejection of pure sacrifice as the dominant quality of contemporary life. Neither wishing nor recognizing things of the spirit, modernity acknowledges only material success.

Religious motifs are not uncommon in modern fiction, but the theme can never be hackneyed as long as the structure of which it is a part is treated imaginatively and convincingly. Hence, we find that although a religious conflict is basic to Graham Greene's novel *The Heart of the Matter*, the experience depicted is altogether dif-ferent from those in West's novels. Both novelists are complementary in that they are concerned with sacrifice; yet they work toward different ends—Greene's, a matter of explicit dogma; West's, of subtle and generalized faith—and provoke different responses.

Although theme is an important aspect of meaning, it is not to be regarded as the total meaning in the work of fiction. It serves as the abstraction or crystallization of the author's ideas. Yet without the support of feeling (mood and tone), of a narrative superstructure (plot, character, and setting), and of esthetic intricacies, theme would be no more than a barren statement—like the statistical description in an almanac of a city we have never seen. Complementing all the other elements which go into the making of a novel, theme is part of a process known critically as *intention*.

The obvious or literal meaning of the term *intention* is deceptive in a critical context because it denotes the author's design before his fulfillment of it. A formal definition, for instance, tells us that intention is "a settled direction of the mind toward the accomplishment of a particular act." This, in a very broad sense, is critically accurate, for we have no doubt that, prior to composition, the novelist *intended* to write a novel, or a poet a poem.* Such information is hardly useful, however; at least, it is information we could have deduced without critical assistance. What a great many readers would like to know is, what effects and meanings did the author intend to impart prior to and during the course of composition? Unfortunately, such knowledge is seldom available to readers, even if the author's ability to reveal it could be assumed. Furthermore, the ultimate usefulness of this kind of insight is both limited and specialized.

Unless we are biographers or literary historians or, for that matter, critics who have mastered all the internal data of a given novel, we must be less concerned with the initiation of the creative process than with its end result. Suppose we have access to memoirs, letters, diaries, recorded conversations, and the like, which reveal the author's thoughts and feelings about a work to be undertaken. And suppose that in these documents he charted the route he would

---

* As Northrop Frye (*Anatomy of Criticism*) says: "If we had the privilege of Gulliver in Glubbdubdrib to call up the ghost of, say, Shakespeare, to ask him what he meant by such and such a passage, we could only get, with maddening iteration, the same answer: 'I meant it to form part of the play.' . . ."

take—foretold his proposed accomplishments—with regard to action, complications, character development, and other essentials for the construction of a novel. Are we to hold him to his preliminary aims, and censure him for departures and discrepancies? Even a scientist at the beginning of an experiment sets forth a schedule of procedure, and anticipates certain results. Yet circumstances may well necessitate modification and alterations in the course of experimentation; and the result, if not identical with the proposed one, may be equally valuable.

A novelist, though having far less occasion than a scientist to commit himself to a strict plan of procedure and anticipated results, generally projects—either methodically or intuitively, consciously or unconsciously—the scheme of his work. But facets of the scheme (or intention) may, for various reasons, change during the course of its development. As Horace (in *The Art of Poetry*) long ago warned his readers:

> For neither always will the minstrel's lyre
> Give back the note his ear and hand require;
> He asks a grave, the chord a sharp remits;
> The archer aims, the bow not always hits.

If out of deference to critical convention, then, we are to use the term *intention*, we must be alert to the ambiguity which may make it a dogma of negative virtue. The reader still in the early stages of his critical indoctrination needs to be reminded that the literal meaning of the word, applied to literature, can be slippery unless it is properly qualified. The danger inheres in what is called *intentionalism* or the *intentional fallacy*, that is, the error of interpreting a work in the light of an author's initiatory motives and attitudes. At the same time, it would be preposterous to assume that what he had in mind during the inception of the novel, or what inspired him to it, has no bearing on the finished product. For this reason, therefore, it is useful to distinguish between private or originating and internal or ultimate intention.

The first, as has been noted, is the concern of the specialist after he has thoroughly familiarized himself with the context of the novel. For example, a critic devoted to an examination of F. Scott Fitzgerald's novels would find many instructive insights in the author's partial, unpublished revision of *Tender is the Night*. Drafted by Fitzgerald after publication of the novel, the revision suggests ways in which he would have improved the original. In effect, the altered version gives us a privileged view of Fitzgerald's originating intention. It is as if we were witnesses during the creation of a new novel. That fact, however, does not alter the condition of *Tender is the Night* as an already completed novel which we may (and generally do) read without reference to what the author had to say about his creative process. The general critic, thus, reads the novel in the form which has been made public and interprets it on the basis of internal or ultimate intention. Considered in this way, intention (to paraphrase John Crowe Ransom, in *The New Criticism*) is the total meaning of the completed work, and it contributes specific or particularized details which were not necessarily part of the conception. The total intention, Ransom points out, is evident only in the final stage, and need not have been known to the author at the time he began to give his conception a logical form.

Dealing with the same problem—and there is no reason why we may not substitute "novelist" for "poet"—Robert Penn Warren (in an essay on *The Rime of the Ancient Mariner*) states: "The implication here [*How do we know that the poet 'intended' certain interpretations?*] is that the process of poetic creation is, shall we say, analogous to the process of building a house from a blueprint: the poet has an idea, the blueprint, and according to it, plank by plank and nail by nail, he makes a poem, the house. Actually, the creation of a poem is as much a process of discovery as a process of making. A poem may, in fact, start from an idea—and may involve any number of ideas—but the process for the poet is the process of discovering what the idea 'means' to him in his total experience. . . . Or a poem may start from a phrase, a scene, an image, or an incident which has, for the poet, a suggestive quality. . . . Then the process for the poet is the process of discovering why the item has caught his attention in the first place. . . . Or the original item may lead to some more or less obscure train of association to another item which will become the true germ of the poem, . . ."

The total intention of the literary work, then, sums up an operation which began with an idea or a suggestion and terminated in its "symbolic potential." This is another way of saying that intention is not the abstract core or germ with which the work begins, but the aggregate of particularized details and responses which give the novel completeness. Intention as we would have it understood here, in short, is equatable with the symbolic achievement or summation of the entire work. Regardless of what the author had in mind or anticipated, the judgment we apply to his work is determined by the internal and structural evidence of the work itself. It is this evidence which supplies us with whatever meaning we are capable of extracting.

Returning to *Miss Lonelyhearts*, for a moment, we see that theme, despite its importance to West's fictional discourse, could hardly be regarded as more than a segment of the total intention. To understand the whole meaning, or intention, we are obliged to assimilate the complex of characterization, symbolism, and feeling, along with theme, which constitute the experience represented by West. Similarly, the meaning of *The Heart of the Matter* is bound up in a variety of elements: not only theme, but a religious conflict, irony, a sinister and oppressive atmosphere, intrigues and complications of plot, and so forth. A well-known novel like Faulkner's *Sanctuary* builds upon gothic horror, upon a mood and tone suggestive of impending doom, frustration, unalleviated evil. But the totality of the novel incorporates these and other elements to reveal an intention concerned with the evil of contemporary life. Interpretations of *Sanctuary* may differ, to be sure, but we seem ultimately to be confronted by a symbolic conflict between order and chaos in which justice and legality succumb to brute force and gangsterism.

The meaning of any serious work of fiction emerges from the interplay of its dominant qualities, to be summed up finally as the author's achievement, his fulfilled intention. As a practical demonstration, let us consider the following short story.

The Forks

by J. F. POWERS

That summer when Father Eudex got back from saying Mass at the orphanage in the morning, he would park Monsignor's car, which was long and black and new like a politician's, and sit down in the cool of the porch to read his office. If Monsignor was not already standing in the door, he would immediately appear there, seeing that his car had safely returned, and inquire:

"Did you have any trouble with her?"

Father Eudex knew too well the question meant, Did you mistreat my car?

"No trouble, Monsignor."

"Good," Monsignor said, with imperfect faith in his curate, who was not a car owner. For a moment Monsignor stood framed in the screen door, fumbling his watch fob as for a full-length portrait, and then he was suddenly not there.

"Monsignor," Father Eudex said, rising nervously, "I've got a chance to pick up a car."

At the door Monsignor slid into his frame again. His face expressed what was for him intense interest.

"Yes? Go on."

"I don't want to have to use yours every morning."

"It's all right."

"And there are other times." Father Eudex decided not to be maudlin and mention sick calls, nor be entirely honest and admit he was tired of busses and bumming rides from parishioners. "And now I've got a chance to get one—cheap."

Monsignor, smiling, came alert at *cheap.*

"New?"

"No, I wouldn't say it's new."

Monsignor was openly suspicious now. "What kind?"

"It's a Ford."

"And not new?"

"Not new, Monsignor—but in good condition. It was owned by a retired farmer and had good care."

Monsignor sniffed. He *knew* cars. "V-Eight, Father?"

"No," Father Eudex confessed. "It's a Model A."

Monsignor chuckled as though this were indeed the damnedest thing he had ever heard.

"But in very good condition, Monsignor."

"You said that."

"Yes. And I could take it apart if anything went wrong. My uncle had one."

"No doubt." Monsignor uttered a laugh at Father Eudex's rural origins. Then he delivered the final word, long delayed out of amusement. "It wouldn't be prudent, Father. After all, this isn't a country parish. You know the class of people we get here."

Monsignor put on his Panama hat. Then, apparently mistaking the obstinacy in his curate's face for plain ignorance, he shed a little more light. "People watch a priest, Father. *Damnant quod non intelligunt.* It would never do. You'll have to watch your tendencies."

Monsignor's eyes tripped and fell hard on the morning paper lying on the swing where he had finished it.

"Another flattering piece about that crazy fellow. . . . There's a man who might have gone places if it weren't for his mouth! A bishop doesn't have to get mixed up in all that stuff!"

Monsignor, as Father Eudex knew, meant unions, strikes, race riots—all that stuff.

"A parishioner was saying to me only yesterday it's getting so you can't tell the Catholics from the Communists, with the priests as bad as any. Yes, and this fellow is the worst. He reminds me of that bishop a few years back—at least he called himself a bishop, a Protestant—that was advocating companionate marriages. It's not that bad, maybe, but if you listened to some of them you'd think that Catholicity and capitalism were incompatible!"

"The Holy Father——"

"The Holy Father's in Europe, Father. Mr. Memmers lives in this parish. I'm his priest. What can I tell him?"

"Is it Mr. Memmers of the First National, Monsignor?"

"It is, Father. And there's damned little cheer I can give a man like Memmers. Catholics, priests, and laity alike—yes, and princes of the Church, all talking atheistic communism!"

This was the substance of their conversation, always, the deadly routine in which Father Eudex played straight man. Each time it happened he seemed to participate, and though he should have known better he justified his participation by hoping that it would not happen again, or in quite the same way. But it did, it always did, the same way, and Monsignor, for all his alarms, had nothing to say really and meant one thing only, the thing he never said—that he dearly wanted to be, and was not, a bishop.

Father Eudex could imagine just what kind of bishop Monsignor would be. His reign would be a wise one, excessively so. His mind was made up on everything, excessively so. He would know how to avoid the snares set in the path of the just man, avoid them, too, in good taste and good conscience. He would not be trapped as so many good shepherds before him had been trapped, poor souls— caught in fair-seeming dilemmas of justice that were best left alone, like the first apple. It grieved him, he said, to think of those great hearts broken in silence and solitude. It was the worst kind of exile, alas! But just give him the chance and he would know what to do, what to say, and, more important, what not to do, not to say— neither yea nor nay for him. He had not gone to Rome for nothing. For him the dark forest of decisions would not exist; for him, thanks to hours spent in prayer and meditation, the forest would vanish as dry grass before fire, his fire. He knew the mask of evil already— birth control, indecent movies, salacious books—and would call these things by their right names and dare to deal with them for what they were, these new occasions for the old sins of the cities of the plains.

But in the meantime—oh, to have a particle of the faith that God had in humanity! Dear, trusting God forever trying them beyond their feeble powers, ordering terrible tests, fatal trials by nonsense (the crazy bishop). And keeping Monsignor steadily warming up on the side lines, ready to rush in, primed for the day that would per- haps never dawn.

At one time, so the talk went, there had been reason to think that

Monsignor was headed for a bishopric. Now it was too late; Monsignor's intercessors were all dead; the cupboard was bare; he knew it at heart, and it galled him to see another man, this *crazy* man, given the opportunity, and making such a mess of it.

Father Eudex searched for and found a little salt for Monsignor's wound. "The word's going around he'll be the next archbishop," he said.

"I won't believe it," Monsignor countered hoarsely. He glanced at the newspaper on the swing and renewed his horror. "If that fellow's right, Father, I'm"—his voice cracked at the idea—*"wrong!"*

Father Eudex waited until Monsignor had started down the steps to the car before he said, "It could be."

"I'll be back for lunch, Father. I'm taking her for a little spin."

Monsignor stopped in admiration a few feet from the car—her. He was as helpless before her beauty as a boy with a birthday bicycle. He could not leave her alone. He had her out every morning and afternoon and evening. He was indiscriminate about picking people up for a ride in her. He kept her on a special diet—only the best of gas and oil and grease, with daily rubdowns. He would run her only on the smoothest roads and at so many miles an hour. That was to have stopped at the first five hundred, but only now, nearing the thousand mark, was he able to bring himself to increase her speed, and it seemed to hurt him more than it did her.

Now he was walking around behind her to inspect the tires. Apparently O.K. He gave the left rear fender an amorous chuck and eased into the front seat. Then they drove off, the car and he, to see the world, to explore each other further on the honeymoon.

Father Eudex watched the car slide into the traffic, and waited, on edge. The corner cop, fulfilling Father Eudex's fears, blew his whistle and waved his arms up in all four directions, bringing traffic to a standstill. Monsignor pulled expertly out of line and drove down Clover Boulevard in a one-car parade; all others stalled respectfully. The cop, as Monsignor passed, tipped his cap, showing a bald head. Monsignor, in the circumstances, could not acknowledge him, though he knew the man well—a parishioner. He was occupied with keeping his countenance kindly, grim, and exalted, that the cop's faith remain whole, for it was evidently inconceivable to him that Monsignor should ever venture abroad unless to bear the Holy Viaticum, always racing with death.

Father Eudex, eyes baleful but following the progress of the big black car, saw a hand dart out of the driver's window in a wave. Monsignor would combine a lot of business with pleasure that morning, creating what he called "good will for the Church"—all morning in the driver's seat toasting passers-by with a wave that was better than a blessing. How he loved waving to people!

Father Eudex overcame his inclination to sit and stew about things by going down the steps to meet the mailman. He got the usual handful for the Monsignor—advertisements and amazing offers, the unfailing crop of chaff from dealers in church goods, organs, collection schemes, insurance, and sacramental wines. There were two envelopes addressed to Father Eudex, one a mimeographed plea from a missionary society which he might or might not acknowledge with a contribution, depending upon what he thought of the cause— if it was really lost enough to justify a levy on his poverty—and the other a check for a hundred dollars.

The check came in an eggshell envelope with no explanation except a tiny card, "Compliments of the Rival Tractor Company," but even that was needless. All over town clergymen had known for days that the checks were on the way again. Some, rejoicing, could hardly wait. Father Eudex, however, was one of those who could.

With the passing of hard times and the coming of the fruitful war years, the Rival Company, which was a great one for public relations, had found the best solution to the excess-profits problem to be giving. Ministers and even rabbis shared in the annual jack pot, but Rival employees were largely Catholic and it was the checks to the priests that paid off. Again, some thought it was a wonderful idea, and others thought that Rival, plagued by strikes and justly so, had put their alms to work.

There was another eggshell envelope, Father Eudex saw, among the letters for Monsignor, and knew his check would be for two hundred, the premium for pastors.

Father Eudex left Monsignor's mail on the porch table by his cigars. His own he stuck in his back pocket, wanting to forget it, and went down the steps into the yard. Walking back and forth on the shady side of the rectory where the lilies of the valley grew and reading his office, he gradually drifted into the back yard, lured by a noise. He came upon Whalen, the janitor, pounding pegs into the ground.

Father Eudex closed the breviary on a finger. "What's it all about, Joe?"

Joe Whalen snatched a piece of paper from his shirt and handed it to Father Eudex. "He gave it to me this morning."

He—it was the word for Monsignor among them. A docile pronoun only, and yet when it meant the Monsignor it said, and concealed, nameless things.

The paper was a plan for a garden drawn up by the Monsignor in his fine hand. It called for a huge fleur-de-lis bounded by smaller crosses—and these Maltese—a fountain, a sundial, and a cloister walk running from the rectory to the garage. Later there would be birdhouses and a ten-foot wall of thick gray stones, acting as a moat against the eyes of the world. The whole scheme struck Father Eudex as expensive and, in this country, Presbyterian.

When Monsignor drew the plan, however, he must have been in his medieval mood. A spouting whale jostled with Neptune in the choppy waters of the fountain. North was indicated in the legend by a winged cherub huffing and puffing.

Father Eudex held the plan up against the sun to see the watermark. The stationery was new to him, heavy, simulated parchment, with the Church of the Holy Redeemer and Monsignor's name embossed, three initials, W. F. X., William Francis Xavier. With all those initials the man could pass for a radio station, a chancery wit had observed, or if his last name had not been Sweeney, Father Eudex added now, for high Anglican.

Father Eudex returned the plan to Whalen, feeling sorry for him and to an extent guilty before him—if only because he was a priest like Monsignor (now turned architect) whose dream of a monastery garden included the overworked janitor under the head of "labor."

Father Eudex asked Whalen to bring another shovel. Together, almost without words, they worked all morning spading up crosses,

leaving the big fleur-de-lis to the last. Father Eudex removed his
coat first, then his collar, and finally was down to his undershirt.

Toward noon Monsignor rolled into the driveway.

He stayed in the car, getting red in the face, recovering from the
pleasure of seeing so much accomplished as he slowly recognized his
curate in Whalen's helper. In a still, appalled voice he called across
the lawn, "Father," and waited as for a beast that might or might
not have sense enough to come.

Father Eudex dropped his shovel and went over to the car, shirt-
less.

Monsignor waited a moment before he spoke, as though annoyed
by the everlasting necessity, where this person was concerned, to
explain. "Father," he said quietly at last, "I wouldn't do any more
of that—if I were you. Rather, in any event, I wouldn't."

"All right, Monsignor."

"To say the least, it's not prudent. If necessary"—he paused as
Whalen came over to dig a cross within earshot—"I'll explain later.
It's time for lunch now."

The car, black, beautiful, fierce with chromium, was quiet as Monsignor dismounted, knowing her master. Monsignor went around to
the rear, felt a tire, and probed a nasty cinder in the tread.

"Look at that," he said, removing the cinder.

Father Eudex thought he saw the car lift a hoof, gaze around, and
thank Monsignor with her headlights.

Monsignor proceeded at a precise pace to the back door of the
rectory. There he held the screen open momentarily, as if remember-
ing something or reluctant to enter before himself—such was his
humility—but then called to Whalen with an intimacy that could
never exist between them.

"Better knock off now, Joe."

Whalen turned in on himself. "*Joe*—is it!"

Father Eudex removed his clothes from the grass. His hands were
all blisters, but in them he found a little absolution. He apologized
to Joe for having to take the afternoon off. "I can't make it, Joe.
Something turned up."

"Sure, Father."

Father Eudex could hear Joe telling his wife about it that night—

yeah, the young one got in wrong with the old one again. Yeah, the old one, he don't believe in it, work, for them.

Father Eudex paused in the kitchen to remember he knew not what. It was in his head, asking to be let in, but he did not place it until he heard Monsignor in the next room complaining about the salad to the housekeeper. It was the voice of dear, dead Aunt Hazel, coming from the summer he was ten. He translated the past into the present: I can't come out and play this afternoon, Joe, on account of my monsignor won't let me.

In the dining room Father Eudex sat down at the table and said grace. He helped himself to a chop, creamed new potatoes, pickled beets, jelly, and bread. He liked jelly. Monsignor passed the butter.

"That's supposed to be a tutti-frutti salad," Monsignor said, grimacing at his. "But she used green olives."

Father Eudex said nothing.

"I said she used green olives."

"I like green olives all right."

"*I* like green olives, but *not* in tutti-frutti salad."

Father Eudex replied by eating a green olive, but he knew it could not end there.

"Father," Monsignor said in a new tone. "How would you like to go away and study for a year?"

"Don't think I'd care for it, Monsignor. I'm not the type."

"You're no canonist, you mean?"

"That's one thing."

"Yes. Well, there are other things it might not hurt you to know. To be quite frank with you, Father, I think you need broadening."

"I guess so," Father Eudex said thickly.

"And still, with your tendencies . . . and with the universities honeycombed with Communists. No, that would never do. I think I meant seasoning, not broadening."

"Oh."

"No offense?"

"No offense."

Who would have thought a little thing like an olive could lead to all this, Father Eudex mused—who but himself, that is, for his association with Monsignor had shown him that anything could lead to everything. Monsignor was a master at making points. Nothing had changed since the day Father Eudex walked into the rectory saying he was the new assistant. Monsignor had evaded Father Eudex's hand in greeting, and a few days later, after he began to get the range, he delivered a lecture on the whole subject of handshaking. It was Middle West to shake hands, or South West, or West in any case, and it was not done where he came from, and—why had he ever come from where he came from? Not to be reduced to shaking hands, you could bet! Handshaking was worse than foot washing and unlike that pious practice there was nothing to support it. And from handshaking Monsignor might go into a general discussion of Father Eudex's failings. He used the open forum method, but he was the only speaker and there was never time enough for questions from the audience. Monsignor seized his examples at random from life. He saw Father Eudex coming out of his bedroom in pajama bottoms only and so told him about the dressing gown, its purpose, something of its history. He advised Father Eudex to barber his armpits, for it was being done all over now. He let Father Eudex see his bottle of cologne, "Steeple," special for clergymen, and said he should not be afraid of it. He suggested that Father Eudex shave his face oftener, too. He loaned him his Rogers Peet catalogue, which had sketches of clerical blades togged out in the latest, and prayed that he would stop going around looking like a rabbinical student.

He found Father Eudex reading *The Catholic Worker* one day and had not trusted him since. Father Eudex's conception of the priesthood was evangelical in the worst sense, barbaric, gross, foreign to the mind of the Church, which was one of two terms he used as sticks to beat him with. The other was taste. The air of the rectory was often heavy with The Mind of the Church and Taste.

Another thing. Father Eudex could not conduct a civil conversation. Monsignor doubted that Father Eudex could even think to himself with anything like agreement. Certainly any discussion with Father Eudex ended inevitably in argument or sighing. Sighing! Why didn't people talk up if they had anything to say? No, they'd rather sigh! Father, don't ever, ever sigh at me again!

Finally, Monsignor did not like Father Eudex's table manners.

This came to a head one night when Monsignor, seeing his curate's plate empty and all the silverware at his place unused except for a single knife, fork, and spoon, exploded altogether, saying it had been on his mind for weeks, and then descending into the vernacular he declared that Father Eudex did not know the forks—now perhaps he could understand that! Meals, unless Monsignor had guests or other things to struggle with, were always occasions of instruction for Father Eudex, and sometimes of chastisement.

And now he knew the worst—if Monsignor was thinking of recommending him for a year of study, in a Sulpician seminary probably, to learn the forks. So this was what it meant to be a priest. *Come, follow me. Going forth, teach ye all nations. Heal the sick, raise the dead, cleanse the lepers, cast out devils.* Teach the class of people we get here? Teach Mr. Memmers? Teach Communists? Teach Monsignors? And where were the poor? The lepers of old? The lepers were in their colonies with nuns to nurse them. The poor were in their holes and would not come out. Mr. Memmers was in his bank, without cheer. The Communists were in their universities, awaiting a sign. And he was at table with Monsignor, and it was enough for the disciple to be as his master, but the housekeeper had used green olives.

Monsignor inquired, "Did you get your check today?"

Father Eudex, looking up, considered. "I got *a* check," he said.

"From the Rival people, I mean?"

"Yes."

"Good. Well, I think you might apply it on the car you're wanting. A decent car. That's a worthy cause." Monsignor noticed that he was not taking it well. "Not that I mean to dictate what you shall do with your little windfall, Father. It's just that I don't like to see you mortifying yourself with a Model A—and disgracing the Church."

"Yes," Father Eudex said, suffering.

"Yes. I dare say you don't see the danger, just as you didn't a while ago when I found you making a spectacle of yourself with Whalen. You just don't see the danger because you just don't think. Not to dwell on it, but I seem to remember some overshoes."

The overshoes! Monsignor referred to them as to the Fall. Last winter Father Eudex had given his overshoes to a freezing picket. It had got back to Monsignor and—good Lord, a man could have his sympathies, but he had no right clad in the cloth to endanger the prestige of the Church by siding in these wretched squabbles. Monsignor said he hated to think of all the evil done by people doing good! Had Father Eudex ever heard of the Albigensian heresy, or didn't the seminary teach that any more?

Father Eudex declined dessert. It was strawberry mousse.

"Delicious," Monsignor said. "I think I'll let her stay."

At that moment Father Eudex decided that he had nothing to lose. He placed his knife next to his fork on the plate, adjusted them this way and that until they seemed to work a combination in his mind, to spring a lock which in turn enabled him to speak out.

"Monsignor," he said. "I think I ought to tell you I don't intend to make use of that money. In fact—to show you how my mind works—I have even considered endorsing the check to the strikers' relief fund."

"So," Monsignor said calmly—years in the confessional had prepared him for anything.

"I'll admit I don't know whether I can in justice. And even if I could I don't know that I would. I don't know why . . . I guess hush money, no matter what you do with it, is lousy."

Monsignor regarded him with piercing baby blue eyes. "You'd find it pretty hard to prove, Father, that *any* money *in se* is . . . what you say it is. I would quarrel further with the definition 'hush money.' It seems to me nothing if not rash that you would presume to impugn the motive of the Rival Company in sending out these checks. You would seem to challenge the whole concept of good works—not that I am ignorant of the misuses to which money can be put." Monsignor, changing tack, tucked it all into a sigh. "Perhaps I'm just a simple soul, and it's enough for me to know personally some of the people in the Rival Company and to know them good people. Many of them Catholic . . ." A throb had crept into Monsignor's voice. He shut it off.

"I don't mean anything that subtle, Monsignor," Father Eudex said. "I'm just telling you, as my pastor, what I'm going to do with the check. Or what I'm not going to do with it. I don't know what I'm going to do with it. Maybe send it back."

Monsignor rose from the table, slightly smiling. "Very well, Father. But there's always the poor."

Monsignor took leave of Father Eudex with a laugh. Father Eudex felt it was supposed to fool him into thinking that nothing he had said would be used against him. It showed, rather, that Monsignor was not winded, that he had broken wild curates before, plenty of them, and that he would ride again.

Father Eudex sought the shade of the porch. He tried to read his office, but was drowsy. He got up for a glass of water. The saints in Ireland used to stand up to their necks in cold water, but not for drowsiness. When he came back to the porch a woman was ringing the doorbell. She looked like a customer for rosary beads.

"Hello," he said.

I'm Mrs. Klein, Father, and I was wondering if you could help me out."

Father Eudex straightened a porch chair for her. "Please sit down."

"It's a German name, Father. Klein was German descent," she said, and added with a silly grin, "It ain't what you think, Father."

"I beg your pardon."

"Klein. Some think it's a Jew name. But they stole it from Klein."

Father Eudex decided to come back to that later. "You were wondering if I could help you?"

"Yes, Father. It's personal."

"Is it matter for confession?"

"Oh no, Father." He had made her blush.

"Then go ahead."

Mrs. Klein peered into the honeysuckle vines on either side of the porch for alien ears.

"No one can hear you, Mrs. Klein."

"Father—I'm just a poor widow," she said, and continued as though Father Eudex had just slandered the man. "Klein was awful good to me, Father."

"I'm sure he was."

"So good . . . and he went and left me all he had." She had begun to cry a little.

Father Eudex nodded gently. She was after something, probably not money, always the best bet—either that or a drunk in the family—but this one was not Irish. Perhaps just sympathy.

"I come to get your advice, Father. Klein always said, 'If you got a problem, Freda, see the priest.' "

"Do you need money?"

"I got more than I can use from the bakery."

"You have a bakery?"

Mrs. Klein nodded down the street. "That's my bakery. It was Klein's. The Purity."

"I go by there all the time," Father Eudex said, abandoning himself to her. He must stop trying to shape the conversation and let her work it out.

"Will you give me your advice, Father?" He felt that she sensed his indifference and interpreted it as his way of rejecting her. She either had no idea how little sense she made or else supreme faith in him, as a priest, to see into her heart.

"Just what is it you're after, Mrs. Klein?"

"He left me all he had, Father, but it's just laying in the bank."

"And you want me to tell you what to do with it?"

"Yes, Father."

Father Eudex thought this might be interesting, certainly a change. He went back in his mind to the seminary and the class in which they had considered the problem of inheritances. Do we have any unfulfilled obligations? Are we sure? . . . Are there any impedimenta? . . .

"Do you have any dependents, Mrs. Klein—any children?"

"One boy, Father. I got him running the bakery. I pay him good—too much, Father."

"Is 'too much' a living wage?"

"Yes, Father. He ain't got a family."

"A living wage is not too much," Father Eudex handed down, sailing into the encyclical style without knowing it.

Mrs. Klein was smiling over having done something good without knowing precisely what it was.

"How old is your son?"

"He's thirty-six, Father."

"Not married?"

"No, Father, but he's got him a girl." She giggled, and Father Eudex, embarrassed, retied his shoe.

"But you don't care to make a will and leave this money to your son in the usual way?"

"I guess I'll have to . . . if I die." Mrs. Klein was suddenly crushed and haunted, but whether by death or charity, Father Eudex did not know.

"You don't have to, Mrs. Klein. There are many worthy causes. And the worthiest is the cause of the poor. My advice to you, if I understand your problem, is to give what you have to someone who needs it."

Mrs. Klein just stared at him.

"You could even leave it to the archdiocese," he said, completing the sentence to himself: but I don't recommend it in your case . . . with your tendencies. You look like an Indian giver to me.

But Mrs. Klein had got enough. "Huh!" she said, rising. "Well! You *are* a funny one!"

And then Father Eudex realized that she had come to him for a broker's tip. It was in the eyes. The hat. The dress. The shoes. "If you'd like to speak to the pastor," he said, "come back in the evening."

"You're a nice young man," Mrs. Klein said, rather bitter now and bent on getting away from him. "But I got to say this—you ain't much of a priest. And Klein said if I got a problem, see the priest— huh! You ain't much of a priest! What time's your boss come in?"

"In the evening," Father Eudex said. "Come any time in the evening."

Mrs. Klein was already down the steps and making for the street.

"You might try Mr. Memmers at the First National," Father Eudex called, actually trying to help her, but she must have thought it was just some more of his nonsense and did not reply.

After Mrs. Klein had disappeared Father Eudex went to his room. In the hallway upstairs Monsignor's voice, coming from the depths of the clerical nap, halted him.

"Who was it?"

"A woman," Father Eudex said. "A woman seeking good counsel."

He waited a moment to be questioned, but Monsignor was not awake enough to see anything wrong with that, and there came only a sigh and a shifting of weight that told Father Eudex he was simply turning over in bed.

Father Eudex walked into the bathroom. He took the Rival check from his pocket. He tore it into little squares. He let them flutter into the toilet. He pulled the chain—hard.

He went to his room and stood looking out the window at nothing. He could hear the others already giving an account of their stewardship, but could not judge them. I bought baseball uniforms for the school. I bought the nuns a new washing machine. I purchased a Mass kit for a Chinese missionary. I bought a set of matched irons. Mine helped pay for keeping my mother in a rest home upstate. I gave mine to the poor.

And you, Father?

Critical Commentary on *The Forks*

If one were to reduce J. F. Powers' story to a simple thematic statement, it might be something like this: the difference in temperament and outlook between Monsignor and Father Eudex is symptomatic of the divided aims of contemporary formal religion. In Monsignor we see the ambitious though frustrated Rotarian in a reversed collar, the extrovert who caters to the material whims of his flock. In Father Eudex, contrarily, we see the simple, unassuming clergyman for whom religion and humanity are virtually synonymous. Monsignor pursues those secularized actions that will satisfy his *amour propre*, but always within the prudential limits of his vocation. But Father Eudex, dedicated to humility and service, is so bent on observing the spirit of his vows that he generally tramples on the so-called refinements extolled by Monsignor.

Powers, whose sympathies are clearly with the junior priest, has magnified the antagonism between the two for dramatic effect. How-

ever, through a point-of-view centered in Father Eudex he has also
conveyed a sense of their seemingly irreparable split on conceptual
grounds. Father Eudex's position is the ennobled one preached by
Christ and recorded in Scripture by St. Matthew. His mission is con-
structive and humane, to teach, heal, and propagate the word of
God. In Father Eudex's sardonic opinion, however, Monsignor has
sacrificed these fundamental selfless duties to a preoccupation with
temporal, newsworthy action. Monsignor "knew the mask of evil already—birth control, indecent movies, salacious books—and would
call these things by their right names and dare to deal with them for
what they were, these new occasions for the old sins of the cities of
the plains." As envisioned by Father Eudex, in short, the priest must
concern himself with individuals before "occasions" and things.
And this Monsignor persistently fails to do.

"The Forks," if not a subtle story, is a well-unified one whose aim
it is to reveal the disparity between religious ideal and expedience.
This aim, which in narrative terms emerges as the conflict between
the two priests, is fulfilled through a progression of revelatory scenes.
The first is expository, introducing the antagonists and establishing
the problem. The next involves the arrival of the check, Father Eudex's assistance with the elaborate garden, and the painful confrontation with Monsignor. From the self-evident contrasts in this scene,
we move quickly to further contrasts in the dining-room scene, seeing Monsignor's worldly elegance opposed to Father Eudex's un-
complicated tastes and table manners. The climax comes with the
departure of Monsignor, in the final scene, and the appearance of
Mrs. Klein.

At least until the concluding scene, then, Powers is more absorbed
by details of character and personality—and the frictions they
cause—than by dramatic, rising action. Indeed, such action as he
represents must for credibility's sake be attuned to the quiet, ordered life of a parish. The two secular figures, Joe and Mrs. Klein,
contribute to the normality of the situation and at the same time
tacitly verify the factions in the ecumenical split. That is, Joe has
good reason to deplore Monsignor's arrogant vanity and to align
himself with Father Eudex, of whose unaffected goodness he is a
beneficiary. But Mrs. Klein, on the other hand, must regard herself

as a victim of the younger priest's impracticality, to say nothing of his uncooperativeness. And in responding adversely to Father Eudex's charitable urgings, she makes plain her affinity with Monsignor's benign worldliness. It is his experience with Mrs. Klein that tries Father Eudex beyond endurance.

The climactic scene with Mrs. Klein does not appear to come to a firm resolution and, consequently, provokes some questions about the intention of "The Forks," and especially about Father Eudex's role in the intention. His prominence in the story, the way in which everything hinges on his reactions and thoughts, and the likelihood that most readers will be drawn to his cause—all these give us comfortable assurance that Father Eudex is the protagonist and Monsignor the antagonist. As the protagonist, however, the junior priest is decidedly lacking in the self-confidence that makes Monsignor dominate every situation in which he participates. For instance, having made the bold (though not really spontaneous) gesture of destroying the check, Father Eudex has grave misgivings. After all, as he himself acknowledges, the money could have been put to good as well as bad use. Earlier, even Monsignor had pointed out, "But there's always the poor."

As a corollary of theme, it may thus be noted, Powers introduces the age-old ethical question: is it proper to apply to good ends money that is tainted or suspect? While he had the check in his pocket, Father Eudex reflected on the question, and though he could not come to a satisfactory decision (should the check be returned? should it go to the strikers' relief fund?) neither did he have to make an irredeemable decision. But once the check was destroyed, even hypotheses became meaningless and he was left with the gloom of self-reproach. "He could hear the others already giving an account of their stewardship, but could not judge them. I bought baseball uniforms for the school. I bought the nuns a new washing machine. I purchased a Mass kit for a Chinese missionary. I bought a set of matched irons. Mine helped pay for keeping my mother in a rest home upstate. I gave mine to the poor. And you, Father?"

But if Father Eudex feels that his own inaction bars him from the right to judge most of the clerical recipients of Rival's bounty, he is far too human to exercise comparable restraint where Monsignor is concerned. There is, in fact, a constant interplay of hostility between the two, with Father Eudex's attitude toward his superior always evident. Monsignor, for his part, retaliates with ironical barbs, meaningful laughs, and the like. To be sure, it would not be seemly for Father Eudex to retort openly, but in his mind at least he always has the last word. As Powers interprets the exchanges between the two priests: "This was the substance of their conversation, always, the deadly routine in which Father Eudex played straight man. Each time it happened he seemed to participate, and though he should have known better he justified his participation by hoping that it would not happen again, or in quite the same way." Silently, however, he ridicules Monsignor's temporal weaknesses: his vanity and posturing, his social and religious snobbery, his doctrinal intransigence ("You'll have to watch your tendencies").

To strengthen and dramatize the conceptual aspect of the conflict, Powers resorts to an accruement of symbols. Textural and intermittent rather than massive, most of the symbols reflect unfavorably on Monsignor and, inevitably, solicit our allegiance to Father Eudex. In the first sentence of "The Forks" we discover Monsignor's most unaustere automobile, "which was long and black and new like a politician's." Thereafter, the sensuous fascination which the car holds for him tells us a great deal about his ostentatiously elegant, virtually sybaritic, appetites. And these in turn go far toward explaining the antipathy between him and Father Eudex, whose yearning for a Model A Ford seems to Monsignor a tasteless breach of the amenities. Additionally, Monsignor's imposing car, as seen through Father Eudex's baleful eyes, suggests—like the formal garden—hypocritical pretense. Monsignor "was occupied with keeping his countenance kindly, grim, and exalted, that the cop's faith remain whole, for it was evidently inconceivable to him that Monsignor should ever venture abroad unless to bear the Holy Viaticum, always racing with death."

Another symbol with overtones comparable to that of the big black car is the tutti-fruitti salad. Thus, while Father Eudex is happy enough to be eating the good solid food, Monsignor grimaces over the unforgivable and alien presence of green olives in the salad. Apart from being an amusing narrative detail, the salad is again emblematic of the schism between the aristocratic and democratic elements of the Church (communistic, the older priest would call the latter). And if Father Eudex's doctrinal and political "tendencies" are suspect, they are no more offensive to Monsignor than his numerous social improprieties, such as shaking hands and wearing only pajama bottoms. It's bad enough to be as badly groomed as a rabbinical student or to read *The Catholic Worker,* but worst of all (and one hears Monsignor sighing), "Father Eudex did not know the forks." The incongruity of this complaint (like the casual shift from overshoes for freezing pickets to strawberry mousse) is forced upon the reader by Father Eudex's despairing recollection of Scripture and the duties of a priest. Symbolically, Monsignor's overly nice insistence on the full armory of silver acts as a goad to Father Eudex. "He placed his knife next to his fork on the plate, adjusted them this way and that until they seemed to work a combination in his mind, to spring a lock which in turn enabled him to speak out."

These, like any good symbols, fit well into the texture of the story, though not always as unobtrusively or as naturally as the meticulous reader would wish. Subject as they are to the author's control, they help to place his intention into a context that is at once fictionally interesting and intellectually provocative. Powers fulfills his large aim of dramatizing the opposition of will and concept within the Church, in a narrative situation that does not impose an unduly cerebral burden on the reader. There are times, indeed, when the ironic tone (e.g., "Father Eudex thought he saw the car lift a hoof, gaze around, and thank Monsignor with her headlights") might be more effective if it were modified. But there are also compensations, especially in the credible depictions of the two priests. In criticizing Monsignor, Powers is not mocking the office he represents but revealing the vulnerability of the man. And Father Eudex, likewise, has his weaknesses, though his attractions are expected to outshine them. Priests for all their awesome responsibilities are human beings. Powers has in effect stripped away the spiritual vestments to show how two men respond to a common cause. The official power and external authority of the Church, he appears to say, rest in the hands of such as Monsignor. But the spiritual vitality of Catholicism, despite (perhaps even because of) self-doubt, inheres in such as Father Eudex.

Symbolism and Allegory

In describing what the novelist has done, the critic relies on the language of exposition. He explains, he interprets, he judges, and in so doing he isolates and abstracts those properties of the novel which emphasize ideas and feelings. As clearly and incisively as his understanding permits, he states the essence of the author's intention. The objectivity insisted upon by his calling binds him to a rational assessment, complete with evidence, of a non-literal composition. The novelist, as has been noted repeatedly, may be motivated by explicit data but constantly thrusts against their limitations, looking for ways of broadening and deepening particularity. The vehicle he has chosen for his concepts is not exact but representational. It is a skillfully ordered aggregation of *symbols* which he has created to connote his understanding of reality.

A symbol is a sign—e.g., an object, a character, an event—through which the author communicates abstract qualities not readily evident in common experience. The symbol, that is, through the power of association, imagination, and suggestion, enables the novelist to go beyond the language of exposition and—if he is successful—uncover the hidden import of his subject. Discussing the value of symbols for Coleridge, Robert Penn Warren explains: "The symbol serves to *combine*—and he italicizes the word—the 'poet's heart and intellect.' A symbol involves an idea (or ideas) as part of its potential, but it also involves the special complex of feelings associated with that idea, the attitude toward that idea. The symbol affirms the unity of mind in the welter of experience; it is a device for making that welter of experience manageable for the mind—graspable."

Warren's statement directs attention to the unifying action of the symbol. Meaning literally to throw together or bring into conjunction, the word *symbol* connotes an act of comparison. As a way of stating resemblances which are not obvious, or of bringing together qualities or concepts which are seemingly dissimilar, the symbol is both figurative and specific. Thus, we can agree with Warren that "it represents a focus of being and is not a mere sign, a 'picture-language.' " The symbol, in other words, is something more than the billboard advertisement which faithfully reproduces an image of a cigarette or an automobile. There is no comparison here, no joining of opposed qualities. The billboard magnifies and literalizes what is already obvious and definite. The literary symbol, on the other hand, is distinguished by some pictorial or imagistic motif created by the author to give shape, order and concentration to the "welter of experience." The symbol, in short, interprets experience; it does not reproduce it.

The symbol, again according to Warren, "is focal and massive." It is concentrated upon the concept and feelings which the author has chosen to place in a narrative context. And it fuses all the latent ideas and emotions into a unity which the mind and instincts can grasp. Through symbolism, the novelist establishes a correspondence between that which is concrete and visible, and that which is intangible and invisible. Used in its fictional context, the symbol pictorializes and particularizes something abstract, for according to strict definition the symbol is an animate or inanimate object. It is a tangible thing "standing for" something which is not tangible, say, a moral, intellectual, or sensuous quality.

While increased range and flexibility of language afforded by symbolism is of immeasurable value to the novelist, he must avoid the trap of inappropriate or excessive symbolism. But there is no sure way to define a principle for symbolic selection and application. One can say only that symbols are never arbitrary; that if they are not inevitable, in the context of their appearance, they are irrelevant. They must be necessary in terms of the author's purpose.

To be sure, a lone symbol may have different meanings for different novelists. Rain, let us say, may be intended by one author to represent despair or gloom, and by another, fertility or growth. Some symbols, furthermore, may be "private." That is, they may have associations for the author which are not immediately evident to the reader. The implications of Stephen Dedalus' name, for example, will be initially foreign to the reader of *A Portrait of the Artist as a*

Young Man or *Ulysses* who does not know something about the Christian martyrs and Greek mythology. Nevertheless, the contextual appearance of "rain" should clarify its relevance and meaning in the particular novel. The significance of "Stephen Dedalus" will emerge from his role in the novel and the "private" symbol (hopefully further illuminated by reference to legend and myth) will become "public," that is, accessible to the reader. A symbol may be obscure, difficult, or ambiguous, but it is self-defeating in its purpose only if it remains permanently elusive.

A symbol may "stand for" something else because we frequently make comparisons and relate general ideas and feelings to specific things. And recognition, even if it is delayed, becomes an important aspect of identifiable meaning and feeling. To take a few common instances, the mark $ may signify not only "dollar" but "money" or "prosperity." Everyone knows that a camera is a piece of photographic equipment. But experience also tells us that, in an appropriate context, the camera may objectify Hollywood. Literary symbols are more complex, of course, but nonetheless accessible when the ground has been broken for their reception.

The object, event, or character, in short, becomes a symbol only when it is caused to exemplify or connote another thing. It is symbolically interesting when it acts not for itself—$ as dollar, or *camera* as camera—but for what its contextual appearance implies, suggests, or dictates. As long as the object fulfills itself without reference to exterior data, it *is* itself and not a symbol.

The complexity of symbolic interpretation poses a demanding critical problem. Even before the critic can say what the symbol means, he is obliged to distinguish between the genuinely symbolic and the merely descriptive or figurative which round out the large narrative framework. This framework—the major, massive symbol consisting of form and meaning—is affected by the selection and ordering of the various materials: character, plot, setting, and so on. The totality, thus, lends itself to a comprehensive interpretation that is grounded in a representational symbolic complex. A story like "The Forks," for example, is not simply a particularized account about two priests. More than that, it supplies a basis for examining their relationship and the spiritual problem uniting them in a context with universal implications. The story supplies, also, within the total structure, what Ransom has called a "fringe of feeling," or "local excitement" of texture (the interior, heterogeneous details of feeling and meaning). These details may then become textural symbols, contributing significantly to the whole meaning of the story.

One of the most important ways to discover meaning in fiction is to examine the interplay and organization of its textural symbols. As we become involved in the often subtle business of specifying and judging them, we also become aware of the depth to which some may extend. We must, of course, observe the contextual limits of the story with which we are working, and by all means avoid irrelevant symbol hunts or assertions of complexity which may not exist. Frequently, however, richly symbolic connotations must be explored on several planes of meaning. Melville's White Whale, for instance, is emblematic of a complex, disturbing vision. It is basic to the plot, and thus has a literal significance. Simultaneously, it functions as a textural symbol which accommodates multiple meanings—moral, philosophical, mystic, among others. These combine as a unified symbolic experience.

That is not to say, of course, that the best symbols are necessarily multilayered ones, or that unilayered ones cannot be exacting. One thinks in this latter connection of textural symbols which, though relatively simple in their presentation, achieve increasing complexity of emotion and meaning through frequent recurrence. The humming of Binet's lathe, as an instance, becomes intensified as Mme. Bovary's decline approaches. Comparably, the sense of time's passage is accentuated in *Mrs. Dalloway* by the periodic tolling of Big Ben. Symbolic repetition acts in Faulkner's *Intruder in the Dust* as a source of characterization. The gold toothpick, the old beaver hat, and the pistol of Lucas Beauchamp, mentioned again and again, are outward signs of his pride and intransigence. The symbolic devices in each of these novels are essentially textural, enriching by their presence the total emotional and intellectual situation. Faulkner's emblems of characterization, in addition, participate directly in the plot and its complications.

Textural symbols as used by skillful authors imbue a narrative situation with buoyancy and energy. They deepen the reader's perception, engaging his mind and imagination at a level far beyond the literal. Recapitulating some instances used earlier in this book, we increase our awareness of the versatility of local, heterogeneous details. Characterization, as an example, can be made symbolic of specific traits, like Esther Summerson's virtue, Dobbins' dogged loyalty, or Mr. Woodhouse's inertness. Each character "stands for" a trait which is his controlling principle. Or the peculiarities of a character may be symbolized through his attire or actions: thus, the childishness of Scratchy Wilson is revealed in his flamboyant clothing; acts of withdrawal and rejection are connoted in Ivan Ivanovich's bathing.

Objects and settings likewise may be converted to significant textural symbolism. The map in "Only the Dead Know Brooklyn" owes its primary interest to the meaning it implies—the disparity between ideal order and confused reality—rather than to objective actuality. The forks in Powers' story *are* table utensils, in terms of narrative realism; but they are also the textural objectification of an idea— the superficiality of Monsignor's religious outlook—and thus intensify the presentation of that idea. We have seen a prolific use of setting, each in symbolic relation to its particular theme and intention: the lowering weather in "Gooseberries" complements the depressing failure of Ivan Ivanovich; the autumn bleakness of *A Farewell to Arms* presages the hardships of war and its threat to human love; the vital changes of season in *My Ántonia* correspond with the changing fortunes of the pioneers; the spoiled lands of *Sons and Lovers* and *Cry, the Beloved Country* are emblematic of society's destructive materialism and its esthetic indifference. One could multiply examples of this order, in which localized symbols work subtly and inferentially with the total intention.

Some authors, on the other hand, abuse their symbolic opportunities, explaining themselves so obviously that symbols lose their suggestive nature and become functional weapons. Witness Frank Norris' graphic representation (in *The Octopus*) of Western exploitation by the railroads:

The protagonist is walking through the still countryside, touched by "the feeling of absolute peace and quiet and security and untroubled happiness and content. . . . But suddenly there was an interruption. Presley had climbed the fence at the limit of the Quien Sabe ranch. Beyond was Los Muertos, but between the two ran the railroad. He had only time to jump back upon the embankment when, with a quivering of all the earth, a locomotive, single, unattached, shot by him with a roar, filling the air with the reek of hot oil, vomiting smoke and sparks; its enormous eye, cyclopean, red, throwing a glare far in advance, shooting by in a sudden crash of confused thunder; filling the night with the terrific clamour of its iron hoofs."

Then comes a vivid depiction of the death of sheep which had strayed onto the tracks in the path of the train. "It was a slaughter, a massacre of innocents. The iron monster had charged full into the midst, merciless, inexorable." All this should be more than enough to convey the emotional and intellectual attitudes of Norris. The symbolic equations are abundantly plain in the contrast between the peace of nature and the mechanical roar of the train; between the "iron hoofs" and the slaughtered sheep. The inhuman character of the train surely requires no further definition. But Norris is a propagandist, and he insists upon spelling out his meaning fully.

Later, therefore, "Presley saw again, in his imagination the galloping monster, the terror of steel and steam, with its single eye, cyclopean, red, shooting from horizon to horizon; but saw it now as the symbol of a vast power, huge, terrible, flinging the echo of its thunder over all the reaches of the valley, leaving blood and destruction in its path; the leviathan, with tentacles of steel, clutching into the soil, the soulless Force, the ironhearted Power, the monster, the Colossus, the Octopus."

The overwrought rhetoric diminishes the textural symbol to bombast. It is made superfluous by expository statement, for its implications have become unimaginatively explicit. A similar failure is evident in Theodore Dreiser's *The Financier,* the story of Frank Cowperwood's rise to economic power. As a young boy, he watches spellbound the gradual dismemberment of a squid by a lobster in a glass tank.

"That's the way it has to be, I guess," he commented to himself. "That squid wasn't quick enough. He didn't have anything to feed on."

He figured it out. The squid couldn't kill the lobster—he had no weapon. The lobster could kill the squid—he was heavily armed. There was nothing for the squid to feed on; the lobster had the squid as a prey. What was the result to be? What else could it be? "He didn't have a chance," he said, finally, tucking his books under his arm and trotting on.

Like Norris, Dreiser wants his symbol, but he wants his explanation too. Consequently, he has enervated a vigorous symbol by virtually extracting its symbolic ingredients. The event must be elaborated in rather bare prose.

It made a great impression on Frank. It answered in a rough way that riddle which had been annoying him so much in the past: "How is life organized?" Things lived on each other—that was it. Lobsters lived on squids and other things. What lived on lobsters? Men of course! Sure, that was it! And what lived on men? he asked himself. Was it other men? Wild animals lived on men. And there were Indians and cannibals. . . .

For days and weeks Frank thought of this and of the life he was tossed into, for he was already thinking of what he should be in this world, and how he should get along. From seeing his father count money, he was sure that he would like banking; and Third Street, where his father's office was, seemed to him the cleanest, brightest, most fascinating street in the world.

Aside from our incredulity at the boy's power of interpreting a physical action as a symbolic condition, we can't help feeling put upon. The atavistic destruction in the tank connotes its meaning, and the author's expository intervention—disguised as fiction—simply creates redundancy. When the symbol is made functional, it loses any kind of satisfying imaginative stimulation. Symbolism, when it is working well, demonstrates the subtle resources of language, drawing upon it for the fullest extension of meaning.

Another specialized strategy for extending meaning is *allegory*, which in an apparently simple story disguises a significant theme.* Its ultimate aim is to work out a lesson on the conscious level, to teach through pictures and stories. While allegory at its best—say,

* For a fuller discussion of Allegory, see *The Order of Poetry*, by Bloom, Philbrick, and Blistein (Odyssey Press, N.Y., 1961).

Pilgrim's Progress, Gulliver's Travels, Moby Dick, or *The Scarlet Letter*—is distinguished by literary excellence, contemporary interest in the mode is minimal. With infrequent exceptions (like George Orwell's *Animal Farm* and *1984,* Huxley's *Brave New World,* William Golding's *Lord of the Flies,* all of Kafka's novels, West's *Miss Lonelyhearts* and *The Day of the Locust*) allegory does not thrive in an atmosphere of critical, intellectual objectivity such as ours. Built upon deeply subjective qualities, it does not satisfy our preference for a didacticism which lies closer to the surface.

As defined by Coleridge, allegory results from "the employment of one set of agents and images with actions and accompaniments correspondent, so as to convey, while in disguise, either moral qualities or conceptions of the mind that are not in themselves objects of the senses, or other images, agents, actions, fortunes, and circumstances, so that the parts combine to form a consistent whole."

Coleridge, though he was not partial to allegory, understood its aims. These are essentially to present at least two meanings: (1) primary, or the literal and figurative surface meaning; (2) secondary, or the abstract moralistic-didactic meaning—secular as well as spiritual. This dualism operates simultaneously, the connotations of the secondary meaning dependent for clarity and interpretation upon the primary. Thus, we may read the allegory for the narrative pleasure it affords, but to stop at the surface is to miss at least half of the intention.

Superficially, *Animal Farm* is a clever and entertaining story. Attentive reading, however, discloses that the narrative is not merely an attractive framework for the exploits of animals which talk and behave like human beings. As in Aesop's *Fables* (though on a more extensive scale) or in the fourth book of *Gulliver's Travels,* the animals personify human traits. Apart from being fictional characters, they are allegorical equivalents of certain moral and political assumptions found in a totalitarian state, in a revolution gone wrong. And Orwell's denunciation of that state is crystallized in its single commandment: ALL ANIMALS ARE EQUAL/ BUT SOME ANIMALS ARE MORE EQUAL THAN OTHERS. *Animal Farm,* then, must be read on at least two levels, literal and allegorical, and its textural details must be taken to illuminate both. In brief, the narrative, descriptive, and symbolic elements work interdependently to provide us with the novel's two layers of meaning.

Prose allegory, then, is a narrative structure whose technical and esthetic details momentarily disguise a non-fictional human condition. It combines the concurrent play of creative and intellective faculties, supplying literal and figurative equivalents for a conceptual interpretation. Joining artistic appeal with rational insights, allegory is an often subtle way of commanding interest and evoking thoughtful responses to dilemmas which may be religious or social, philosophical, spiritual, or political. The possible limitation of allegory as a fictional mode inheres in its ultimate subordination of the imaginative quality to the intellectual and didactic.

For a practical consideration of some of the preceding remarks, we turn now to a short story by Nathaniel Hawthorne.

Wakefield

by NATHANIEL HAWTHORNE

In some old magazine or newspaper I recollect a story, told as truth, of a man—let us call him Wakefield—who absented himself for a long time from his wife. The fact, thus abstractedly stated, is not very uncommon, nor—without a proper distinction of circumstances—to be condemned either as naughty or nonsensical. Howbeit, this, though far from the most aggravated, is perhaps the strangest, instance on record, of marital delinquency; and, moreover, as remarkable a freak as may be found in the whole list of human oddities. The wedded couple lived in London. The man, under pretence of going a journey, took lodgings in the next street to his own house, and there, unheard of by his wife or friends, and without the shadow of a reason for such self-banishment, dwelt upwards of twenty years. During that period, he beheld his home every day, and frequently the forlorn Mrs. Wakefield. And after so great a gap in his matrimonial felicity—when his death was reckoned certain, his estate settled, his name dismissed from memory, and his wife, long, long ago, resigned to her autumnal widowhood—he entered

the door one evening, quietly, as from a day's absence, and became
a loving spouse till death.

This outline is all that I remember. But the incident, though of
the purest originality, unexampled, and probably never to be repeated, is one, I think, which appeals to the generous sympathies of
mankind. We know, each for himself, that none of us would perpetrate such a folly, yet feel as if some other might. To my own con-
templations, at least, it has often recurred, always exciting wonder,
but with a sense that the story must be true, and a conception of
its hero's character. Whenever any subject so forcibly affects the
mind, time is well spent in thinking of it. If the reader choose, let
him do his own meditation; or if he prefer to ramble with me through
the twenty years of Wakefield's vagary, I bid him welcome; trusting
that there will be a pervading spirit and a moral, even should we
fail to find them, done up neatly, and condensed into the final
sentence. Thought has always its efficacy, and every striking incident its moral.

What sort of a man was Wakefield? We are free to shape out our
own idea, and call it by his name. He was now in the meridian of
life; his matrimonial affections, never violent, were sobered into a
calm, habitual sentiment; of all husbands, he was likely to be the
most constant, because a certain sluggishness would keep his heart
at rest, wherever it might be placed. He was intellectual, but not
actively so; his mind occupied itself in long and lazy musings, that
ended to no purpose, or had not vigor to attain it; his thoughts were
seldom so energetic as to seize hold of words. Imagination, in the
proper meaning of the term, made no part of Wakefield's gifts. With
a cold but not depraved nor wandering heart, and a mind never feverish with riotous thoughts, nor perplexed with originality, who could
have anticipated that our friend would entitle himself to a foremost
place among the doers of eccentric deeds? Had his acquaintances
been asked, who was the man in London the surest to perform nothing today which should be remembered on the morrow, they would
have thought of Wakefield. Only the wife of his bosom might have
hesitated. She, without having analyzed his character, was partly
aware of a quiet selfishness, that had rusted into his inactive mind;
of a peculiar sort of vanity, the most uneasy attribute about him; of

a disposition to craft, which had seldom produced more positive effects than the keeping of petty secrets, hardly worth revealing; and, lastly, of what she called a little strangeness, sometimes, in the good man. This latter quality is indefinable, and perhaps non-existent.

Let us now imagine Wakefield bidding adieu to his wife. It is the dusk of an October evening. His equipment is a drab great-coat, a hat covered with an oilcloth, top-boots, an umbrella in one hand and a small portmanteau in the other. He has informed Mrs. Wakefield that he is to take the night coach into the country. She would fain inquire the length of his journey, its object, and the probable time of his return; but, indulgent to his harmless love of mystery, interrogates him only by a look. He tells her not to expect him positively by the return coach, nor to be alarmed should he tarry three or four days; but, at all events, to look for him at supper on Friday evening. Wakefield himself, be it considered, has no suspicion of what is before him. He holds out his hand, she gives her own, and meets his parting kiss in the matter-of-course way of a ten years' matrimony; and forth goes the middle-aged Mr. Wakefield, almost resolved to perplex his good lady by a whole week's absence. After the door has closed behind him, she perceives it thrust partly open, and a vision of her husband's face, through the aperture, smiling on her, and gone in a moment. For the time, this little incident is dismissed without a thought. But, long afterwards, when she has been more years a widow than a wife, that smile recurs, and flickers across all her reminiscences of Wakefield's visage. In her many musings, she surrounds the original smile with a multitude of fantasies, which make it strange and awful: as, for instance, if she imagines him in a coffin, that parting look is frozen on his pale features; or, if she dreams of him in heaven, still his blessed spirit wears a quiet and crafty smile. Yet, for its sake, when all others have given him up for dead, she sometimes doubts whether she is a widow.

But our business is with the husband. We must hurry after him along the street, ere he lose his individuality, and melt into the great mass of London life. It would be vain searching for him there. Let us follow close at his heels, therefore, until, after several superfluous turns and doublings, we find him comfortably established by the fireside of a small apartment, previously bespoken. He is in the

next street to his own, and at his journey's end. He can scarcely
trust his good fortune, in having got thither unperceived—recol-
lecting that, at one time, he was delayed by the throng, in the very
focus of a lighted lantern; and, again, there were footsteps that
seemed to tread behind his own, distinct from the multitudinous
tramp around him; and, anon, he heard a voice shouting afar, and
fancied that it called his name. Doubtless, a dozen busybodies had
been watching him, and told his wife the whole affair. Poor Wakefield! Little knowest thou thine own significance in this great
world! No mortal eye but mine has traced thee. Go quietly to thy
bed, foolish man; and, on the morrow, if thou wilt be wise, get thee
home to good Mrs. Wakefield, and tell her the truth. Remove not
thyself, even for a little week, from thy place in her chaste bosom.
Were she, for a single moment, to deem thee dead, or lost, or last-
ingly divided from her, thou wouldst be wofully conscious of a
change in thy true wife forever after. It is perilous to make a chasm
in human affections; not that they gape so long and wide—but so
quickly close again!

Almost repenting of his frolic, or whatever it may be termed, Wakefield lies down betimes, and starting from his first nap, spreads forth
his arms into the wide and solitary waste of the unaccustomed bed.
"No,"—thinks he, gathering the bedclothes about him,—"I will not
sleep alone another night."

In the morning he rises earlier than usual, and sets himself to consider what he really means to do. Such are his loose and rambling
modes of thought that he has taken this very singular step with the
consciousness of a purpose, indeed, but without being able to define
it sufficiently for his own contemplation. The vagueness of the project, and the convulsive effort with which he plunges into the execu-
tion of it, are equally characteristic of a feeble-minded man. Wakefield sifts his ideas, however, as minutely as he may, and finds himself curious to know the progress of matters at home—how his exemplary wife will endure her widowhood of a week; and, briefly,
how the little sphere of creatures and circumstances, in which he
was a central object, will be affected by his removal. A morbid vanity, therefore, lies nearest the bottom of the affair. But, how is he to
attain his ends? Not, certainly, by keeping close in this comforta-

ble lodging, where, though he slept and awoke in the next street to
his home, he is as effectually abroad as if the stage-coach had been
whirling him away all night. Yet, should he reappear, the whole
project is knocked in the head. His poor brains being hopelessly puzzled with this dilemma, he at length ventures out, partly resolving to
cross the head of the street, and send one hasty glance towards his
forsaken domicile. Habit—for he is a man of habits—takes him by
the hand, and guides him, wholly unaware, to his own door, where,
just at the critical moment, he is aroused by the scraping of his foot
upon the step. Wakefield! whither are you going?

At that instant his fate was turning on the pivot. Little dreaming
of the doom to which his first backward step devotes him, he hurries away, breathless with agitation hitherto unfelt, and hardly dares
turn his head at the distant corner. Can it be that nobody caught
sight of him? Will not the whole household—the decent Mrs. Wakefield, the smart maid servant, and the dirty little footboy—raise a
hue and cry, through London streets, in pursuit of their fugitive lord
and master? Wonderful escape! He gathers courage to pause and
look homeward, but is perplexed with a sense of change about the
familiar edifice, such as affects us all, when, after a separation of
months or years, we again see some hill or lake, or work of art, with
which we were friends of old. In ordinary cases, this indescribable
impression is caused by the comparison and contrast between our
imperfect reminiscences and the reality. In Wakefield, the magic of
a single night has wrought a similar transformation, because, in that
brief period, a great moral change has been effected. But this is a
secret from himself. Before leaving the spot, he catches a far and
momentary glimpse of his wife, passing athwart the front window,
with her face turned towards the head of the street. The crafty nin-
compoop takes to his heels, scared with the idea that, among a thousand such atoms of mortality, her eye must have detected him. Right
glad is his heart, though his brain be somewhat dizzy, when he finds
himself by the coal fire of his lodgings.

So much for the commencement of this long whimwham. After
the initial conception, and the stirring up of the man's sluggish
temperament to put it in practice, the whole matter evolves itself in
a natural train. We may suppose him, as the result of deep delibera-

tion, buying a new wig, of reddish hair, and selecting sundry gar-
ments, in a fashion unlike his customary suit of brown, from a Jew's
old-clothes bag. It is accomplished, Wakefield is another man. The
new system being now established, a retrograde movement to the
old would be almost as difficult as the step that placed him in his
unparalleled position. Furthermore, he is rendered obstinate by a
sulkiness occasionally incident to his temper, and brought on at
present by the inadequate sensation which he conceives to have
been produced in the bosom of Mrs. Wakefield. He will not go back
until she be frightened half to death. Well; twice or thrice has she
passed before his sight, each time with a heavier step, a paler cheek,
and more anxious brow; and in the third week of his non-appearance
he detects a portent of evil entering the house, in the guise of an
apothecary. Next day the knocker is muffled. Towards nightfall comes
the chariot of a physician, and deposits its big-wigged and solemn
burden at Wakefield's door, whence, after a quarter of an hour's visit,
he emerges, perchance the herald of a funeral. Dear woman! Will she
die? By this time, Wakefield is excited to something like energy of
feeling, but still lingers away from his wife's bedside, pleading with
his conscience that she must not be disturbed at such a juncture. If
aught else restrains him, he does not know it. In the course of a few
weeks she gradually recovers; the crisis is over; her heart is sad, perhaps, but quiet; and, let him return soon or late, it will never be
feverish for him again. Such ideas glimmer through the midst of
Wakefield's mind, and render him indistinctly conscious that an almost impassable gulf divides his hired apartment from his former
home. "It is but in the next street!" he sometimes says. Fool! it is
in another world. Hitherto, he has put off his return from one particular day to another; henceforward, he leaves the precise time un-
determined. Not tomorrow—probably next week—pretty soon. Poor
man! The dead have nearly as much chance of revisiting their earthly
homes as the self-banished Wakefield.

Would that I had a folio to write, instead of an article of a dozen
pages! Then might I exemplify how an influence beyond our control lays its strong hand on every deed which we do, and weaves its
consequences into an iron tissue of necessity. Wakefield is spellbound. We must leave him, for ten years or so, to haunt around his

house, without once crossing the threshold, and to be faithful to his wife, with all the affection of which his heart is capable, while he is slowly fading out of hers. Long since, it must be remarked, he had lost the perception of singularity in his conduct.

Now for a scene! Amid the throng of a London street we distinguish a man, now waxing elderly, with few characteristics to attract careless observers, yet bearing, in his whole aspect, the handwriting of no common fate, for such as have the skill to read it. He is meagre; his low and narrow forehead is deeply wrinkled; his eyes, small and lustreless, sometimes wander apprehensively about him, but oftener seem to look inward. He bends his head, and moves with an indescribable obliquity of gait, as if unwilling to display his full front to the world. Watch him long enough to see what we have described, and you will allow that circumstances—which often produce remarkable men from nature's ordinary handiwork—have produced one such here. Next, leaving him to sidle along the footwalk, cast your eyes in the opposite direction, where a portly female, considerably in the wane of life, with a prayer-book in her hand, is proceeding to yonder church. She has the placid mien of settled widowhood. Her regrets have either died away, or have become so essential to her heart, that they would be poorly exchanged for joy. Just as the lean man and well-conditioned woman are passing, a slight obstruction occurs, and brings these two figures directly in contact. Their hands touch; the pressure of the crowd forces her bosom against his shoulder; they stand, face to face, staring into each other's eyes. After a ten years' separation, thus Wakefield meets his wife!

The throng eddies away, and carries them asunder. The sober widow, resuming her former pace, proceeds to church, but pauses in the portal, and throws a perplexed glance along the street. She passes in, however, opening her prayer-book as she goes. And the man! with so wild a face that busy and selfish London stands to gaze after him, he hurries to his lodgings, bolts the door, and throws himself upon the bed. The latent feelings of years break out; his feeble mind acquires a brief energy from their strength; all the miserable strangeness of his life is revealed to him at a glance: and he cries out, passionately, "Wakefield! Wakefield! You are mad!"

Perhaps he was so. The singularity of his situation must have so moulded him to himself, that, considered in regard to his fellow-creatures and the business of life, he could not be said to possess his right mind. He had contrived, or rather he had happened, to dissever himself from the world—to vanish—to give up his place and privileges with living men, without being admitted among the dead. The life of a hermit is nowise parallel to his. He was in the bustle of the city, as of old; but the crowd swept by and saw him not; he was, we may figuratively say, always beside his wife and at his hearth, yet must never feel the warmth of the one nor the affection of the other. It was Wakefield's unprecedented fate to retain his original share of human sympathies, and to be still involved in human interests, while he had lost his reciprocal influence on them. It would be a most curious speculation to trace out the effect of such circumstances on his heart and intellect, separately, and in unison. Yet, changed as he was, he would seldom be conscious of it, but deem himself the same man as ever; glimpses of the truth, indeed, would come, but only for the moment; and still he would keep saying, "I shall soon go back!"—nor reflect that he had been saying so for twenty years.

I conceive, also, that these twenty years would appear, in the retrospect, scarcely longer than the week to which Wakefield had at first limited his absence. He would look on the affair as no more than an interlude in the main business of his life. When, after a little while more, he should deem it time to reënter his parlor, his wife would clap her hands for joy, on beholding the middle-aged Mr. Wakefield. Alas, what a mistake! Would Time but await the close of our favorite follies, we should be young men, all of us, and till Doomsday.

One evening, in the twentieth year since he vanished, Wakefield is taking his customary walk towards the dwelling which he still calls his own. It is a gusty night of autumn, with frequent showers that patter down upon the pavement, and are gone before a man can put up his umbrella. Pausing near the house, Wakefield discerns, through the parlor windows of the second floor, the red glow and the glimmer and fitful flash of a comfortable fire. On the ceiling appears a grotesque shadow of good Mrs. Wakefield. The cap, the nose and chin, and the broad waist, form an admirable caricature, which dances, moreover, with the up-flickering and down-sinking blaze, almost too merrily for the shade of an elderly widow. At this instant a shower chances to fall, and is driven, by the unmannerly gust, full into Wakefield's face and bosom. He is quite penetrated with its autumnal chill. Shall he stand, wet and shivering here, when his own hearth has a good fire to warm him, and his own wife will run to fetch the gray coat and small-clothes, which, doubtless, she has kept carefully in the closet of their bed chamber? No! Wakefield is no such fool. He ascends the steps—heavily!—for twenty years have stiffened his legs since he came down—but he knows it not. Stay, Wakefield! Would you go to the sole home that is left you? Then step into your grave! The door opens. As he passes in, we have a parting glimpse of his visage, and recognize the crafty smile, which was the precursor of the little joke that he has ever since been playing off at his wife's expense. How unmercifully has he quizzed the poor woman! Well, a good night's rest to Wakefield!

This happy event—supposing it to be such—could only have occurred at an unpremeditated moment. We will not follow our friend across the threshold. He has left us much food for thought, a portion of which shall lend its wisdom to a moral, and be shaped into a figure. Amid the seeming confusion of our mysterious world, individuals are so nicely adjusted to a system, and systems to one another and to a whole, that, by stepping aside for a moment, a man exposes himself to a fearful risk of losing his place forever. Like Wakefield, he may become, as it were, the Outcast of the Universe.

Critical Commentary on *Wakefield*

Repeatedly throughout this story, Hawthorne emphasizes his didactic concern over the situation he has invented. He trusts "that there will be a pervading spirit and a moral, even should we fail to find them, done up neatly, and condensed in the final sentence." We need have no fears, however, for in that final sentence he has summed up the protagonist's dilemma, announcing him to be "the

Outcast of the Universe." And this tersely accurate description has been anticipated by several other statements which we may take to be expressive of the author's personal attitude. "Thought," he says, "has always its efficacy, and every striking incident its moral."

Hawthorne takes pains to enforce the efficacy of his thoughts and the morality of his incidents. Indeed, his presence in the narrative is an ever-constant reminder of salutary purpose. Although the format is a fictional one, the first-person mode of address holds us rather rigorously to a philosophical outlook. Thus, he presents the bare outline of what is purported to be a factual occurrence, but quickly engages us in an interpretation. ". . . the incident, though of the purest originality, unexampled, and probably never to be repeated, is one, I think, which appeals to the generous sympathies of mankind. We know, each for himself, that none of us would perpetrate such a folly, yet feel as if some other might."

What, literally, is the folly? Simply that Wakefield, on a whim that had been in his mind for some time, leaves his home without preparing his wife for a prolonged absence. Instead of going on a journey, as he had said he would, he takes up residence in rooms "previously bespoken. . . . in the next street to his own, and at his journey's end." What began as a silly escapade goes on—unaccountably and irrationally—for a period of twenty years.

At first, Wakefield justifies his action as curiosity "to know the progress of matters at home—how his exemplary wife will endure her widowhood of a week; and, briefly, how the little sphere of creatures and circumstances in which he was a central object, will be affected by his removal. A morbid vanity, therefore, lies nearest the bottom of the affair." But, as Hawthorne explicitly tells us, "a great moral change has been effected" in Wakefield, and he cannot reënter his own home. This inner metamorphosis, this "great moral change," is the crux of Wakefield's dilemma, and it is the issue which Hawthorne has chosen to treat allegorically.

The moral problem is an acute one whose implications are universal rather than local. The time of the story is deliberately indeterminate and the London setting vague enough to be unrestrictive. But the narrative situation and its allegorical equivalents are relatively simple, even obvious. Throughout, Hawthorne has avoided exterior complications, and he has supplied easily accessible references to the allegory. In fact, he urges the moral upon us through pointed exposition which tends to leave the story texturally thin.

The interior details are kept to an essential minimum, because the allegorical scheme insists that the generalized moral not be subordinated to distracting particulars. Nevertheless, a few textural symbols in the short story reveal Hawthorne's attention to an artistic as well as didactic purpose. Apart from giving "Wakefield" a tangible narrative form, they appeal to the reader's emotions, and they enhance the moral. The London setting, for example, is identified in a few phrases and allusions, but further elaboration is unnecessary. The name "London," the largest metropolis in the world at the time of writing, could be counted on to call forth an image of its vastness and impersonality. For the average American reader, furthermore, London would convey the physical remoteness characteristic of the entire story.

London is symbolically important as an objective detail, but it has an even larger allegorical significance, which Hawthorne states. "We must hurry after Wakefield along the street, ere he lose his individuality, and melt into the great mass of London life. It would be vain searching for him there." Later, after the chance meeting with his wife, Wakefield's expression is so wild "that busy and selfish London stands to gaze after him." Yet he is still frighteningly alone. "The life of a hermit is nowise parallel to his. He was in the bustle of the city, as of old; but the crowd swept by and saw him not."

Hawthorne's business, as he tells us, "is with the husband," and the husband's actions, though ultimately the core of the allegory, provide the most obvious textural symbols. The first action comes with his deplorable decision to desert his wife temporarily. The successive actions coincide with his repeated inability to controvert his decision. These are physical deeds, congruous with the development of the narrative and of our mood toward Wakefield. More importantly, however, they objectify moral assumptions much greater than Wakefield as one isolated human being. "Poor Wakefield!" Hawthorne warns. "Little knowest thou thine own insignificance in this great world!"

Wakefield's conduct carries an allegorical lesson. Having surrendered one's moral obligation to a vain, selfish fancy, the individual must be blamed for initial responsibility. But the step once
taken is irrevocable. "Then might [Hawthorne] exemplify how an
influence beyond our control lays its strong hand on every deed which
we do, and weaves its consequences into an iron tissue of necessity." Wakefield, in effect, ceases to be a specific person and becomes
a moral exemplum of human failure. "Let us call him Wakefield,"
but the name is unimportant, and his action as fact "is not very uncommon." Wakefield is Anyman, and all people should take heed.

Although Hawthorne endows his protagonist with attributes
which may make Wakefield's actions credible, he does not permit
him to be more than a personification, a shadowy, allegorical figure.
Combining omniscience with the first-person point-of-view, Hawthorne flatly states that "no mortal eye but his has traced Wakefield," that is, understands his motives and their implications. Wakefield represents for Hawthorne's Puritan conscience some of man's
most venal faults: craftiness, pettiness, secrecy, vanity, intellectual
slothfulness, infidelity (as deadly in their way as the Seven Deadly
Sins). And he detests him, as a type, accordingly.

Beyond these moral failures, however, Hawthorne represents
Wakefield as a madman, or at least mentally incompetent. Contemptuously, he alludes to his "feeble mind," to his "dizziness," to his
"poor brains." A twentieth-century reader, steeped in Freudian
terminology, might be tempted to exonerate Wakefield on these
grounds. Hawthorne, however, is concerned with a moral not a psychological disorder, and finds Wakefield guilty of abrogating a God-
given responsibility to himself and his fellow man. At the same
time, he intimates that Wakefield himself does not understand the
monstrousness of his behavior.

The victim of the breach is Mrs. Wakefield, likewise a personification, whose fidelity and loyalty are foils to her husband's unenviable
traits. By her very nature, however, she is unable to recognize his
spiritual disease. She is saddened by his loss, but not inconsolable.
"And, let him return soon or late, her heart will never be feverish for
him again." The grim joke is on Wakefield, for when he does return
—unmotivated by love or generosity—the relationship between them

can never be the same as it was twenty years before. She is left with the memory of his ambiguous smile, the symbol of an insuperable barrier.

Point by point, then, Hawthorne has established a ratio between literal event and allegorical meaning, giving every physical detail an interior meaning. "Wakefield! whither are you going?" The question following Wakefield's desertion is rhetorical. The moral change is spelled out. "It was Wakefield's unprecedented fate to retain his original share of human sympathies, and to be still involved in human interests, while he had lost his reciprocal influence on them." And finally the thematic statement: "Amid the seeming confusion of our mysterious world, individuals are so nicely adjusted to a system, and systems to one another and to a whole, that, by stepping aside for a moment, a man exposes himself to a fearful risk of losing his place forever." Thoughtless and irrational, Wakefield violated a divine ordinance, and the price is the sacrifice of his happiness— and his wife's.

Glossary of Critical Terms

(The use of small capital letters for a term in context indicates that it is listed separately.)*

Aesthetic distance: Connotes a separation between practical or "real" experience and that revealed in the novel. The reader, though not wholly detached from his personal self, is enabled to effect enough of a severance to assure him that he is dealing with art and not with just another aspect or IMITATION of reality. Also called (by Edward Bullough) "psychical distance." Pp. 19, 51.

Allegory: Pp. 145, 217-19, 227-31.

Anacoluthon: P. 75.
See PLOT.

Angry Young Men: Term applied to contemporary British writers who are dissatisfied with the traditions and manners generally associated with the Establishment. They tend toward harshly realistic (though often cynical or comic) depictions of lower- and middle-class subjects. Their attitudes are characteristically militant or rebellious. P. 58.

Antagonist: Pp. 24, 87, 100, 108.
See PROTAGONIST, CHARACTER and SETTING.

Arrangement: P. 56; ch. 5.
See SELECTION.

Atmosphere: Pp. 145-46.
See SETTING.

---

* The esthetic and technical implications of certain terms (e.g., EXISTENTIALISM, NATURALISM, REALISM) should be explored more fully than is possible in a critical glossary, or even within the scope of this book. Their presentation here is necessarily simplified.

Bildungsroman or **erziehungsroman:** The English counterpart of this German-designated mode is "the novel of adolescence." Having to do with the formation or development of a youthful protagonist (e.g., Samuel Butler's *The Way of All Flesh*), the *bildungsroman* is a novel of initiation and education.

Causality: Pp. 63-4.

Character and **characterization:** Pp. 20, 57-8, 60-1; ch. 2.
Kinds—
"flat" and "round" (pp. 20-1, 22, 24, 36-40, 52).
"static" and "dynamic" (p. 25).
"explicit" and "implicit" (pp. 26-7, 28).
"hero" and "villain" (pp. 23-4).
"protagonist" and "antagonist" (pp. 24, 87, 88, 108).
See also DIALOGUE, SETTING, POINT-OF-VIEW, STREAM-OF-CONSCIOUSNESS, IMPRESSIONISM.

Climax: Subsequent to the ascending movement of the PLOT, its highest point of tension or crisis; the final moments before a turn in the situation. Pp. 64, 66, 100.
See RESOLUTION.

Coincidence: Pp. 86, 87.

Communication (also **fallacy of communication** and **heresy of communication**): P. 13.

Complication: Pp. 64-5.
See PLOT.

Conflict: Contention between opposing forces, sometimes described as "crisis," "contrast," "struggle," and "opposition." In most PLOTS essential to the action. Pp. 65, 145-46.
See SETTING.

Contrapuntal technique: Pp. 75-7.
See PLOT.

Credibility: Pp. 10, 22-3, 65.
Cf. probability and inevitability.

Description: Particularizing details of CHARACTER, SETTING, etc., to evoke a sense of objective reality. "Description may be either direct, or indirect (by suggestion); enumerative (by cumulative details), or impressionistic (by few, but striking details)." Generally, in modern fiction, assimilated with character and action as close part of the narrative progression. (See Shipley, ed. *Dictionary of World Literature*.)

Dialogue: Pp. 25-6, 39.
See CHARACTER and PLOT.

Digressions and **relevance:** Pp. 72-3, 75.

Dynamic: see CHARACTER.

Empathy: Imaginative transference of one's own feelings into the situation or character portrayed. A concept long familiar in the study of art, but borrowed in modern times from German psychologists, who designated the involuntary response as *Einfühlung*. Cf. SYMPATHY ("an affinity, association, or relationship between things so that whatever affects one, similarly affects the other or others."—Webster). P. 23.
See SELF-IDENTIFICATION.

Episodic technique: Pp. 68-71.
See PLOT.

Epistolary technique: Pp. 152-3.
See POINT-OF-VIEW, PLOT.

Existentialism: Though derived ultimately from the thought of the Danish philosopher Sören Kierkegaard (1813–55), existentialism as a literary and philosophical movement has become current in France and elsewhere since about 1945 under the leadership of Jean-Paul Sartre. It is concerned with existence as a practical (as opposed to abstract) condition, and the view that man has a capacity to liberate himself from the void (*néant*) into which he is born. He may live throughout his life, barely conscious of himself. Sometimes, however, he becomes aware of the lonely, subjective nature of the self; and he paradoxically contemplates his ability to exercise choice—to liberate himself from the void—with despair. Characterized by irrational acts of violence, by moral anguish (*angoisse*) and by a sense of *absurdité*. (See Paul Harvey and Janet E. Heseltine, *The Oxford Companion to French Literature*.) P. 58.

Experience: Pp. 60-1, 62, 79-80, 109-10, 123-24, 211-12.
Cf. REALISM, REALITY.

Exposition: Explanation or conveyance of important information, generally about what precedes the narrative situation but is essential to our understanding of it—e.g., details of CHARACTER, MOTIVATION, or action. P. 211.
See PLOT.

Fable: Pp. 184-86.
See THEME and INTENTION.

Fact and **truth:** Pp. 7, 9-11.

Fiction, definition of: Pp. 4-5, 7; ch. 1.

Foreshadowing: Anticipation, generally implied subtly, of events to come. P. 52.
Cf. SUSPENSE.

Gothic and **gothicism:** P. 87.
Terms derived from medieval art, originally as applied to irregular (as opposed to classically regular) architectural style. Then attached to fictional mode—"Gothic Novel" (e.g., Horace Walpole, *The Castle of Otranto*; Matthew Lewis, *The Monk*; *et al.*)

—in 18th century. Characterized by supernatural and eerie events, accompanied by sense of horror for its own sake, ruined abbeys, etc. In contemporary usage, gothicism connotes macabre and fearsome effects.

Hero: Pp. 23-4.
See VILLAIN and CHARACTER.

Imagination and **invention:** Pp. 9-10.

Imitation: Pp. 56-7.
See PLOT.

Impressionism: P. 28.
"A type of REALISM the aim of which is to render the immediate sense impression of the artist apart from any element of inference or study of detail."—Webster. Practiced in fiction by Joseph Conrad, Ford Madox Ford; at times by Thomas Wolfe, Virginia Woolf, James Joyce, *et al.*

As described by Ford (*Joseph Conrad: A Personal Remembrance*): "It became very early evident to us that what was the matter with the novel, and the British novel in particular, was that it went straight forward, whereas in your gradual making acquaintanceship with your fellows you never do go straight forward." Our initial reaction to an individual is likely to be modified or even altered as we come to know him better. "To get such a man in fiction you could not begin at his beginning and work his life chronologically to the end. *You must first get him with a strong impression, and then work backwards and forwards over his past.*" We come to know individuals *"in various unordered pictures."* Conrad and Ford *"saw that life did not narrate, but made impressions on our brains."*

Intention: Pp. 19, 188-91.
Cf. "intentionalism," "intentional fallacy"; also "originating" and "total" or "ultimate" intention; author's "purpose" and "achievement." See DIGRESSIONS.

Interior monologue: Pp. 77-80.
See STREAM-OF-CONSCIOUSNESS.

Irony:
Statements and conditions whose literal presentation is deliberately contrary to the effects actually intended. The reversals may be achieved by hyperbole, understatement, depreciation, contradiction. *Dramatic irony* (sometimes *tragic irony*) reveals to the reader the true state of affairs, contrary to the expectations or assumptions of the CHARACTERS in the story.

Judgment: P. 13.

Kunstlerroman: From German, a novel which depicts the growth of an artist, generally in the face of familial and social hostility. A famous example is Joyce's *A Portrait of the Artist as a Young Man.*

Linear technique: Pp. 66, 71, 100.
See PLOT.

Looping chronology: Pp. 73-5.
See PLOT.

Melodrama: Derived from theatrical usage. Emphasizes sensationalism and extremes of emotion at the expense of CREDIBILITY. P. 102.

Mood: Pp. 128-35, 143-44.
See TONE, SETTING, POINT-OF-VIEW.

Motivation: Causes or circumstances which explain why CHARACTERS act as they do, providing bases for CREDIBILITY.
See PLOT and CONFLICT.

Movement and **progression:** Pp. 20, 60.

Myth: A way of saying or telling in narrative form. It can be an objectified rendering of abstract values, ideas, or emotions; or the imaginative interpretation of historically real men and actions. It translates the unseen, the remote, and the impalpable into sensory experience, casting them into forms or correspondences to be coped with imaginatively and rationally. (For a full discussion, see *The Order of Poetry*, pp. 52 ff.) Pp. 102-4.

Naturalism: In fiction, a literary movement which observes the principles of philosophical naturalism. Characterized by a deterministic (hence, often pessimistic) view of life. It is dedicated to presenting existence with scientific detachment, emphasizing material phenomena and repudiating the possibility of supernatural phenomena. Owing to its rigorously limited subjects—the seamy side of life, psychologically and biologically determined CHARACTERS, etc.—has been called "slice of life," *tranche de vie*. Initiated in 19th century by Zola, the Goncourts. Carried on by Frank Norris, Jack London, Theodore Dreiser, James Farrell, *et al*. Much indebted to the theories of Darwin, Freud, and Marx. Naturalistic writers, though professing to suspend judgments, frequently imply strong protest. P. 7.

Novel, definition of: Pp. 5-7, 11-12; ch. 1.

Novella or **novelette:** A prose narrative, intermediate in length between the NOVEL and the SHORT STORY (often arbitrarily set at about 15,000 words). E.g., Faulkner's *The Bear*, James' *The Beast in the Jungle*, Joyce's *The Dead*, etc. P. 5.

Objective correlative: Phrase made famous by T. S. Eliot in a discussion of *Hamlet* (*Selected Essays*, 1932). "The only way of expressing emotion in the form of art is by finding an 'objective correlative'; in other words, a set of objects, a situation, a chain of events which shall be the formula of that *particular* emotion; such that when the external facts, which must terminate in sensory experience, are given, the emotion is immediately evoked. If you examine any of Shakespeare's more successful tragedies, you will find this exact equivalence; you will find that the state of mind of Lady Macbeth walking in her sleep has been communicated to you by a skillful accumulation of sensory impressions; the words of Macbeth on hearing of his wife's death strike us as if, given the sequence of events, these words were automatically released by the last event in the series. The artistic inevitability lies in this complete adequacy of the external to the emotion. . . ." Pp. 108, 130-31.

Organic and **organicism:** Metaphoric way of arguing for the inseparability of the various parts of the novel; its identity as a unified, living (as opposed to mechanical) thing.
See INTENTION.

Personification: The transference of human traits or emotions to inanimate or non-human objects, beings, forces, or abstract ideas.
See ALLEGORY.

Picaresque: From Spanish *picaro* > "rogue," as exemplified in *La vida de Lazarillo de Tormes* (*ca.* 1554), and carried on in Le Sage's *Gil Blas* (1715–35), Thomas Nash's *The Unfortunate Traveller* (1594), Defoe's *Moll Flanders* (1722), etc. In its origins, the picaresque was a type of novel or mode of storytelling—generally EPISODIC—the PROTAGONIST of which was a socially parasitic rascal from the lower classes. P. 69.
See PLOT.

Pleasure: Pp. 14-15.

Plot (action, events, incidents): Ch. 3.
See ANACOLUTHON, CAUSALITY, CONTRAPUNTAL, DIALOGUE, DIGRESSIONS and RELEVANCE, EPISODIC, LINEAR, MOVEMENT and PROGRESSION, PICARESQUE, SCENIC, STORY, STREAM-OF-CONSCIOUSNESS, TIME.
See also POINT-OF-VIEW.

Point-of-View (focus of narration, angle of vision, central intelligence; sometimes **persona, voice, mask**): Pp. 12, 147-57, 177-78; Kinds—
    omniscient (pp. 147-50).

3rd person (pp. 150-51).
1st person [narrator] (pp. 151-52).
1st person [observer] (pp. 153-54).
epistolary (pp. 152-53).
multiple (p. 154).
stream-of-consciousness (pp. 77-80, 157-61).

Protagonist: Pp. 24, 88
See ANTAGONIST and CHARACTER.

Realism and **reality;** cf. **verisimilitude** and **truth** as opposed to illusion: Faithful rendering of actuality, attention to detail. Generally intended to give the impression of objective reproduction, although due allowance must be made for artistic licence and interpretation. In literary history, realism was often associated with lower- and middle-class life, but the term is no longer thus restricted. Rather, it connotes *all* aspects of EXPERIENCE and CHARACTER. A realistic movement began in the 19th century, to show life as it is. (See Flaubert's *Madame Bovary;* cf. NATURALISM.)

Relevance: Pp. 71-2.
See DIGRESSION.

Resolution or **denouement;** sometimes, in tragedy, the **catastrophe:** Resolution, literally, is the working out, the unravelling or the solution of the situation. Following the CLIMAX, an event or events reveal the outcome of the PLOT and its COMPLICATIONS. Pp. 64-5, 66.

Roman à clef or **livre à clef:** A "novel with a key," that is, a work in which real, contemporary persons are portrayed under fictitious names. A central character in Maugham's *Cakes and Ale,* for instance, has been identified as the British author Hugh Walpole, and another in Huxley's *Point Counter Point* as D. H. Lawrence.

Romance: Distinguished by Clara Reeve (*The Progress of Romance,* 1785) from NOVEL: "The word *Novel* in all languages signifies something new. It was first used to distinguish these works from Romance, though they have lately been confounded together and are frequently mistaken for each other. . . . The Romance is an heroic fable, which treats of fabulous persons and things.—The Novel is a picture of real life and manners, and of the times in which it is written. The Romance in lofty and elevated language, describes what never happened nor is likely to happen.—The Novel gives a familiar relation of such things, as pass every day before our eyes, such as may happen to our friend, or to ourselves; and the perfection of it, is to represent every scene, in so easy and natural a manner, and to make them appear so probable, as to deceive us into a persuasion (at least while we are reading) that all is real, until we are affected by the joys or distresses, of the persons in the story, as if they were our own."

According to Hawthorne (in the preface to *The House of Seven Gables*): "The latter form of composition [novel] is presumed to aim at a very minute fidelity, not merely to the possible, but to the probable and ordinary course of man's experience. The former [romance]—while, as a work of art, it must rigidly subject itself to laws, and while it sins unpardonably so far as it may swerve aside from the truth of the human heart—has fairly a right to present that truth under circumstances, to a great extent, of the writer's own choosing or creation."

As seen by Fanny Burney (in her preface to *Evelina*, 1778), ". . . the fantastic regions of Romance, where Fiction is coloured by all the gay tints of luxurious Imagination, where Reason is an outcast, and where the sublimity of the *Marvellous* rejects all aid from sober Probability." Pp. 4-5, 23.

Scenic technique: Pp. 67-8.
See PLOT.

Selection: P. 56; ch. 5.
See ARRANGEMENT and TONE.

Self-identification: Pp. 22-3.
See EMPATHY.

Sentimentality: P. 88.

Setting: P. 20; ch. 4.

Short story: Pp. 3-4.

Static: P. 25.
See CHARACTER.

Story: Pp. 62-3.

Stream-of-consciousness (interior monologue; associationism): Pp. 77-80, 157-61.
William James (*The Principles of Psychology*, Ch. IX, "The Stream of Thought") describes "Five Characters in Thought": "How does it go on? We notice immediately five important characters in the process. . . .

"1) Every thought tends to be part of a personal consciousness.

"2) Within each personal consciousness thought is always changing.

"3) Within each personal consciousness thought is sensibly continuous.

"4) It always appears to deal with objects independent of itself.

"5) It is interested in some parts of those objects to the exclusion of others, and welcomes or rejects—chooses from among them, in a word—all the while."

* * *

"Consciousness, then, does not appear to itself chopped up in bits. Such words as 'chain' or 'train' do not describe it fitly as it presents itself in the first instance. It is nothing jointed; it flows. A 'river' or a 'stream' are the metaphors by which it is most naturally described. *In talking of it hereafter, let us call it the stream of thought, of consciousness, or of subjective life.*"

Henri Bergson (*Creative Evolution*) pictures life as a cosmic river "of *current passing from germ to germ through the medium of a developed organism.* It is as if the organism itself were only an excrescence, a bud caused to sprout by the former germ endeavoring to continue itself in a new germ. The essential thing is the *continuing progress*, indefinitely pursued, an invisible progress, on which each visible organism rides during the short interval of time given it to live." Quoted by Harry Hartwick (*The Foreground of American Fiction*) as one of the influences on stream-of-consciousness. See CHARACTER and PLOT.

Style: Pp. 135-37.

Surprise and **coincidence:** Pp. 86, 87.

Suspense: P. 65.
Expectation enforced by uncertainty and anticipation. A means of developing and maintaining interest while we advance toward the outcome of the situation. See FORESHADOWING.

Symbolism: Pp. 15-16, 24-5, 36-40, 56, 209-10, 211-17.
See CHARACTER, PLOT, SETTING, TEXTURAL SYMBOLISM.

Sympathy: See EMPATHY.

Technique: P. 16.

Textural symbolism: Pp. 213-15, 229.
See SYMBOLISM.

Theme: Pp. 145, 183-88.
See SETTING.

Time (time-sequence; time-shift; "looping chronology"): Pp. 63, 73-5, 124.
See PLOT and MOOD.

Tone: Pp. 128-35, 144-45.
See MOOD and SETTING.

Villain: Pp. 23-4.
See HERO, ANTAGONIST, and CHARACTER.

Bibliography

(A Selected List of Books for Further Study.
Many of the titles are available in paperback.)

Aldridge, John W., *After the Lost Generation* (New York, 1958).
    ed., *Critiques and Essays on Modern Fiction 1920–1951*
    (New York, 1952).
Allen, Walter, *The English Novel: A Short Critical History* (New
    York, 1955).
    ed., *Writers on Writing* (New York, 1948; 1949).
Allott, Miriam, *Novelists on the Novel* (New York, 1959).
Beach, Joseph Warren, *The Twentieth Century Novel: Studies in
    Technique* (New York, 1932).
Booth, Wayne C., *The Rhetoric of Fiction* (Chicago, 1961).
Cary, Joyce, *Art and Reality: Ways of the Creative Process* (New
    York, 1958).
Cowie, Alexander, *The Rise of the American Novel* (New York,
    1948).
Daiches, David, *The Novel in the Modern World* (Chicago, 1939).
Edel, Leon, *The Modern Psychological Novel* (New York, 1955).
Forster, E. M., *Aspects of the Novel* (New York, 1954).
Hartwick, Harry, *The Foreground of American Fiction* (New York,
    1934).
Hoffman, Frederick J., *Freudianism and the Literary Mind* (New
    York, 1959).
James, Henry, *The Art of the Novel*, with an introduction by
    R. P. Blackmur (New York and London, 1934).
    The Future of the Novel, ed. Leon Edel (New York, 1956).
Leavis, F. R., *The Great Tradition* (New York, 1954).
Lubbock, Percy, *The Craft of Fiction* (New York, 1957).

O'Connor, William Van, ed., *Forms of Modern Fiction* (Minneapolis, 1948).

Richards, I. A., *Principles of Literary Criticism* (New York, 1924).

Shipley, Joseph T., ed. *Dictionary of World Literature* (New York, 1953).

Thrall, W. F., Hibbard, A., and Holman, C. H., *A Handbook to Literature* (New York, 1960).

Van Ghent, Dorothy, *The English Novel: Form and Function* (New York, 1953).

Wellek, René, and Warren, Austin, *Theory of Literature* (New York, 1949).

Woolf, Virginia, *The Common Reader* (New York, 1953).